SOVEREIGN SCHOOLS

How Shoshones and Arapahos
Created a High School on the
Wind River Reservation

MARTHA LOUISE HIPP

UNIVERSITY OF NEBRASKA PRESS   LINCOLN

Library of Congress Cataloging-in-Publication Data
Names: Hipp, Martha Louise, author.
Title: Sovereign schools: how Shoshones and
Arapahos created a high school on the Wind
River Reservation / Martha Louise Hipp.
Description: Lincoln: University of Nebraska Press,
[2019] | Includes bibliographical references and index.
Identifiers: LCCN 2018025843
ISBN 9781496208859 (cloth: alk. paper)
ISBN 9781496213624 (epub)
ISBN 9781496213631 (mobi)
ISBN 9781496213648 (pdf)
Subjects: LCSH: Wyoming Indian High
School—History—20th century. | Arapaho
Indians—Education (Secondary)—Wyoming—
Wind River Indian Reservation—History. | Shoshoni
Indians—Education (Secondary)—Wyoming—
Wind River Indian Reservation—History. |
Wind River Indian Reservation (Wyo.)
Classification: LCC E97.6.W9+ |
DDC 371.215/08997354078763—dc23
LC record available at https://lccn.loc.gov/2018025843

Set in Questa by E. Cuddy.
Designed by N. Putens.

CONTENTS

ILLUSTRATIONS

PREFACE

Native Americans began a movement for control of their schools in the mid-1960s. This book is about that movement with a focus on the epic struggle of the Wind River Indian Reservation people to establish their public school. Their story is a microcosm of the complex social and political circumstances that begged change; a courageous few faced and acted to overcome barriers of prejudice, economic deprivation, and discrimination that had been in place for more than one hundred years.

My work to record this history began in November 2000 as a winter storm brought darkness early; its winds were blowing sparse snow and sleet straight across the barren ground. All the same, a small group of Elders, Indian and non-Indian, gathered in the semi-darkness to meet with me at the old Choke Cherry Café, not far from the reservation school where I worked. I was first on the short agenda and so knew that they were waiting for me to speak when it grew quiet; I explained that I had come to ask for suggestions for a required school and tribal community research project. Elder Gerald Sage (1938–2012) responded after another quiet wait; he said the history of the Wyoming Indian High School was an interesting one—one that I could help preserve. The other Elders agreed.

I agreed to do my part without realizing the enormity of what I had taken on. I feel that I owe anthropologists an apology for getting into their field with so little appreciation of their knowledge and work. It can no longer be said that I lack that "appreciation." This project has taken eighteen years. I have read many books, articles, legal documents, and minutes of meetings and most important, I have taken the care and time needed to piece together newspaper stories and the academic work of historians and anthropologists with what the Elders told me. Local museum photographs and the remnants of the old boarding schools confirmed their existence, as did the heartache that remained of their trauma. I took the word of the Elders; it was internally consistent (with emotion and story line), and they were consistent with one another and with other evidence including that from other Native American areas and sources.

Interviewees recommended one another for their experience and interest and were not scientifically selected. I usually simply took notes but sometimes used tape recordings; those were transcribed by Barbara Sage (see below). Helsha Acuña, professor of Native American studies at Central Wyoming College, provided training sessions about how to prepare for the interviews. I used some of my own training as a psychologist to be an intense listener.

Many questions and concepts for this study were not formulated ahead of time. Rather, as I researched the basic facts of Wind River and local town educational history I learned of several areas in need of further study. I had not known, for example, the extent of prejudice and discrimination in this Rocky Mountain region until informed about it by interviewees and newspaper accounts; I had not known the threat that non-Indian education could pose to Indian identity; I had not known that the concept of self-determination included "Indian control of Indian schools." These concepts are central to the story.

The concept of self-determination did not mean a rejection of "educated Indians," as Indians were called by the Arapahos when they had succeeded in white-run schools. Otherwise, the tribal people on the Wind River Reservation would not have fought so hard and so long for a public school. They recognized the need to be able to deal with the white-dominated world. In fact, that motivation is explicit in the school's mission statement and by the school's icon: the image of Cleaver Warden, one of the most prominent among the Arapaho men educated at the boarding school in Carlisle, Pennsylvania. A Southern Arapaho, Warden served as interpreter to and from non-Indians for the Northern Arapahos (Northern and Southern Arapaho language were the same), which itself was highly important and necessary to Arapaho survival in the early 1900s but also was influential in their political activities (see chapter 6). The Arapahos have long admired Warden's capabilities and strive to see their children gain the power of non-Indian knowledge and to blend it with their own.

I want to thank the many individuals and groups who provided me with this Wind River education. Early support for my work time as psychologist for the Wyoming Indian School District 14 (2000–2007) to do home visits, interviews, and related activities came from Lonn Hoffman (1958–2004), superintendent of the Indian schools. He required school-related research by all professional employees. Because of his support and the tribal Elders' desire to have the story told, dozens came forward to be interviewed.

The first group I want to thank are the students, teachers, and staff at Wyoming Indian High School, where I came to appreciate Arapaho and Shoshone culture. The names of those who made essential contributions, if not listed here, are given when their part of the history appears in the main text.

Marilyn Groesbeck, a teacher and school board member during the school's early years, provided an outline for the study and a list of possible interviewees. The child of a local homesteading family, she had once planned to write this book herself. The basic history was first told to me by Barbara Sage, a Shoshone tribal member and reservation rancher with a master's degree in political science from Utah State University. She did further studies in curriculum and instruction at the University of Wisconsin and in American Indian policy at the University of Arizona. She aided me with many hours of research, particularly from the local newspapers. One of the papers, the *Lander Journal*, called the *Wyoming State Journal* in the 1970s, proved an outstanding resource, one that often provided a window into Indian and non-Indian views of circumstances and events. It won several top national awards during the years of our story for its coverage of news and for column writing by Editor Bill Sniffin.

Sage was a member of the Wind River Indian Education Association (WRIEA), the group that pushed for political advances on the reservation and in Fremont County as well as in the state of Wyoming and at the federal level. Surviving members of this organization, including their attorney, Michael Gross, provided invaluable information about the politics and motivations of that time period. Gross provided a sequence of events in a long email. His copious legal files and Indian education publications were fundamental to my understanding of the story. Later, attorneys John G. Ghostbear and Kirke Kickingbird provided their files regarding an Indian lawsuit against the U.S. Department of Education, which were also essential to my grasp of events.

Other sources became important as current issues were explored. Wyoming's Fremont County coroner, Ed McAuslan, supplied a categorized listing of death statistics from the Wind River Indian Reservation and Fremont County for a five-year period. Epidemiologist Cheryl Beseler, PhD, of Colorado State University, then provided a statistical comparison of rates of death for Native American and white residents by gender. The resulting facts are an invaluable addition to an understanding of the effects of past traumas on today's reservation people and schools.

Financial support for interview research and conferences came from the Wyoming Council for the Humanities and the Federal Programs Office. Their support was very helpful in documenting events at the local and national levels.

Scholarly works specific to education on this reservation in the 1970s are essential and rare. Elders and the Wyoming coordinator of Indian education published one of the most important works in 1972, *The Wind River Reservation Yesterday and Today* (later revised by the Curriculum Development Workshop). It is the only book where the specific locations and dates of establishment and closings of the various reservation schools can be found. Two University of Wyoming master's theses gave essential leads and documentation of events. One, by Edward Duncombe, tells of the Episcopal Mission at Ethete on the reservation and of the work of his father, an Episcopal priest and a significant figure in the reservation history. The other, from the early 1970s, is "A Study of the Progress, Methods, and Opinions Concerning the Development of a Unified School District on the Wind River Indian Reservation," by Victor Zerga, a superintendent of these schools. Zerga gave interviews for this book; Duncombe, who was a teenager in the Lander high school during the events of this story, provided not only descriptions of that time but, three decades later, his invaluable professional editing skills. A most basic book among all is that by Loretta Fowler, *Arapahoe Politics, 1851–1978*. I could not have provided major portions of the context for this story without Fowler's book.

Then I want to thank the several people who were kind enough to read earlier drafts and not be too discouraging. Reviewers pointed to the need to inform readers better early in the story about the history and placement of crucial locations. Late in the process, Ardy Sixkiller Clarke, PhD, professor emeritus at Montana State University, prompted further organization and addition of contextual information.

And importantly, I want to thank Matt Bokovoy, acquisitions editor for the University of Nebraska Press, for helping me change my long held manner of communication to more effective methods; in other words, for editing my work. I learned from working with him that "editing" is far more than word choice, syntax, and paragraph placement. Although it is all of that, Matt's in-depth understanding of the content and feeling for how best that can be conveyed made for a more readable and meaningful work. He sometimes understood the depth of the content better than I did; he knew the relevant literature and suggested it to me. I must say that editing is also being a diplomat. Gradually I learned that I was safe when I saw an email from him and began really learning from what he had to say.

Closer to home, Carol Atkinson, PhD, a friend and psychologist colleague of many years, was interested in my project and heard my complaint about the difficulty in preparing a manuscript for publication.

In spite of knowing well the time and effort that would be required, she volunteered her considerable editing skills. I believe that the project and my novice capabilities may have required more than she anticipated, but all the same she stayed with it—and me—to the end some five years later. She was capable of piercing to the core of the meaning of a phrase to ask a question, goading me into doing more research, or of suggesting that somehow the meaning had escaped her, goading me into greater explanatory effort. In either case, as a result the work became more focused and contained added interest. I must also admit that her astute interventions probably saved a few paragraphs from disaster. I will always be grateful to her for her generosity; she provided her experience and natural editing expertise in many hours of work over these years. In the end, our joint efforts won the praise of a reviewer regarding its editing, and the work among the three of us—Carol, Matt, and me—won unanimous approval for acceptance for publication by the University of Nebraska Press editorial advisory board.

I have remained in contact with several of the interviewees for this book, and they have continued to be informative, as the epilogue reflects. Recently Ethete residents honored me for writing this book: they held a "giveaway," a ceremony that was of benefit to me and perhaps half of the attendees. I danced with the families, visited, and feasted on their abundant foods. The heartwarming welcomes from interviewees and work associates of years ago buoyed my heart.

And the long-term patience and editorial contributions of family members, most notably my husband, Richard, are deeply appreciated. To my grandsons, James and Miles, whose school events I sometimes missed while writing (and who are now grown), I offer my sincere apologies.

ABBREVIATIONS

AAIA	American Association on Indian Affairs
AIM	American Indian Movement
BIA	Bureau of Indian Affairs
CDW	Curriculum Development Workshop
CICSB	Coalition of Indian Controlled School Boards
CS-T	*Casper Star-Tribune*
FCRC	Fremont County Reorganization Committee
HEW	Department of Health, Education and Welfare
JOM	Johnson-O'Malley Act
LVHS	Lander Valley High School
NARF	Native American Rights Fund
OEO	Office of Economic Opportunity
ONRR	Office of Natural Resources Revenue
PIE	Parents Interested in Education
WIHS	Wyoming Indian High School
WRIEA	Wind River Indian Education Association
WRIR	Wind River Indian Reservation
WRNA	Wind River Native Advocacy
WRSAEA	Wind River Shoshone and Arapaho Education Association
WSJ	*Wyoming State Journal*

Introduction

"English" invaders believed that with a Euro-American education Indians would shed their cultural identity, assimilate, and ultimately become so mixed as to be invisible. Mission schools would "civilize" and Christianize the Native child and eliminate the "Indian problem." But Native Americans didn't acclimate to the "civilizing" notions of the invaders. They came home from the boarding schools and "returned to the blanket." The state enrolled the next generation of Indians in local town high schools. The aim in writing this book was to document one tribal people's strategy, progress, and setbacks in their fight to take control of their children's education, as well as documenting the racism and discrimination that made their struggle so difficult.

The tribes had long understood education as the mechanism by which culture could be either maintained or destroyed. They well knew why Euro-Americans wanted to assimilate their children; the Indians' western lands were the "Indian problem," as broken treaties had shown. These were dangerous times for Native Americans; the tribes were subjugated and yet terrified after massacres and further threats of mass murder. And so Arapaho leaders sent the strongest peace signal possible: the sacrifice of their children's Native childhood.[1]

The Arapaho leaders placed thirteen of their own children on a train, sending the first to the Indian Industrial School at Carlisle, Pennsylvania, in 1881. Chief Black Coal, the principal Arapaho leader of the nineteenth century, stated, "[We have] given our children, whom we love, into [government] hands. We wish also to assure you by this that we never more want to go on the warpath, but always to live in peace." Two boys were sent with peace pipes to be given to the president and to the secretary of war. They were little warriors. The Carlisle school returned five of the children "alive and in good health" and eight with chronic illnesses, from which several died (the exact number is not known). The Indian Industrial School closed in 1918.[2]

When the main part of our story begins the government no longer required Wind River Indian Reservation parents to send their children to boarding schools. But Native Americans faced another obstacle to cultural continuance in the mid-1960s—border town high schools run by non-Indians. These schools treated American Indian history and culture as nonexistent and, in many instances, treated Indian students as interlopers. The Indian students felt and saw the racism that remained. But that did not mean that the townspeople wanted to segregate the Native American students into a reservation school; *quite the reverse*. Having Native teenagers in their high schools provided Indian federal education funds to their schools. They wanted the money but did not seem concerned about what Indian students wanted or needed.

Events in the Wind River Reservation area illustrate the struggle for "Indian control of Indian education," as advocates described their cause. Margaret Connell Szasz, in *Education and the American Indian: The Road to Self-Determination since 1928*, gives an invaluable account of the purpose and meaning of the national movement for the Indian people; the Bureau of Indian Affairs (BIA) and the public schools gave Native Americans no voice in their children's education and no place for their cultures.[3] Overall, the bureau and the states had failed. The Wind River people's efforts to reclaim their children's education were similar to other Native efforts in the 1970s, when there was broad agreement about the need to establish Indian schools where an expression of indigenous culture would not be silenced. The interviews of the Wind River people here, along with other sources, describe the actions that they and other Native Americans took and how government officials, the state, the border towns, and reservation non-Indians reacted.

The Shoshones and Arapahos sought educational sovereignty; they intended to establish their culture and their identity in schools that they would control. In 2000 they hoped that their story would raise awareness and add an important piece to Native American history. I came on this history serendipitously (see preface). It was near perfect to serve as an example of the national struggle.

Many of the adult and elderly interviewees were students in Wind River Reservation boarding schools. The intent and origin of the schools as well as the abridgement of Indian land and resource rights described in chapter 1 provide the historical background for an understanding of their generation's struggle for self-determination in education. The Wind River boarding schools closed later than most; the Government Boarding School closed in 1955 (high school classes there ended in 1942), and the mission schools closed between 1945 and 1966. After that there was no reservation high school.

Chapter 2 stands alone to explain national Native American efforts for self-determination; their efforts and concepts are central to the Wind River story. The chapter shows how the self-determination theme was in many ways synchronistic with the tumultuous times of the 1960s. Those times, well covered by the media, culminated in recognition of the problem and sympathetic action at the highest levels of government. A congressional report, still relevant today, described the BIA and state educational failures that had hindered tribal people for generations. Other U.S. government actions favorable to self-determination were taken by the Supreme Court in 1954 (*Brown v. Topeka Board of Education*) and Congress in 1964 (the Civil Rights Act). President Nixon's 1970 "forked tongue" speech about "self-determination" gave Native Americans false hope yet played into their politically savvy hands. Finally, the chapter outlines the first direct action taken across the country by Indigenous people to establish self-determination through Indian schools.

Chapter 3 is the first of the book's core chapters directly describing the Wind River story. Interviewees remembered details of their poverty and extent of the surrounding prejudice that motivated those who, night after night, discussed their quandary. They were most bitter about the control that non-Indians held over their resources, but that was not a winnable battle, and in many ways not a top priority. They hired an attorney and took on the fight to control their schools.

The Wind River microcosm and the national macrocosm run parallel and unite at times. Tribal people across the country were impacted by Nixon's policy betrayals, and little money was available for local Indian education in 1971. BIA officials jealously fought the Arapahos, Shoshones, and other Plains tribes to keep control of Indian schools.

Throughout the struggle Wind River people had to fight the non-Indian and "mixed-blood" reservation residents, some of whom worked together in the county's School Redistricting Committee. As emerges in later chapters, the state's education officials and judges all the way up the ladder seemed to be sometimes for and sometimes against an Indian school. But Wind River Native American motivation was high; maintaining culture and tribal identity rose above all else. Self-determination was central to these goals.

The Wind River group found friends in the Coalition of Indian Controlled School Boards, a *Washington Post* writer, and with the Episcopal Church (at least for a time). Tribal Elders were eloquent speakers and diplomats, as this epic story shows. These skills and the spiritual strength and social confidence needed in the struggle are striking given the background history and the prejudice that surrounded these Native Americans at the time. The violence, as was documented in a border town school, make their courageous attitude even more remarkable.

Certainly there are enough problems to make this story interesting. At the national level, Native Americans had reason to be deeply disappointed—and defeated. President Nixon went back on his much proclaimed 1970 promise of self-determination and withdrew federal support. At the same time, new state law that called for educational equality, described in chapter 5, did not counteract an important non-Indian policy; the state legislature assumed that county towns would control the Indian schools indefinitely. Additionally, income from oil and gas resources on the Wind River Reservation, which was adequate to support Indian schools, instead provided income to the "mixed-blood" and non-Indian reservation school districts, while Indian districts were cut off from large portions of this income; two of the three Indian districts had almost none. Despite the unfairness of this particular inequality, the non-Indian community organized to fight the equal distribution of tax base money. Prejudice meant that abuses of power in the Rocky Mountain region were hardly noticed—except by Native Americans.

Wyomingites, like many others, had not given up assimilationist goals in the 1970s. That is, in their eyes the sooner reservation land and resource rights were no longer held by Indians, the better. However, as the middle chapters show, the Indian school's Fremont County opponents were divided. They were stuck in obstinate squabbles over the Native Americans' tax base, and their angry conflicts left some friends for the Indians. But there was also strife on the Native American side between some of the "mixed-blood" factions (aligned with whites) and advocates of a reservation school. Local newspaper stories played up this conflict—the strife was portrayed as a "split" between the tribes. The stories also portrayed a potential school in the reservation's Indian area as "segregation." Group meeting minutes and newspaper stories document the shocking details of the prejudice that justified suppression of tribal culture.

The Wind River Indians managed to get a BIA school after some high drama in Washington DC. But strong opposition did not end. Revealing the strength of the Wind River people in fighting back against the opposition in Fremont County, they took the fight to the state capitol en masse and celebrated Indian style when they knew they had won. But opposition in the county continued. Newspaper stories, although sometimes revealing a bias for the non-Indian, were extremely helpful in providing the timeline for and events of the clash between the county and the state, which now took the Indians' side over the Indian school.

Termination policy had threatened withdrawal of federal services, such as health services and education, and of federal management of trust property (which entailed at least some protection of Indian ownership) in the 1950s.[4] In the 1970s there was another convergence of the local story with the national. All Native Americans experienced the consequences of federal policy and its vagaries. When Nixon's insincerity and actual opposition to Indian empowerment were apparent before the end of his presidency, the Coalition of Indian Controlled School Boards with their Native American lawyers became essential. The attorneys' provision of legal records and journal articles was invaluable to this story.

There were, of course, variations in the development of Indian schools across the country. The new Wyoming state law accounted for some of those differences, although the story soon gets back to the same old theme—control of Indian resources. As stated, the school became a BIA school, but the new state law required the county committee to draw boundaries within each county for equitable and efficient school districts. If Wind River people were to get a *public* school district, it would remove some of the resources from non-Indian control, and the BIA school would probably cease to exist. The present book tells how all of that worked out.

Fortunately, Indian leadership was experienced and insightful. The leaders fought battles at one governmental level and, when those seemed lost, switched to another. They were fighting a moving and evolving target; the BIA, (sometimes) insubordinate to the president, opposed Indian control of their schools, and state officials were sometimes for and sometimes against it, but it was local entities, in spite of their own conflicted self-interests, that formed the most determined opposition. Indian leadership emerged in several venues. The struggle of the two tribes of the Wind River Reservation with the towns, the state, and the nation that surround them is not an unusual one for Native Americans. All were motivated to fight for the right to continuance of identity and culture. The expression of self-determination through Indian schools was a natural means to that end.

But administrative control of Indian schools, as promised by Nixon, was no panacea; financial control of education at the state level resulted in alien standards and unrealistic goals, often placing the burden upon the student. Happily, the last chapter tells how Indian teachers and the omnipresent Indian school environment accomplish much of what was intended. The epilogue describes some of the broader effects of the high school that became central to overcoming an otherwise poverty-ridden reservation life.

In this story the strength of American Indians arises from their support for one another and in their capacity for perseverance. These strengths saved their identity. When their adversaries became discouraged, and could no longer deal with the struggle, they took over and won a better world for their children.

Twentieth-century Arapahos and Shoshones valued a Euro-American education and the ability to speak the English language, although the Arapahos did not want individuals to benefit for themselves alone but for the tribe as a whole, and traditional ways were to be put first. This pragmatic value may not have existed and the Wind River story might never have happened except for events on the Cimarron Trail in 1831. There a fur company trapper en route to Santa Fe spotted a young boy, lost for many days after chasing a rabbit far downriver from his Arapaho parents' migrating camp. The trapper ran to tell the head of his company, Thomas Fitzpatrick; they captured the boy, and Fitzpatrick carried him to the wagons for food. It was a Friday, which seemed a perfect name. Fitzpatrick, delighted by Friday, took him to St. Louis and enrolled him in a Catholic boarding school. Friday stayed for at least two years. He became fluent in English and for a time lost his ability to speak Arapaho. He and Fitzpatrick made return trips to the West, and many years later Arapaho traders saw them and thought Friday might be the lost boy. His parents had never given up hope that he was still alive. They were reunited, and Fitzpatrick gave Friday the choice of whether to return to his parents, who entreated him to stay with them. After some days Friday gave in. He became a warrior and later would have been shot and killed except for the failure of a Ute Indian's gun. He immediately shot the Ute but ever after was a pacifist. As such, he changed his name to "The Man Who Sits in the Corner and Keeps His Mouth Shut," also interpreted as "Sitting in the Meek." He became an

intermediary, later to be demoted to interpreter (likely because of his friendship with whites). Still, he was immeasurably important to the tribe as their only English speaker until his death in 1881. A U.S. military official said he spoke English "like a college student." Friday was among those leaders who sent their children or grandchildren to the East, as described in chapter 1. One of two grandsons, Little Plume, or "Hayes," never returned (see epilogue). But there were many descendants; Friday's son, Bill, an army scout, was "successful enough to be given five wives," all sisters.[5] Some of the names of the numerous Fridays on the Wind River today are to be found in the story to follow, along with those of many other Wind River Reservation families.

1. Little Plume or "Hayes," son of Friday, April 15, 1882, gravestone at the Carlisle Indian Industrial School in Pennsylvania. Photograph by Kay Karol Horse Capture. Courtesy of Gloria Goggles, Wind River Indian Reservation.

1

Precursors

Massacres, "Agreements," Boarding Schools, and Strategies for Survival

The Northern Arapahos, the Sioux, and the Northern Cheyennes signed an agreement with the U.S. government in 1876 to leave the Black Hills and no longer wage war. They had to sign; they were dying of starvation and exposure. The "agreement" forced them to forfeit "all claims and hunting privileges in the land outside of the reservations" (apparently in retribution for the Sioux massacre of Custer and his men at the Little Bighorn), and so they were essentially confined on reservations. The government was to provide each tribe with an agency, a few employees, and a school with a teacher—rations too, if they sent their children to school. Avoiding this was not really an option on the Wind River Reservation where so little game remained. Black Coal (with Friday as his interpreter), was an intermediary for the Arapahos until his death in 1893. He was referred to by the agent as "great chief Black Coal—(who) at all times urged his people to send their children to school." Black Coal's urgings for schooling were a sign of peaceful cooperation, a necessity in this time of "war" and annihilation.[1]

For nearly a decade before the 1876 agreement the Arapahos had encountered the power of overwhelming numbers and advanced weaponry intermingled with offers for white man's education; the 1864 Sand Creek massacre and mutilation of the dead bodies of Arapaho and Cheyenne men, women, and children (Sand Creek at Fort Wise, designated by government officials as a safe haven) was followed by the Fort Laramie Treaty of 1868, the first treaty to include education.

It and the first Plains Indian treaty, the Fort Laramie (or Horse Creek) Treaty of 1851, failed as soon as they encountered settler hostilities for the lands and resources. President Grant's Peace Policy emphasized peace with church-run schools, but the "Indian wars" did not end. The U.S. military pursued reservation Northern Cheyenne and Sioux Indians "up and down" the Powder River country north and west of the Black Hills (in the territories of Montana and Wyoming) during the 1876–77 winter. Gunshots killed many; perhaps more (women, children, babies, and elderly) froze to death in the deep snow. The massacre at Wounded Knee was yet to come.[2]

The context for the Native American experience in the first white schools was complicated and traumatic. The dominant society deliberately used education to eradicate tribal cultures and spearhead what was then thought of by some as a humanitarian movement to stop the killing and assimilate Indian people. This chapter is background for the core narrative of this book.

Protestant evangelical reformers and Catholics each sought the solution to the "Indian problem" through education. But prejudice in its most brazen forms along with ignorance of the central importance of tribal identity and culture diminished their perception of the humanity of Native Americans. Church leaders promised to instill the work ethic and patriotism—a good fit with the congressional intent of the individualization and Americanization of the noble and ignoble "savages."[3]

And so the government contracted to help the churches finance schools—"contract schools," as they came to be called. Government teachers and matrons required the children to maintain the schools through their own labor to prepare them to become self-supporting individuals and no longer a "burden" on the government. Most important to the Protestant reformers was the means to "correct all evils": individual salvation. Indians, through developing patterns of individualism, would be freed from "the bondage to the tribe" and would become individual citizens "like all the other races in this country." People on the frontier engendered and supported the government policy; they assumed that tribal lands and resources would be put up for sale if tribal people would give up their communal life, disperse, and assimilate.[4]

As the 1880s came to an end the government was directing the majority of its funding to the Catholics (thanks to presidential politics and lobbying by the Washington DC Bureau of Catholic Indian Missions), a source of great resentment among the predominant Protestants. Catholic immigration had steadily increased since the 1870s, and the Protestants saw a threat to their domination. They used the Catholic leaders' declaration of the infallibility of the pope as an anti-Catholic propaganda tool and "Americanism" as a front for the animosity that they felt against the Catholics. Native American children were affected by this conflict. Under pressure, Congress gradually eliminated direct appropriations for contract schools during the 1890s. After that the church-run schools continued to have access to per pupil funding through Indian treaty rights; the large congressional appropriations went to the "strongly Protestant" government schools.[5]

But Catholic schools did not suffer for lack of funding. Wealthy Catholics gave large donations that provided for the construction of buildings and paid teachers' salaries. Katharine Drexel and her sisters, children of a "wealthy Philadelphia financier," were among the donors. Katharine gave thousands to St. Stephen's on the Wind River Reservation. Additionally, Indian treaty rights provided St. Stephen's, like other Catholic schools, with federal Indian funds. The Catholics did not ask the tribal council for their approval for the use of Indian federal trust funds (where past experience suggested that they would not be accommodated) but instead asked Arapaho families to give permission to use the communal federal funds after "a feed."[6] The immediate need for food prevailed.

Indian boarding schools were the most important tool of the western assimilationist movement. There were four such schools on the Wind River Indian Reservation. The government independently funded only one, known as the Wind River Government Boarding School. Catholic and Episcopal priests carried out the churches' and the government's missions at the other three—to Christianize and "civilize" the Indian, with western expansion in mind.[7]

The Rev. John Roberts, an Episcopalian, was the first missionary to arrive on the Wind River Indian Reservation, then called the Shoshone Indian Reservation. He came to Wyoming Territory seeking more meaningful work after an assignment in the Bahamas (where most were already converted) and began his work with a few student boys almost immediately. The boys chased skunks when free; the smelly odor permeated his one-room cabin. They slept on a carpet "padded with straw underneath." His betrothed followed him from the Bahamas three years later, by which time he had transformed from a clergyman dressed in tropical "whites" to a mountain man covered in furs and frost. They married on Christmas day at 4:00 p.m., the day she arrived after a five-thousand-mile journey. Their first home was in the one-room adobe boarding school at Fort Washakie. There he worked mainly with the Shoshones at the base of the Wind River Range of the Rocky Mountains.[8]

Reverend Roberts had reached Fort Washakie in 1883 when an arctic storm dropped the temperature to sixty degrees below zero. The sled driver offered him a coat as they began the 150-mile trip from Green River, "Got you a coat? That ain't no coat, get you an extry one off'n m'bed." Roberts saw suffering from exposure at stage stations along the way and one stage driver frozen to death. The young Roberts officiated at the driver's burial in the deep snow. Roberts later attributed his survival to his constant digging of snow drifts away from the path of the horses and the sled upon which he rode. When they finally reached a point overlooking the Shoshone encampment, he and the driver saw what appeared to be fields of Japanese lanterns—an illusion created by teepees with sagebrush fires burning inside. The Indians had moved all their teepees closer to the agency for better access to rations.[9]

A Catholic priest, Father Joannes Jutz, wisely planned his trip for the springtime of the following year but in so doing lost his chance to settle in with the Shoshones—"first come, first gained," he observed. Seeing the circumstance, he immediately traveled twenty-seven miles from the western side of the reservation to the southeast corner where

2. Shoshone Indian Mission-Church School for Girls at Fort Washakie, Wyoming (1900–1945), 2009. Photograph by author.

the Arapahos reside—the "Arapahoe" area, as it is spelled there. That night the reverberations of a "big base [sic] drum" and the "ghostly incantations" of medicine men ministering to an ill woman kept him awake. The very next morning he performed Mass under the observant and ritually experienced eyes of Chief Black Coal, his two wives, and two children.[10]

Father Jutz helped construct a convent on the triangular delta between the Little and Big Wind Rivers where he could barely see the Wind River Range of the Rocky Mountains across the wide expanse of arid sagebrush and prairie lands. The convent crumbled the next spring from torrents of mountain snow-melt breaking through its walls and washing away the sands at its base.[11]

The Catholics took years to open St. Stephen's Catholic Mission School. Several groups of teaching nuns arrived but soon left again; eventually the Sisters of St. Francis came from Philadelphia and stayed well into the 1960s in spite of the "difficulty and hardship."[12]

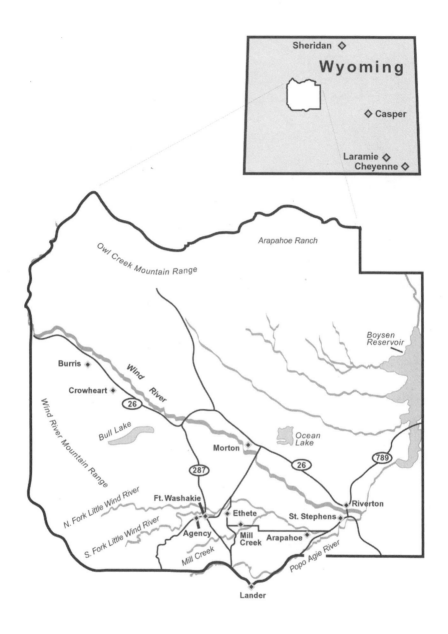

3. Wind River Reservation. Reprinted from Anderson, *The Four Hills of Life.*

President Arthur assigned the care of the Wind River Indians to the Episcopal Church. Roberts, who had been sent to the Wind River to establish an Indian mission, worked with the U.S. Indian agent (later agents were titled "superintendents") to establish the reservation's government school, a low, dimly lit adobe building built by 1884. Its "heavy iron bars" on its few windows kept hostile intruders out and the unruly boys in at night.[13]

The government school held up to ninety Arapaho and Shoshone boarders by the fall of 1886. The government replaced the adobe building with a new "bright and airy" building with dormitories in 1892. But Roberts's dream was to establish a church school. The Shoshone chief Washakie gave 160 acres to bring the dream to fruition; the Shoshones laid the cornerstone in 1889. Roberts's school was the Shoshone Episcopal Mission School and was for girls only. There he worked, preaching, teaching, and farming until he died at the age of ninety-six. He was never able to raise the money to include boys but believed that the girls should come first since they were the home makers who would acculturate others with "civilization" when they returned to the camps.[14]

The Wind River boarding schools, with the exception of Roberts's mission school, were culturally repressive and harsh in their treatment of children. The trauma from early childhood separation from parents followed by abusive treatment and illness can hardly be overstated. An Arapaho woman, hearing a "white-washed" boarding school account of "procurement" of children cried, "They came shouting and pounding on the door! Parents were terrified." Some tried to hide their children in the sage-covered hills, but without food, water and shelter that could not have lasted for long. Strangers in long black dresses came on wagons and took them away as young as age four. The feisty ones immediately jumped out of school windows and tried to run away. Their language, only partially learned, was usually stunted for lack of usage and for inculcated shame; it could not be spoken in three of the four schools.[15]

St. Stephen's Catholic school held 58 students on average in 1893, and the new Government Boarding School had an average of 174 children by 1896. Deadly epidemics spread rapidly and with "peculiar severity" in the wet and cold; 80 of the 174 were "sick in bed" all at one time with measles. Trachoma, a painful and in those days incurable eye disease that could lead to blindness, also plagued the students. Fifty-one percent of the students on the Wind River Reservation had it in 1912, the highest rate among all reservations. After tuberculosis, officials considered trachoma to be the most serious of the diseases that spread among the students. The government school had a 50 percent death rate until 1901, when "after much delay" the government granted Roberts's requests to allow children to visit their homes.[16]

Roberts allowed the building of teepee playhouses at the Shoshone Episcopal Mission School where the girls played Indian games and sang Indian songs. They also kept their long braids. Perhaps it was that he had five young children or that he had seen so many die. The school was relatively small, about twenty-five students in 1896.[17]

Helen Cedartree in *Wind River Memories* describes a second Episcopal Mission boarding school, St. Michael's, located six miles east of the Shoshone school in the sage-covered plains of the Arapaho settlement known as Ethete ("Where they shed their coverings"). The Episcopalians established the mission in 1913 on land that they purchased from Arapaho leaders Yellow Calf and Seth Willow. A few boys attended St. Michael's Mission School at first; it was mainly for girls until the church completed a building for boys in 1918. The teachers made certain that the boys in attendance before 1918 were kept separate from the girls at night; the girls slept in four one-story buildings (fifteen to twenty-five in each), while the boys slept in the church on hammocks that were tied to the rafters.[18]

Schools were not the only tool used to assimilate Indians. Congress passed the General Allotment Act in 1887 (the Dawes Act) to end tribal ownership of land and assign it to individual Native Americans or heads of households. Protestant reformers were the moving force behind the bill; it was assumed that individual ownership would "substitute white civilization for his (communitarian) tribal culture."[19] The Dawes Act also promised other benefits; it made possible the sale of Native American land piece by piece. The non-Indians used their laws to claim what they had promised to the Native Americans and left them impoverished.

Two-thirds of all reservation lands, those of the greatest value, were sold under the Dawes Act. In March 1905 Congress ratified an agreement that made 1.3 million acres of desirable Wind River "surplus" reservation lands with federally backed irrigation projects available for settler purchase. According to Fowler in *Arapahoe Politics*, the government negotiator, James McLaughlin, "informed the tribes" that there had been a Supreme Court decision that gave the tribes no choice; it was "a courtesy that they were discussing the matter at all." These lands in the northeastern triangle of the reservation were over one-half of the then approximately 2,354,000-acre reservation. Irrigation ditch work permitted the Arapahos to move to camps on the family's allotment in the summer, and when the water was shut off in the wintertime they moved back to areas near the river for access to water. The government restored most of the land to the reservation in 1939, but the 171,000 acres not restored, termed the "Riverton Reclamation Project," are still populated mostly by non-Indians. The tribes are buying it back as it becomes available. This land runs from the center of the reservation to its eastern side, approximately ten miles northeast of Ethete. It is politically important to this story because of its non-Indian occupancy. Riverton itself is a "doughnut hole" inside the southeast corner of the reservation. Its population of nearly eleven thousand is approximately 85 percent non-Indian. Riverton was determined by the EPA to be a legal part of the reservation in 2013, but that was not the final decision; a three-judge panel of the Tenth Circuit Court of Appeals ruled in 2017 that Congress did intend to "diminish the size of the reservation" based on the 1905 McLaughlin "agreement," which removed Riverton from the reservation to the state up to the present time. The tribes are appealing that decision to the full twelve-judge Tenth Circuit Court.[20]

Native Americans are constantly reminded, by white and "mixed-blood" ownership of reservation land, of their need to remain vigilant and educationally accomplished regarding their legal status. Prejudiced perceptions had imparted a special disregard for ordinary rights, disregard that furthered indigenous impoverishment. Non-Indian resentment of Indian ownership most certainly played its part in the twentieth-century prejudice and conflict over Indian control of a school. It was prejudice that, in spite of the following history, allowed members of the two Wind River tribes to join in their struggle for the school.

When Meriwether Lewis and William Clark came through the Rocky Mountains in 1805 with Sacajewea as their guide, she found her brother, Câmeahwait, "gaunt with starvation." As *Letters of the Lewis and Clark Expedition* describes, "She ran and embraced him & threw her blanket over him & cried profusely." Câmeahwait advised Lewis and Clark on directions for their journey as the hard frosts of August warned the expedition to hurry out of the mountains.[21] Chief Washakie and Sacajewea are sources of great pride and give historical roots to the Eastern Shoshones of the Wind River. A majestic statue of Sacajewea stands in the Fort Washakie cemetery where metal headboards lean into the earth and plastic roses fade.

Indian and settler hostilities culminated in the Bear River massacre of 249 Shoshones and Bannocks in late January 1863. Six months later the government assigned the Wind River Shoshones 44,672,000 acres of territory in the first Treaty of Fort Bridger. Several government agreements reduced the acreage of the treaty to "about one-twentieth that size" by 1905, just one hundred years after the Lewis and Clark expedition came through the Rocky Mountains. The first Fort Bridger treaty allowed telegraph lines, an overland stage, and the possibility of construction of a railroad in Shoshone country. The second Fort Bridger treaty, in 1868, exchanged the 1863 treaty territory for far less for the Shoshones with the promise that "the United States now solemnly agrees that no persons except those herein designated (the 'Shoshonee') . . . shall ever be permitted to pass over, settle upon, or reside in the Territory described for the use of said Indians." But government troops escorted the Arapahos onto this Shoshone territory for permanent residence in 1878. Thirteen years later the Shoshone chief Washakie in a letter to the president of the United States expressed his feelings about the U.S. government betrayal: "We do not concede that the Arapahos have a right to one foot of the land on this Reservation."[22] It is this betrayal for which *some* Shoshones held *the Arapahos* responsible in the 1970s.

Prehistoric independence had left an imprint that is not easily erased. The Shoshones unified under Chief Washakie; the Arapahos consolidated through the consensus gained in lengthy group discussions. Elders, whom the Arapahos saw as closest to the Supernatural, held the greatest influence in the discussions. They were not unilaterally in charge; Black Coal once refused to agree with Chief Washakie about an important land concession unless he had the backing of Arapaho leadership. He said that if he did, "some of them would kill me!"[23]

The federal government was at times indecisive about how it should rule the sometimes unruly Native Americans. U.S. Supreme Court chief justice John Marshall commented in 1831 that the Native American's "relation to the United States—resembled that of a ward to its guardian." But in 1832 Marshall vindicated the Cherokee in their fight against intrusions by non-Indian Georgians and made it clear that their protections by the federal government, as guaranteed in treaties, did not take away their nationhood, or "right to self-government."[24] Marshall may have been among the first to validate Native thinking about self-determination.

Government officials wanted to put an end to government responsibility for its "wards" through the "efficiency and businesslike management" of the country's Progressive era of the early 1900s. But that would not have been in the best interest of the tribes. The Arapahos selected their Council of six based on preferences of the Elders. The Council vote was "nearly always unanimous." The two tribes used jointly convened councils to their advantage when the Wind River superintendent tried to force their disintegration through the establishment of the Joint Business Council. They were masters at maintaining the appearance of agreement while turning things on their heads. The Shoshone and Arapaho councilmen "formed an alliance," as requested, but did this, according to Fowler, "in order to increase their effectiveness as advocates for Indian interests." The superintendent was not happy but the tribes joined in subverting his attempts at retribution. The commissioner refused several times over the years to approve a Joint Council constitution in spite of the original federal objective, perhaps not wanting too much tribal independence or sovereignty.[25] The commissioner's edginess in this regard suggests that he knew government officials had never really succeeded in taking self-determination from the tribes. Their unification strategy had worked to maintain their independence of federal rule.

Fowler details additional Arapaho strategies that were particularly sophisticated. First, they learned that the church could be helpful; they enlisted the aid of the Catholics (local priests and the Bureau of Catholic Indian Missions) to prevent the superintendent (with whom the priests also were not happy) from choosing unwanted representatives to negotiate for them in Washington DC on an important issue, land leasing. The superintendent made his appointments but was soon removed. The tribes also learned that being skeptical of government offers could work to their benefit; they rejected the Indian Reorganization Act, passed under President Roosevelt's commissioner of Indian Affairs, John Collier. As a result, they were "never subject to political reorganization" under the act, as were most other plains tribes.[26]

The mid-1930s were pivotal for the Arapahos in their transition from pure traditionalism toward the use of the abilities of younger "educated Indians." These were men (usually) who, as Fowler relates, "could serve the ends of the tribe in its dealings with Whites." They understood white society but remained loyal to the Elders and Arapaho values. They were better able to negotiate with the federal government. But the transition was not without turmoil; the younger and Elder Arapahos discussed differences passionately and openly. The solution that they accepted made use of contemporary knowledge and continued Elder executive powers. The Arapaho ability to use dual perspectives (as in worshiping the Christian God and returning to Indian ceremonials afterward), to assess circumstances, and to act in unity remained intact decades later when they decided to fight for a school.[27] In the meantime, federal promises continued with double talk and double standards for Native Americans.

The U.S. government granted citizenship to individual Native Americans when they received Dawes Act allotments and to the remaining Native Americans in 1924. But citizenship for Native Americans did not automatically mean voting rights. The 1924 act left American Indian enfranchisement to the states, and several western states prohibited Indians outright from voting; a Wyoming literacy law was left in place stating that in order to vote one had to be able "to read the constitution of this state." This requirement, which made it easy to declare Native Americans incompetent to vote, was reenacted in 1943 and again in 1951. The state did not repeal the test until after literacy requirements were banned in 1970 amendments to the U.S. Voting Rights Act. Note that this was a year during which the Arapahos and Shoshones were making legal and legislative arguments for their school.[28]

Wind River Indian children attended the government or mission boarding schools in 1924. They lived on non-taxable land and so the state did not provide them with a public school. Three to four miles from Ethete were the "Upper" and "Lower" Mill Creek areas (referring to elevation), each with an elementary school funded by the county. The state consolidated these schools with St. Michael's Mission School in 1957 to form Mill Creek Public School District 14, a district that is central to this history.[29]

Elder Verna Thunder (b. 1927), a student in the 1930s, said in an interview for this book that the county's Mill Creek schools were "just for the white rancher kids. Later on they [Native American students] went but in our time we just went to the boarding schools." I asked, "And why was that?" Verna replied, "They came and got you!"[30] Verna's strong seventy-nine-year-old voice conveyed her anger. The government had deprived her of essentials to her childhood—family comfort and care. A few years before Verna's birth, things had begun to change at the national level.

Indian defense societies struggled to defend Indian religious and land ownership rights in the 1920s. Public attention to the injustices placed Interior Secretary Hubert Work under pressure to reform federal policies. He had reservations about these policies himself and requested a private institute study of Indian Affairs in 1926. The investigation, ironically titled "The Problem of Indian Administration" (as opposed to the then commonly use phrase "the Indian problem"), was known as the Meriam Report for its lead investigator Lewis Meriam. The

1928 report strongly criticized all aspects of Indian policy, particularly regarding health care, land allotment, and education. Descriptions of the latter were most disturbing. The Meriam Report exposed the boarding schools' deplorable conditions: jail-like detention areas, poor nutrition, and lack of sanitation; overcrowding in dormitory rooms— many closed off from light and air; and child labor, "primarily for the support of the institution." But Congress continued to resist closing boarding schools for years "because they constituted a significant boost to the economies of the communities in which they were located." Only twelve of seventy-seven boarding schools ceased operations between 1928 and 1933 *while the number of students continued to increase.*[31] Boarding schools on the Wind River Reservation did not close until decades after the Meriam Report was published, although Indian students began to attend non-reservation high schools once funds became available in the mid-1930s.

The Meriam Report aroused widespread public sympathy for Native Americans. Franklin Roosevelt appointed John Collier as the commissioner of Indian Affairs shortly after his election in 1932. Collier closed many boarding schools and sought guidance from anthropologists rather than from the missionaries. This perhaps better than any other action symbolized the takeover by the progressives from the "old reformers," the Protestant Christians. The large number of Catholics migrating into the United States had reduced Protestant influence and "the increasing secularization of American society" in the 1920s brought a close to the Protestant era.[32]

Congress passed the Johnson-O'Malley Act early in Collier's tenure. This short piece of legislation provided funding for Indian services and education but did not assure Native American influence in the use of those funds. It gave federal funds to states with little specificity—a move toward integration of services and assimilation of the Indian.[33] Officials in border towns were motivated to provide a high school education for Native American students with the increase in funding.

Indian high school students in Wyoming had several unsatisfactory choices—they could leave for distant boarding schools or attend the local boarding schools that were open until midcentury, as described in the introduction. They also could attend the high schools of Fremont County, schools that did not follow Collier guidelines to integrate the Indian students' out-of-school experience. Instead the state simply passed Native student education and enculturation from the federal and church schools to local Euro-American administrators and teachers. Border town schools put the federal Native American funds into the *general* budget.[34]

Most Wind River Indian Reservation elementary students still lived in its four boarding schools in the mid-1930s. These had changed little since the previous century. Reservation Elders remember that high school grades were added to the Government Boarding School near Fort Washakie in the late 1930s but ended around 1942. St. Stephen's did not offer high school classes until 1957. These, the last high school classes on the reservation, closed in 1966. The Episcopal Mission School at Fort Washakie did not offer high school classes except for their "equivalent" classes taught by the older girls. High school grades were offered at St. Michael's Episcopal Mission beginning sometime in the early 1930s and lasted until the school closed in 1957.[35]

No one prepared Indian students for off-reservation high school before transportation was initiated to Lander, one of the largest towns in Fremont County, with just over seven thousand people in 1970. It was a quiet agricultural and mining center that provided a library, hospital, banks, grocery stores, and overnight stays to tourists on their way through the prairie to Yellowstone. Independent-minded owners lived in plain one-story houses near the broad main street. At the turn of the century the railroad had brought in some two-story houses to be put together by the numbers from kits. Gardens and spruce trees flourished in the long summer days of northern sun. A scattering of churches held their particular moral ground.[36]

It was a conservative town where many people favored long-held ways of thinking and doing things; few of its teachers were trained in or experienced with tribal culture, history, or language.[37] Native American students, just beginning to emerge from extreme poverty, faced cultural invisibility and indifference along with outright prejudice and discrimination in these newly mixed-race schools.

Many of our interviewees attended the boarding schools at St. Stephen's Catholic Mission or St. Michael's Episcopal Mission. Lloyd Dewey (1922– 2008) lived in the southeastern Arapahoe area near St. Stephen's Mission on an unmarked road, part of a network of dirt roads and occasional long, uneven driveways. His house, its sun-faded blue-gray paint blending into the sage, sat opposite a wide gully. The fences held a few years of tumbleweeds and no one had plowed the fields. The house seemed deserted in the warm spring of my first visit; the stairs were extremely worn and the day so still that I hesitated to knock. Lloyd's wife Edith opened the door; he, being blind, wore dark glasses and sat in a chair immediately to my right.

Edith always attended Lloyd. He looked and acted much like descriptions of his great-grandfather, the fiery Arapaho chief Sharp Nose.[38] Like him, Lloyd was lean, a bit stern, and not much for small talk. He was, however, fluent in English and Arapaho. A pleasant sage-scented breeze came through the southern window's sheer curtains where Edith sat and talked with me. I already knew that Lloyd had attended high school in Lander beginning in 1936, and during my first visit I soon asked how he was treated there. He responded: "I wasn't treated very good. They still had that notion that we were dumb and we were dirty. But I was a good student. I carried four subjects, Latin, English, General Science and Mathematics and I excelled in all of them. I was a straight A student."

When I asked if the teachers were surprised by his performance, he said:

Well it was more derogatory than anything else. They thought I was copying from the other kids. I tried to prove to them that I wasn't but they insisted that I did. So then I was put, put down. They put me by myself. The same room it was, I was maybe two or three desks away from the rest of them. And I continued bringing up my grades, kept my grades up there. . . . Sometimes during that time we had history.

And it wasn't the history I knew. I argued with the teachers and they didn't like it so I'd get called to the principal's office and they'd dress me down. They said, "How do you know so much?" I said . . . "Well, I don't, I don't know that much." I said, "American history, I learned from my father. He went to school in Carlisle, Pennsylvania. That's where he got his education." And then around the time I wasn't going to school is when I learned my American history.

I commented that apparently his history was "a different account than some of the Lander teachers had," and he responded with a chuckle: "Well, whatever it was they didn't like it!"[39]

Lloyd's testimony revealed contradictory attitudes and feelings about the non-Indian education that they received. As others stated (see later interviews) there was a deep sense of loss and abandonment associated with the years spent in boarding schools, both local and distant. Yet the Arapaho felt pride about the knowledge held by those who returned from the Carlisle Indian Industrial School, as is implied in Dewey's statement. This feeling contrasted with the feelings about the Lander high school. Interviewees seemed to have a lasting sense of degradation that they felt there. Most important is how Arapahos felt and still feel about the continuance of their culture; non-Indian education was considered an additional set of knowledge, not a replacement.

Lloyd remembered that all Arapaho and most Shoshone students dropped out of the Lander school. He felt he was treated better at the Jesuit St. Stephen's elementary boarding school than at Lander's high school: "They were more tolerant. . . . They listened to us. . . . We were more or less learning all the same thing."[40]

He said he had been told that he could go to college after graduation from the Lander high school. However, he became ill with poliomyelitis and was forced to drop out of high school in March 1937. He recovered and worked in the Civilian Conservation Corps in 1938. Later he became director of the tribally owned Arapaho Ranch, but he never returned to school.[41]

St. Stephen's Mission School changed personnel after Lloyd Dewey's elementary school attendance and deepened its determination to rid the tribal communities of their cultural ways and beliefs. Their methods directly attacked tribal spiritual beliefs, leaving "deep scars within the (tribal) community." The Indian office's efforts were in concert with the church's efforts: since 1883 it had urged tribal courts (in which judges were appointed by reservation agents) to prohibit the Sun Dance and other ceremonies.[42]

The courts were successful at some agencies but not at the Wind River. But Father Prendergast, superior of the mission at St. Stephen's, prohibited Wind River Catholics from taking part in these ceremonies during the 1940s and, according to a Jesuit historian, withheld sacraments from those who did take part. Interviewees for this book remembered that if they took part in the Sun Dance, St. Stephen's priests would excommunicate them and even deny funeral rites for their children. At the same time each of the mission schools, hungry for students with their $125 per year federal government payments, did what they could to recruit and retain the students.[43]

The Catholic and Episcopal missions developed an antagonistic competition. The Catholics found the "large number" of Catholic students enrolled in St. Michael's to be "a thorn in our side." The Episcopalians complained that "gross intimidation" was being used on Arapaho families to urge their re-baptism in the Catholic Church. A Catholic priest in a half admission responded claiming there had been "no unfair methods, no intimidations other than the warning any zealous priest may give as occasion seems to demand." He questioned the validity of baptisms "conferred by a protestant minister."[44]

The methods used at St. Stephen's Mission only alienated its students. Bernadine Friday (1932–2009) described how for speaking their own language, students were hit hard on the hands with a ruler or a paddle in staccato blows, "and then they'd take us upstairs to the dormitory and make us kneel down. It was really hard to be afraid all the time—to speak or anything." Nelson White (b. 1939) was kept at St. Stephen's Mission for months at a time from age seven. He began school "without a word of English," and the teachers could not speak Arapaho. The children of mixed marriages, known as "the breeds," provided translation. The nuns ignored or dismissed Nelson's cultural ways.[45]

The parents of Nelson White and his brother Crawford (b. 1942) lived near Ethete, but the brothers' grandparents lived in the St. Stephen's area, so they were enrolled at St. Stephen's. Crawford seemed particularly anguished at his parents' decision: "I don't understand why my parents sent us over there. I never understood that." But his parents had five children in their one-room log house, and when his aunt was killed in a car accident, seven more came to live with them.[46]

Crawford and Nelson were at Nelson's home with Nelson's wife Bonnie when I arrived to photograph them. Crawford seemed in a stern mood and I was nervous anyway; the lighting was poor under shade trees' sprinklings of shade or in the open sun, where everyone had to squint. I did not notice until the photograph of Crawford was developed that the gold stitching on his wool baseball cap said "Purple Heart—Combat Wounded," a painful reminder of the war that overlay the early pain of deprivation and the struggle to survive.

Indian education was above all intended to teach Indians to be self-supporting. It was Congress that set a precedent for the "proper care, support, and education" of Indian students to be given "in exchange for their labor," as was done in an "outing system" at the Indian Industrial School in Carlisle, Pennsylvania. Nelson and Crawford rose at 4:30 a.m. to do various assigned chores—that is, to feed hogs, milk cows, can vegetables, cut ice blocks from the river, or mop the floor—all under the threat of going to Hell if they failed to pray each morning in the church. Conversion failed. Today Nelson, a deeply spiritual Arapaho man, is "Keeper of the Pipe," the Flat Pipe being the Arapahos' most sacred object.[47]

Teachers used paddles and belts to punish students in off-reservation schools during those years, but Nelson White described teachers who had "different kinds of whips"—they administered severe beatings with long strips of rubber tire tube tied on a wood handle. Crawford described being beaten with a rubber hose and whacked on the head with

4. Crawford White, 2009. Photograph by author.

a ruler. Gerald Sage (1938–2012) and Hubert Friday (b. 1936) in a panel discussion described the same abusive punishment except that besides students being beaten with the hose on the back or legs, a barber's strap was also used at St. Michael's. Elder Burton Hutchinson (1929–2011) in a separate interview, pointed out that their coach, "Coach Wilson," who "came and taught us football and basketball," was also their teacher and barber. Panel members pointed out, "He's the one who used to do the 'whippin.' Used to call him 'Rubber Hose Wilson.'"[48]

The abusive treatment may have heightened the anger against and competitiveness with whites. Coach Wilson began the long tradition of winning streaks for Wyoming Indian basketball. "We beat Riverton, we beat Lander and all of the schools around here," said Starr Weed (1918–2015), team member at the Fort Washakie government school. They were team members in school as well. Hutchinson described the students' secret comradeship: when they sat out on the grass, "We'd all speak Arapaho (laughter).—We just had to watch our teachers. They come by you have to talk English."[49]

Elder interviewee Caroline Goggles (1930–2014; her surname Iron Eyes was converted to Goggles at the Carlisle Indian Industrial School) told about a nun from St. Stephen's who, in contrast to the abusive Coach Wilson, kept track of children after they left the mission and gave them rides to the Lander high school. Caroline added that when Indian students were concerned about the registration fees, the nun said, "Don't worry about it" and paid the fees herself. Caroline gave the nun's name and place of origin, "Sister Marian from the East," and recognized her as a "good person" who had the central Arapaho virtue of "pity."[50]

But Caroline's experience was generally the same as that of the others; she too was prohibited from speaking her home language at St. Michael's. She recalled that when youths reached the age of sixteen years, "You couldn't get those kids to go to school." Verna Thunder (b. 1927) mentioned her despair and loneliness at St. Michael's several times:

Sunday evenings we would come back. Kids would be cryin'. The younger ones would be cryin'. It would be awfully lonely—on Sunday evenings. I still think about those times on Sunday evenings. I used to just dread Sunday evenings when we'd have to come back to the school. And some things still come to me. The things we were forbidden to do or when I think about them, it makes me sad. My older sisters went there too. I guess it was similar.[51]

The powerful hands of a dominant and foreign society placed these young children in institutions with no semblance of home and no arms to be held by except those of another child—perhaps in sleep. Schools run by Native people would have provided a familiar language, food, and the smiles and laughter of community where the children would have been comfortable and better able to learn.

Six-year-old Bernadine Friday (1932–2009) was so desperate to leave St. Stephen's that she walked in her sleep out of the dormitory room and down the stairs dreaming that she was running home. She described her first day's experience as follows:

> They took me over there and I didn't know. We left the house and they took me up to the mission. . . . Took me up there on the wagon, my grandpa and grandma, and then when that sister came and that lady—she was interpreter—she was talkin' Arapaho . . . and then grabbed my hand. She said "we're goin' into the other room" and so we went into that next room and then, then my grandpa and my grandma left, I guess. When I came back out they were gone. I start lookin' for them and here they, they told 'em to go on 'cause I would be crying. I cried anyway. I tried to get away but then— kept me there. . . .
>
> After they did that well the next day they, uh, started cleaning me up and I had long hair and long braids and here they cut my hair real short and then they went and changed my clothes too. I had long squaw dress on and then, they put slippers on me and little short dress and then when my grandma came back she seen how I looked and she got mad 'cause you know we're not supposed to cut our hair. . . . At night when we'd go to bed a bunch of kids would be cryin' in that dormitory wantin' to go home but we were all in that dormitory.

Bernadine and her cousin managed to sneak out of the school and run home many times by way of a ditch. Her father wanted them to stay home, but he and her grandmother were warned by a cousin: "'If you don't send these kids to school, you're goin' to jail. They're goin' to put you in jail' . . . so then we'd have to go back and when we got back to the school we'd get punished again."[52]

The harm done by the boarding schools can hardly be overstated. Native people remain bitter over seeing the culture of their home community completely discounted. And the fact that boarding school personnel were unable to understand or translate their language is the likely groundwork of schoolroom difficulties that Native American children have to this day. They carry forward generation by generation the damage done by the pain of the early absence of family and home language along with the abuse (including sexual, as is now admitted by the Jesuits) in the schools. They had adequate cause to reject non-Indian schools altogether. But as Anderson points out in *The Four Hills of Life*, the Arapaho tribe, like others, had observed since first contacts with whites the need to appropriate their powers of literacy so as to deal with them.[53] They also needed schools of their own to carry forth identity, culture, and expression of their values.

New laws and intentions for assimilation made for stark shifts in experience for many more Native students in the mid-twentieth century. Congress passed two "Impact Aid" supplemental Johnson O'Malley Act laws in 1950. Impact Aid provided school construction and operating funds to districts that schooled students who lived on non-taxable land (military or reservation). Congress's intent was that more reservation children would be prepared to attend the local town schools—such as at Lander and Riverton.[54]

You might have found several Arapaho boys sitting in the Noble Hotel lobby asleep if you were looking for lodging in Lander on a late winter's night in the 1950s. Harold Del Monte, owner of the Noble Hotel, the best hotel in Lander, was sympathetic to the reservation people and allowed the boys to stay there without question. He had gone with Elders and Council members to Washington where a white man could be of use in getting the attention of congressional representatives in the 1940s. It was a good thing that Del Monte was sympathetic; the school left basketball players from the reservation area to fend for themselves without transportation after athletic activities or games. Gerald ("Jerry") Sage described it this way, "We slept, but sitting up—just to get to play ball." The situation confirmed feelings about his status: "By the time we went to high school we were sort of ashamed of being Indian from what they (at St. Michael's Mission) taught us. When we did something they didn't like they would say, 'White people don't do that.' . . . They pushed us toward the White ways. We called it 'white-washed.'"[55]

But Arapaho standards are higher than white standards in some matters; the Arapaho consider either playing with food or using foul language to be a disgrace. Jerry and his friends once walked into the Lander high school cafeteria and discovered "they were using rough language. (Another time) they were having a food fight! We could never do something like that!"[56]

Sage attended an out-of-state high school before going to Lander, as did many others. He first attended Hare Episcopal Mission in Mission, South Dakota. He became lonely for his parents and ran away soon after arriving. His parents came to find him, and once they did, "There was no way I was going to let them go without me coming back."[57] That is how he came to enroll at Lander's Fremont County Vocational High School (FCVHS), as it was then named. He lived more than fifteen miles from Lander.

Language difficulties did not matter as much in athletics as in academics, and Native American boys could find some joy in taking part in basketball. They stayed and played and after the early afternoon games, they hitchhiked home. Sometimes government workers stopped for them along the long and narrow road to Fort Washakie. Forrest Stone (1927–2003), FCVHS student and son of the Wind River Reservation superintendent (1935–44), described it: "During the war years, gas was at a premium. Government cars would give a ride. Don't know if that was permissible but with transportation being scarce we did it, I know."[58]

Native American reservation residents Darwin (1933–2010) and Sandra St. Clair (1936–2005) spotted reservation boys hitchhiking home from the Lander high school one spring day in the late 1960s. Chester Armajo and Jerry Brown often walked or ran back to the reservation. Sandra explained, "They had just won the conference championship for cross-country for Lander high school and they were getting ready to go to state, which they eventually won, but anyway they were having to hitchhike home." The St. Clairs gave them a ride, beginning a frequent afternoon pastime.[59]

The in-school library presented another problem that sometimes involved long walks for rural students. It was small and limited. Students who lived in town used the town's library after hours for more complicated projects, but that was not possible for the reservation students. Caroline Goggles said they were permitted to go there during their study hour. They had to hurry: "Three of us would run down there." I questioned her about the long run and she laughed and added: "You had to walk fast anyway!" Caroline attended FCVHS from 1944 through 1948 and raised several successful professional and political leaders on the Wind River Reservation, but she herself never graduated.[60]

A privately owned bus dropped students off at their homes after regular school hours and picked them up in the mornings if they lived on the main road to Ethete. The rest had to be at the Ethete crossroads to meet the bus. Vera Trosper (1948–2011), Wyoming Indian High School secretary, explained in 2006, "The guy that owned the bus lived there at the gas station—in a trailer. Clark Heinrich. That's why we had to go down there in the morning to catch the bus." The bus "had a little stove with a pipe" for ventilation.[61]

The generation before Vera's also rode the Heinrich bus, sometimes driven by Clark's father, John Heinrich, and sometimes by his trailer live-in Sam Harisawa, the son of a Japanese reservation resident, Bill Harisawa. Caroline Goggles said that it was believed the government had relocated the elder Harisawa with his family to the large northern Wyoming "internment" camp, Heart Mountain, during World War II. The Harisawas settled on the reservation where they made a living farming after the war. And thus American refugees, robbed of everything, found a home with those who shared their fate.[62]

The Lander school did not make the bus with its little stove available to Native American athletes after school, but students from Lander appreciated their basketball skills. Gerald Sage pointed out, "We had white girl friends." Only their parents and sometimes the white boys objected. Hubert Friday (named to the Alumni Hall of Fame in 2004 and holder of several Lander all-time records), still handsome in his seventies, explained: "But the bad part is, the girl liked me, you know, and I'd take 'em to the show and dance but her mother . . . when I'd take her home, the parents say, 'I don't want you to see my daughter no more.'" Gerald Sage interjected, "The kids themselves really weren't that prejudiced." The women also remembered that friendships between Indian high school girls and the town girls in the mid-1940s were usually positive.[63]

It was adult prejudice that closed the doors. Hubert Friday, Wyoming's Outstanding Athlete in 1956, reported, "I had a lot of offers—Montana State, Iowa State, Kansas, BYU, but (to go there) I had to join the church, and UCLA. The assistant coach (from the University of Wyoming) came out and had me sign." However Friday went to Laramie two weeks before school started and the head coach "wouldn't talk to me," and the assistant coach told him that he had to go to a junior college. Most of his adult life, Friday, for fear of humiliation, "never told nobody, I just kept it to myself."[64] He went to Northwest Community College in Powell, Wyoming, and came back to work in several roles at the elementary school near Ethete.

The BIA asked the tribes "to accept state jurisdiction" over reservation schools in the mid-1950s when termination of BIA services seemed imminent. The Shoshone General Council did so. The Arapaho, long dissatisfied with their children's education, had through their General Council in 1946 requested that the superintendent of the reservation and the commissioner of Indian Affairs "provide public schools for Arapahoe children at the earliest possible date." Wyoming was able to tax reservation corporate income and equipment (not reservation land values) "for support of public schools" once the tribes gave permission to the state to put public schools on the reservation. The legislature passed this means of raising revenue in the 29th legislative session, and voters ratified the bill in 1948.[65] The passage of decades did not alleviate for Native Americans the significance of the state's use of reservation income.

The potential for tribal employment was a double-edged sword for the Arapahos from the beginning of the termination period. They took control of hiring managers for their 383,500-acre ranch from the BIA in 1951. The manager was then likely to hire tribal labor. As a result of the improved economic conditions, the Wind River tribes were among those identified for "termination" in 1954—they were deemed capable of using tribal or private resources to pay for services long held as a federal responsibility. Congressional proposals and legislation for a policy of termination (urged by proponents for Indian assimilation) presented a huge threat to Indian people. Their lands would be no different than any others, taxed by local entities. As a corollary to "termination" the BIA's "Branch of Relocation" aided removal of thousands of tribal people to urban areas. The tribes sent English-speaking Council members Nell Scott and Robert Harris as their representatives to Washington DC.[66]

The tribes' faith in Councilwoman Scott to deal with Congress was well deserved. English was her only language; she, like the first Friday, could well mediate for her people. And she, a "half-breed," was an "educated Indian," able to deal with whites but loyal to basic Indian values. Showing that she was brave, she was a trainer of a wild moose named Nancy that she and her husband often took to rodeos for its performances. However, she said that the key to their success in Washington was much "cry(ing) on the shoulders" of congressmen. There they put a stop to Congress's application of the national policy of termination to their people. The poorly educated condition of Wind River people provided the argument that halted their termination and allowed their survival.[67]

The amazing courage of these Council people was only the surface manifestation of the determination held by the Wind River tribal people to regain control over their lives. They had never succumbed in spirit to military defeat. This chapter has documented several tribal strategies that protected their cultures—internal continuance for each and an alliance of the two, collaboration with a church, and use of the white world's education—strategies that remained alive and continued to serve as models in the 1970s. Tribal people across the country had never given up their deeply felt need to establish actionable control—self-determination for their peoples through their schools.

2

Self-Determination

A Twentieth-Century Use for the Schools

The Society of American Indians was the first national pan-Indian organization, its members known as "the red progressives." The society used "self-determination" as a slogan during the years of progressivism and reform of the early 1920s. A century of oppression by the dominant society gave the phrase a profound and generalized meaning. However, the reformist concepts soon gave way to internal tribal loyalties and external pressures. Federal policy of the 1930s under the Indian Affairs Commissioner Collier at least encouraged "limited powers of self-government," but the strength of the concept of self-determination was impeded by the division of reservations into factions, a world war, and the 1950s congressional press for termination.[1] It did not resurface again politically until the 1960s. Then it gained an explicit focus when Native Americans began to take over their schools. National civil rights struggles culminated in Supreme Court, congressional, and presidential actions that, intentional or not, generated strength for this Native American cause.

The struggle for civil rights had intensified in the 1950s. Both African Americans and Native Americans fought injustice, inequality, and racial discrimination but with strikingly different objectives. African Americans, plagued by the racist exploitation of the "separate but equal" ruling in *Plessy v. Ferguson* (1896), sought integration into white facilities, including the schools. Native Americans, who had been fighting integration into white culture through the schools for decades, fought for separation. In 1954 the Supreme Court ruled in *Brown v. Board of Education of Topeka* that when states provide education for children, that education must be "available to all on equal terms."[2] This phrase, "available to all on equal terms," later proved to be central to Wind River legal arguments.

However, that decision was far removed from the day to day problems encountered by Wyoming's Native Americans, who in the 1950s still had no sewer or water treatment and were afflicted with unchecked communicable diseases. In an interview for this book, Arapaho tribal member Caroline Goggles (1930–2014) remembered the time when there still was "no piped water" on the Wind River Reservation, let alone television. She stated quietly, "We were too poor."[3]

The 1960s saw the development of militant Indian advocacy. The National Congress of American Indians was an "outspoken advocate" of Indian rights early in the 1960s, as described by Francis Paul Prucha in *The Great Father*. Other Indian advocacy organizations amplified Indian demands for self-determination. One, the National Indian Youth Council, gained publicity for Indian rights in "fish-ins" in Washington State in 1964. The pan-Indian occupation and seizure of Alcatraz at the end of the decade succeeded in gaining even more publicity and sympathy for their cause. One well-publicized story was that the Native Americans (many of them students in the area) made a facetious offer: "to buy (the island) for $24 worth of beads." The ongoing struggle for justice by African American and other disadvantaged minority groups energized that of the Native Americans. They needed reforms at the national level to achieve ordinary rights and greater control over their lives. The federal government's trust responsibilities appeared to validate the fight to protect tribal assets and resources, but government paternalism at times jeopardized self-determination (see chapter 7). The National Tribal Chairman's Association asserted that trust responsibilities were intended to *prevent* "further erosion of tribal sovereignty." Native American activists saw trust responsibilities as including "education, health care, and other social services." The legal representative for the Department of the Interior did not.[4]

The years of effort by activists led to the drafting of the Civil Rights Act in 1964 under President John F. Kennedy. The legislation endured a record-breaking filibuster after Kennedy was assassinated but was finally passed under President Lyndon B. Johnson's leadership. In the Elementary and Secondary Education Act the next year (1965) Congress allocated Title I funds for disadvantaged children, including Indian children who lived on or off reservations.[5]

The Rev. Martin Luther King Jr. implored the holders of power for equality for all underclasses when he delivered his "I Have a Dream" speech to a quarter of a million people gathered at the Washington Monument in 1963. Life was lived "on a lonely island of poverty in the midst of a vast ocean of material prosperity" in American Indian as well as in African American homes; these brown-skinned minority peoples were "still languishing in the corners of American society . . . exile(s) in (their) own land."[6]

Plains Indians, like African Americans, were known for their "burning eloquence" and valued oral tradition into contemporary times:

> [It was] '66, '68 when the Martin Luther King era became nationally televised—with TV in every home by now, with his making speeches about civil rights . . . at the base of Washington Monument, about him having his dream. And about the same time everyone in America has that in mind. So civil rights is prime time. So about that time we start making our way into this capital, our nation's capital. And then we voice our concerns and it is difficult to really convince anyone because we are a small minority.[7]

The American Indian Movement (AIM) was founded in 1968 to help Native Americans living in Minneapolis–Saint Paul. The movement soon spread to other distressed Indian urban areas and to reservations, where AIM became widely known for its 1973 occupation of Wounded Knee on the Pine Ridge Indian Reservation. AIM leaders chose Wounded Knee, the site of a devastating massacre in 1890, as a symbolic site to "dramatize their opposition to the BIA (Bureau of Indian Affairs) and their demand for self-determination and a return of tribal sovereignty," as described by Colin Calloway in *First Peoples*. Their efforts gained national media attention, although Lakota philosopher/historian Vine Deloria Jr. criticized them for not resolving deeper issues—perhaps too much to ask. AIM did gain public awareness of their plight. According to Calloway, AIM "demonstrated dramatically that Indian-U.S. relations would continue to be marked by conflict as long as American society encroached on Indian resources and denied Indian rights."[8]

President Johnson addressed Congress regarding Native Americans and Alaskan Natives just as AIM was founded. He spoke of the indigenous peoples as "the forgotten Americans" and emphasized their right to "self-determination."[9]

Some six months before Johnson's 1968 speech Senators George McGovern, Robert F. Kennedy, and Walter F. Mondale initiated a study of Indian education. Kennedy headed the study's subcommittee. The subcommittee's purpose was to "examine, investigate and make a complete study of any and all matters pertaining to the education of Indian children." The study, *Indian Education: A National Tragedy—A National Challenge*, which became known as the Kennedy Report, took two years. Senator Wayne Morse of Oregon took over after the assassination of Senator Robert Kennedy in June 1968, until January 1969, when Senator Edward Kennedy became chairman.

The report's focus on education—its purpose being central to U.S. assimilationist policy—was of key importance. Margaret Connell Szasz, in *Education and the American Indian: The Road to Self-Determination since 1928*, summed up the report as follows: "The Kennedy Report was as grave a censure of federal Indian policy as the nation had ever witnessed. Perhaps the fact that many of its recommendations had been made in the Meriam Report some forty years earlier guided the extraordinarily negative conclusions that it drew. It concluded that the 'dominant policy of the Federal Government towards the American Indian has been one of coercive assimilation,' and that this policy 'has had disastrous effects on the education of Indian children.'"[10]

The report included a four-part summary, beginning with the policy of "coercive assimilation." The subcommittee stated in part 1 that this policy had resulted in:

A. The destruction and disorganization of Indian communities and individuals.
B. A desperately severe and self-perpetuating cycle of poverty for most Indians.
C. The growth of a large, ineffective, and self-perpetuating bureaucracy which retards the elimination of Indian poverty.
D. A waste of federal appropriations.

An important finding was that the national policy of assimilation had left the nation "massively uninformed and misinformed about the American Indian, and his past and present." Such misinformation alone had created "prejudice, racial intolerance, and discrimination towards Indians far more widespread and serious than generally recognized."[11] The third section of the report was focused on the "disastrous effects" of U.S. policy on Native American education:

A. The classroom and the school becoming a kind of battleground where the Indian child attempts to protect his integrity and identity as an individual by defeating the purposes of the school.
B. Schools which fail to understand or adapt to, and in fact often denigrate, cultural differences.
C. Schools which blame their own failures on the Indian student and reinforce his defensiveness.
D. Schools which fail to recognize the importance and validity of the Indian community. The community and child have retaliated by treating the school as an alien institution.
E. The dismal record of absenteeism, dropouts, negative self-image, low achievement, and, ultimately, academic failure for many Indian children.
F. A perpetuation of the cycle of poverty which undermines the success of all other federal programs.

The final part of the report concluded that the causes of all of these failures had been the "continuous desire to exploit, and expropriate, Indian land and physical resources" as well as a "self-righteous intolerance of tribal communities and cultural differences."[12]

The Kennedy Report was instrumental in encouraging the Wyoming Wind River Native American project for Indian control of their schools that had already been initiated. There were a total of sixty recommendations, among them that the curriculum of predominantly Indian schools "include substantial information about Indian culture and history and factual material about contemporary Indian life." The report also recommended that teachers be trained in the "native language of their Indian students" and that the parents of Indian students be involved and given "an important voice—both at the national and local levels. Whenever Indian tribes express the desire, assistance and training should be provided to permit them to operate their own schools under contract." A result of the report was that it became more difficult to ignore parents who showed up at Senate office doors. "The 1969 Report of the Special Senate Subcommittee became the single most important contemporary document in Indian education, and so it remains," wrote the Wyoming Indian project's attorney, Michael P. Gross, in 1978.[13]

The 1934 Johnson-O'Malley Act (JOM), perhaps inadvertently, provided the legal rationale for Indian control of schools on the Wind River and other reservations; it gave authority to the secretary of the interior, "at his discretion, to enter into a contract or contracts" with states, territories, or "through the qualified agencies of such State or Territory," to provide Indian education and various other medical, agricultural, and social services. Therefore JOM contracts could be made through the BIA *with other entities*. As Arapaho tribal member William C'Hair said, the JOM Act was "the only avenue open until the Indian Self-Determination and Educational Assistance Act was passed" in 1975 (discussed in chapter 9).[14] Tribal people carefully studied and used the JOM Act; after its passage, schools were established on some reservations and the hope for "self-determination" was kept alive on others.

Native Americans first established BIA and Office of Economic Opportunity (OEO) "demonstration project" schools in the mid-1960s. The Navajos established a bilingual/bicultural demonstration project at Lukachukai, Arizona, which they relocated to Rough Rock, New Mexico. There it became the Rough Rock Demonstration School in 1966, "the first Native controlled school in modern times." It set precedent for Native Americans to manage funds directly provided from the OEO and the BIA. The Pima Tribe established a pre-K to third grade BIA school on the Gila River Indian Reservation at Blackwater, Arizona, in the 1960s, with a local school board, but without "formal budgetary, planning or policy-setting control." The Navajos founded a second school at Ramah, New Mexico, in 1970 using the Rough Rock model. This was the first tribally administered school system since the 1890s to offer a high school. It was established with OEO, BIA, and private funding.[15]

While, according to Szasz, tribal efforts for self-determination in education "appear to have been centered in the Southwest," the movement in actuality "was spread across the country." The initial projects were summer programs in central Washington State aimed at remediation and college preparation for Yakama students who were dealing with cultural barriers to their progress; one project for the Yakama was a cultural recovery program in a public school. In the Olympic Mountains of western Washington, Quinault students learned about their culture, including arts and crafts; in California, "many small groups of Indians" fought textbook battles that were finally won in the courts; in Montana the Blackfeet added their history to the curriculum; Maine's Indian Department of Education added the Independent International Indian High School in 1970. The high school drew its student body from thirty-five reservations where populations totaled 20,000. The Cree and Chippewa tribes at Rocky Boy Reservation in Montana also managed to gain board control of their school in 1970, a school on their reservation that had previously been controlled by the school board of a town thirty miles away. Aided by their congressional delegation, they supported their school with grants from the Department of Health, Education and Welfare and the BIA until 1971, when Impact Aid money provided more permanent funding.[16]

The Miccosukee, a tribe of some five hundred individuals in the Florida Everglades, took over all of their existing BIA services in May 1971, including a school, with the help of their tribal chairman Tiger Buffalo, attorney Bobo Dean, and Micmac tribal member and BIA official Alexander McNabb. This school was in its infancy with only two grades; the Miccosukee majority had rejected "white man's education" until the late 1960s. Three other tribal communities were working for Indian control in 1971: the Northern Cheyennes in Busby, Montana, the Oglala Sioux on the Pine Ridge Indian Reservation, and the Navajos at Rock Point in Arizona.[17]

Congress passed an amendment to the Impact Aid legislation in 1972 that provided additional funding for local (often non-reservation) elementary and secondary schools in order to meet the "special educational needs" of Native American children, prompting border town attention to maintaining Native American enrollment.[18] However, a few reservation schools continued to be established.

The Navajos elected their own school board in 1972 and gained administrative control of the Rock Point elementary boarding school with a government contract in 1973. The Northern Cheyennes took control of the Busby School, a boarding school, in 1972. On the Wind River Indian Reservation, Ethete, Fort Washakie, and Arapaho parents had begun seeking solutions to their school dilemmas in 1967. They knew they faced a long, if not impossible journey; they were surrounded by communities hungry for their federal funds and politically armed with rhetoric against Indian control. Wind River Indians needed to show irrefutable evidence of their capacity to manage a school if they were to be trusted with its control. The Wind River Shoshone and Arapaho Education Association published a "Fact Sheet" in April 1971 that described the need for an Indian-controlled school and the steps already taken. The publication argued for an "independent school . . . (with) a democratically chosen school board" and enumerated failures in the local public schools, where there was "lack of Indian control." They and many other tribes were in agreement on this matter. Indian control of Indian education, often infused with Indian culture and language, had become a national movement, inseparable from the concept of self-determination.[19] The Nixon administration apparently knew about the indigenous sentiment for self-determination and began using this for its own goal, assimilation.

Those who were in charge of assimilation of the indigenous peoples seemed to believe that Indian objections to white-style education might dissipate if their state-run schools were administered by American Indian school boards—with the appearance of American Indian control. But state oversight of content and teaching processes could eventually erode away all knowledge of tribal history and culture. The Indians' feeling for the land of their ancestors would lose its meaning.

Richard Nixon used "self-determination" in a proposal that implied his support for the efforts that were being made to establish the Indian schools mentioned. Nixon's "Special Message to the Congress on Indian Affairs" on July 8, 1970, laid out broad hopes for "self-determination without termination." He gave an unprecedented show of understanding throughout the entirety of his message: "We must make it clear that Indians can become independent of Federal control without being cut off from Federal concern and Federal support."[20]

However, Nixon did not propose true autonomy in Indian schools, even in his most pro-education statements. He proposed that Johnson O'Malley funds go directly to local schools to be used for Indian students or to the Indian school districts *where their school boards functioned like other school boards* "throughout the nation"; in other words, under control by the state (see Castile's discussion following).[21] Nixon's proposal led to confusion and conflict about the administrative control of Indian education as well as its financing: would Indian funds, such as JOM money or money from taxation of local resources, be used for state-controlled education?

George P. Castile pointed out that "self-determination," as described by Nixon, was only a shift to Native American *control of some of the administrative functions*, a shift toward the "limited 'autonomy' characteristic of ethnic relations in many socialist nations." Roxanne Dunbar Ortiz and others suggested that self-determination was used as a distraction by Nixon, a "less threatening" issue than were the "anti-war and Black liberation movements," although Ortiz also noted that the attention thereby gained for self-determination could "broaden" its political effects. But apparently Nixon's policy advocates believed that a shift to Indian control, with financial resources doled out conditionally, would be the most expedient way to erode Native American resistance to melding into the larger society—an "enlightened social policy" in Indian affairs.[22]

Nixon and his speech writers appeared to attempt to appease his base by proposing complicated, little understood but life changing policy in areas other than Indian education. He introduced one little known policy change by explaining at length a "conflict of interest" between certain government authorities (the Departments of Interior and Justice) and the tribes. This he followed with the proposal for an Indian Trust Counsel Authority, "to assure independent legal representation for the Indians' natural resource rights," *to be governed by presidential appointees.*[23] The president would surely have less control with the Departments of Interior and Justice standing in the middle.

Nixon's proposal to return the sacred Blue Lake lands to the Taos Pueblo Indians in New Mexico (lands that had been taken to create a national forest) is better known. This he portrayed as "an important symbol of this government's responsiveness to just grievances," which indeed they were. But in the same speech Nixon urged that for the sake of "economic development," ninety-nine-year leases on tribal lands be available "for commercial, industrial and recreational development." Elected tribal council members might feel pressured to lease the land in circumstances of extreme need; in 1970 the average annual income of families on 80 percent of reservations was $1,500. Nixon pointed out that his proposed leases would be better than selling the land outright, certainly an undesirable comparison.[24] Ninety-nine-year leases to out-side entities would likely force families, multiplied by the third or fourth generations, off the reservations. Such leases could have accomplished all that the infamous Dawes Act had sought.

President Nixon's definitions of "Indian self-determination" along with his land proposals would seem to have kept huge constituencies and powerful congressional leaders happy.[25] But his banner message, that of "self-determination" for Indians, seems to have gone too far for his political friends. Even the ostensibly less threatening educational issues proved to be a problem for Nixon's base (see chapter 4).

Nixon's first venture into Native American policy might well stand out among all of the other instances of deviousness for which he became infamous. However, his apparently magnanimous attitude toward Indians served his political purposes; they were a very small minority in the United States, less than half of one percent in 1990, when larger minority groups were seeking change. American Indians were certainly skeptical of any political promise, but in this case they accepted the "gift" of a slogan that they already owned, turned it around, and used it themselves. As Castile said, sometimes being used as a symbol can itself be used.[26]

The Shoshones and Arapahos were already active on the Wind River Indian Reservation working for self-determination in their children's schools by the time of Nixon's speech. The following chapter shows those beginnings.

3

Why the Wind River People Wanted a School

Late 1960s

Tribal protests concerned local and regional conflicts until events of the civil rights movement in the 1960s. Then Native Americans began to work to put an end the government's assimilationist policies and establish self-determination in education. This brought unity. Arapaho tribal member Ben Friday Jr. (1933–2003), a foreman for U.S. Steel and a uranium surface mine worker in Riverton, Wyoming, was one of the organizers on the Wind River Indian Reservation at Ethete.[1]

I met "Jr. Ben," as he was called by his family, at his home in Ethete in 2001. There the receding autumn light angled across and warmed the deep blue and red furnishings of their living and dining room. A family member had told me that he had cancer but still I was taken aback to see how weak and thin he was. The illness appeared to be no hindrance to him. He gave me the gentle Arapaho handshake and, with a smile, offered a comfortable chair. There I heard about the political strife involved in establishing an Indian school: "Those are the years I hate to think about. Often we were up until 3:00 a.m. In '66 to '67 everything was going on." I met Caroline Goggles (1930–2014) a few weeks later. She also welcomed me into her home along Blue Sky Highway. She was frail and became blind over the years of our acquaintance. But from the beginning she was cheerful and wanted to tell me how the struggle began: "We had no facilities so we asked Saint Michael's." The small mission sanctuary built with large pieces of stone from their mountains was at the center of the sprawling Ethete area. It proved to be there for their use. Ben Friday Jr. was a member of Saint Michael's Episcopal Mission and keeper of the books.[2]

I also met Alberta Friday (b. 1931) early in the development of this project. She was a Shoshone/Bannock member of the Shoshone Fort Washakie school board and a teacher of Arapaho children at a Mill Creek elementary school in the 1950s. She remembered Elder Theresa White Wolf, who "never missed a meeting," along with the other people from Ethete village (a condensed area of government housing) who walked a considerable distance through winter's snow to be at the St. Michael's meetings. Alberta pointed out that the stereotype is that "Indians are not interested in education [but in fact] they saw it as the one way to improve their children's future."[3]

One of the first things that brought the Wind River tribal people's attention to their schools was an attempt by white teachers to "reorganize" the Indian school money for the purpose of providing their own children with three separate schools. According to Ben Friday Jr., "The educated ones fought back."[4]

Ethete became the center for much of the Arapahos' cultural and political life during the 1950s. St. Stephen's and Arapahoe near Riverton, known as "Lower Arapahoe," had served as a subagency to Fort Washakie, nearly thirty miles distant. The distribution of allotments in the early 1900s encouraged some of the Arapahos to move westward. Then as cars replaced trains, Ethete became more convenient as a tribal center, not far from the Shoshones' Fort Washakie; each was about sixteen miles from Lander. And being physically closer to the Shoshones than was Lower Arapahoe, Ethete was in a better position to establish relationships with them and with their white relatives. As a prime example, anthropologist Jeffrey D. Anderson described Ben Friday Sr., or Chief Friday, who lived in his camp near Fort Washakie, as a "transculturalized Arapaho." Paradoxically, Ethete's strength also came from its strong traditional identity; in the 1960s the Sun Dance grounds were permanently established there. The Episcopal Mission encouraged Arapaho religious practices. The religions, in contemporary terms, had an "interfaith alliance"; attendees took part in the ceremonies of each system at religious events. As a result, some from St. Stephen's shifted their allegiance to the Ethete Episcopal Church. In short, Ethete was a natural for the emergence of reservation political activism in the 1960s concerning the schools. As Chippewa tribal member Jerome Buckanaga wrote in 1978, "The education of Indian children has never been above politics. People who argue that schools are not political institutions do not follow school board elections, attend meetings, and probably have never tried to bring substantial changes to a school."[5]

As stated in chapter 1, Ethete was in the Mill Creek Public School District 14, which was an elementary district, like the others in the predominantly Indian areas on the reservation. The other two Indian districts were centered at Fort Washakie (District 21) and at Arapahoe (District 38). There were other reservation districts (see map), but these were predominantly or politically non-Indian in their makeup. Indian children of high school age often attended the nearest high schools: Mill Creek and Fort Washakie students were nearest to Lander, and Arapaho students were nearest to Riverton. Otherwise, as described later, they went to boarding schools or to no school at all.

Ben Friday Jr. ran for election to the Mill Creek school board against non-Indian incumbent John Wunder in 1968, and won. Allison Sage Sr. (d. 1998) had for some time been on the board but with the checkerboard of white and Indian ownership of reservation land, this was the first time that the three-member Mill Creek school board had a Native American majority. The new board members worked well together, according to Friday, and decided to go to the Wyoming State Legislature to ask for a reservation high school. They were rebuffed with a discriminatory rationale: the legislature did not see the need to pay construction costs for a high school *on the reservation*. Friday remembered their finality: "They said we had no land, no building, no money. . . . 'Get land, buildings and money, then we'll talk to you about a school.'" The schools, after all, as Buckanaga put it, were usually "one of the chief instruments of domination used by the American society at large."[6]

Ben Jr. still felt the sting of the rejection in December 2002: "This is why

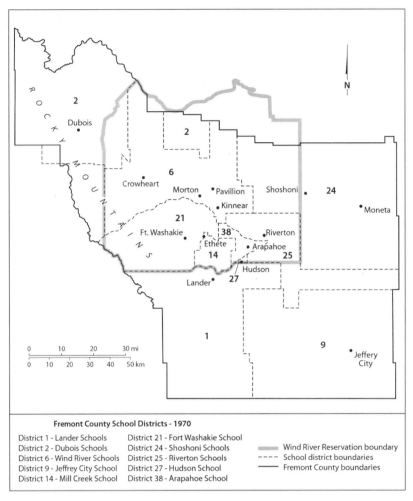

5. Fremont County, Wyoming, with school districts (1970) and Wind River Indian Reservation boundaries superimposed. Created by Bill Nelson Maps. District map located at State of Wyoming Archives, Cheyenne.

we were going to Washington—to get the money."[7] He died within weeks of telling me this. The evening before his death he was in a deep sleep; I was at his bedside with his family and a rancher from nearby. Crystalized moisture filled the sky and became a deep fuchsia over the mountains to the west in the narrow timeframe of dusk before dark. The family stood outside and tearfully watched the sky until darkness had fallen.

The operation of an Indian school would only be possible with federal money. The Arapahos were unemployed and underemployed, and as their population increased in the late 1960s, the meager oil and gas payments were unsteady or in decline. The tribes had little control over the leases made to national corporations—often mismanaged by the BIA. "Whenever there [was] a little gathering," angry discussions about "the Indians [not] getting any money," came up. Ben Friday Jr. had told me about these discussions that were a part of the early meetings about funding for the school. Congress did not pass a law until 1982 to establish oversight of this vast source of income to the tribes.[8]

Revenue payment rules divided the income in half between the tribes, but their numbers were uneven, which resulted in monthly payments that were lower for the individual Arapahos ($38 each in 1970) than for the Shoshones ($50 each). The Arapahos numbered 2,850, approximately 800 more than the Shoshones at that time; the total average overall income per person was approximately $107. They had begun directly receiving revenue payment of per capita incomes only eleven years earlier after an act of Congress. With a bemused smile, Ben Friday had told me, "It was all about money. There is hardly any money here."[9] The Ethete and Arapahoe school district per-student income was by far the lowest in the county.

Federal Native American educational funds across the nation flowed into the border town schools. The federal government sent the money to the states, which sent it to local districts, where the funds were placed in general budgets. Michael Gross wrote, "Indian children bring millions of federal dollars into public schools each year. Without these Indian dollars, many public schools would not be able to afford carpets in their libraries or fancy audio visual equipment." Yet, as another legal scholar, Daniel Rosenfelt, observed, there was a fallacious belief in the non-Indian population that Native Americans contributed nothing to the operation of the schools. He added that "disparities in educational programs" provided to Indians exceeded "most of the overt discrimination formerly practiced against blacks in the Deep South."[10]

Non-Indian encroachments on the Wind River Reservation separated the wealth of their districts from Indian populated areas and made for additional disparities. The wealthiest *on-reservation* district lay just some ten miles northeast of Ethete in the Riverton Reclamation Project (see chapter 1), where the mostly non-Indian settlements of Kinnear, Morton, and Pavillion lay. The tribal people who attended the late night meetings "wanted to have all the Indian reservation to be one district," according to Caroline Goggles, a means to solving the discrepancy problem. An early 1970s letter to the Elliott Foundation, in a plea for financial help, expresses the hope that "taxes taken off the reservation by the state be returned to us (the tribal community) so that we could run our own schools." A reservation school district could provide not only an Indian education but direct returns for the tribal community—jobs up and down the economic ladder.[11] This was true not only for the Ethete area but for St. Stephen's as well.

But the Indian people came to feel that it was unrealistic to expect to achieve a unified control of schools across the entire reservation; this idea was at a later point dropped. Any such effort would have brought statewide opposition. They were fighting an uphill battle as it was. William C'Hair of the St. Stephen's–Arapahoe area described their situation: "Very few people wanted to be involved. It was too dangerous. The feeling was: 'risky.' People felt it was too great a cause—un-accomplishable. We were howling at the moon."[12] However, local town attitudes about race, prevalent in their schools, could not be ignored.

Chris Goggles (1924–2001), a grandparent counselor at the high school, explained: "Prejudice was in the towns. So they would go away to boarding school or [their parents would] keep them home."[13]

Lander had not always been the quiet town described in chapter 1. A near riot had occurred less than one hundred years earlier when a Catholic priest from St. Stephen's Mission gave a "fatal sermon" on "the laws and obligations of marriage." He left Wyoming entirely after the sermon, and the town gained the reputation among the priests of being a "Hell Hole." It was a military outpost, Fort Auger, its unruly solders kept to remind the Indians of white control.[14]

Lander's history did not just lurk in the background. The ancestors of many whites of the area had passed down the blessings of their superiority easily and naturally. Thus an undercurrent of disrespect of American Indians was common in Lander in spite of its civilized and peaceful appearance.

A peak Lander event was its annual "One-Shot Antelope Hunt." The hunt was held in the field as antelope season opened. A participant would receive "the highest form of ridicule" if he missed his shot at the antelope, as described in the *Wyoming State Journal* (*WSJ*) of Lander. The rules required unsuccessful shooters to wear dresses and flowered shawls, a style combination often worn by elderly Shoshone and Arapaho women, and to "dance with the squaws." The "squaw dance," as it was called, involved the costumed hunters dancing with the women who had dressed them.[15]

Local residents greatly celebrated the hunters in banquets and newspaper stories. They were astronauts, governors, and business executives from across the region and beyond. The news placed much attention on the involvement of several Shoshone families, possibly to quiet any objections, and, justified the male-only hunting activities as "Indian tradition." In actuality the hunt began in 1939 or 1940 with the jesting of two white men. Indian families did not fail to notice the ridicule and implied contempt for their culture.[16]

Wind River parents feared Lander high school's "open campus" policy for the risks that it posed. The minority status of their children could make them vulnerable to fights or accusations in the town. The parents objected without effect.[17]

Those Indian people who pursued a higher education were outraged over the border town discrimination. The more distant *Casper Star-Tribune* (*CS-T*) reported on the situation as problematic in 1966. University of Wyoming student Iva St. Clair gave a statement that a paper submitted to the State Department of Education by Lander high school counselor Don Wolcott "attacked the Indians using everything from genetics to morals. . . . He contended that the Indian parents can't control their children, the children have no respect for their elders, and that the Indian families are permissive. This is the thinking of a man who handles every Indian entering the Lander schools."[18]

Wyoming Indian High School's social studies teacher, Pamela St. Clair Gambler (b. 1961), noted in 2006 that discrimination existed at the reservation's Black Mountain, a ranching area some fifty-seven miles north of Lander (twenty miles north of Crowheart). She was one of just a few Native Americans during her first years at the one-room Crowheart elementary school. "I didn't know I was different until I went to school. [There], I got hit on the back, if I did anything wrong, hand slapped or hit across the knuckles." And, even though her scores were the highest in the class, "I was never complimented."[19]

Other researchers found attitudes of prejudice across the region. Murray and Rosalie Wax described the classroom status for the Lakota (South Dakota) child in the early 1970s as being lower caste, causing psychological pain, avoidance, and inattention. These conditions, not to mention language and cultural differences, led teachers to assign them to low ability groups. Once students were thus classified, teachers identified the minority children with that ability level, maintaining the pariah status for the culture as a whole. The self-concept of Native American children decreased with number of years of schooling.[20]

Any "special attention" can create further shame in an environment that humiliates. Alberta Friday described a Lander school situation in which the student felt so demeaned by the process of being singled out for testing that when given test blocks to put in order, "he said he 'just moved them around' as if he was illiterate." Eventually his mother removed the boy from the Lander high school and sent him to Flandreau boarding school in South Dakota. In a second circumstance described by Friday, a boy who was enrolled in the Lander high school for four years did not pass a class. He finally dropped out and went to a boarding school, where he graduated after four more years.[21] There may be more to the story than this, but it seems that when he was in an environment that celebrated other cultural ways and never his own, he felt invisible or worthless and was unable to learn.

William C'Hair pointed out that children with disabilities were also misclassified: "And many of these children—some were handicapped, maybe not severely. Some, they needed a pair of glasses. . . . Some couldn't see the old-fashioned blackboards. Some of them might have a hearing impairment . . . and then these things were undetected . . . when they asked questions, when they asked for explanations or to repeat something, well they were made to feel as if they were stupid and so they just give up."[22]

Some students did not give up entirely. They left for out-of-state boarding schools. Sandra C'Bearing (b. 1954), who served for many years on the Wyoming Indian Schools' Board of Directors, told how as a Lander freshman student, "I used to sit in the back of the classroom. I would put up my hand, 'I know, I know,' but I never, never got called upon." It was the same for all Native American students, according to C'Bearing (an earlier reservation superintendent may have abbreviated the family surname "Coal Bearing" carelessly to "C'Bearing"). "We'd raise our hands and they'd never call on us."[23]

When teachers and students were choosing class officers, Sandra went to the class sponsor to say, "Yeah, I'd like to do that," but she was told: "We're having try-outs for the tiger [the class mascot]. You could try out for that. That way, no one could see you." Sandra told the sponsor, "No, I don't want to be the tiger, dancing around."[24]

Sandra felt, "I'm here but I'm not here. What am I doing here? I'm not allowed to participate. In the morning, we would gather across the street. That's where the Indian students were." The Lander school kept its politically useful myth of uniformity while segregation was internal—not unlike the "desegregated" schools available to black students in the late 1970s.[25]

Sandra's parents wanted to keep her at home and in the Lander school, but at the end of her first year Sandra had had enough. She gathered with other Arapaho students in the fall to get on a bus to Flandreau, South Dakota. The bus picked up Indian children along the way, and the ride took so long that Sandra's fear grew into a feeling that they were going in the wrong direction—she began to cry before the next day's mid-morning arrival. However, this boarding school had learned to accommodate American Indian teenagers. Indian staff brought in pie and popcorn and stayed with them "'til 2:00 in the morning—'til everything was quiet and then go to bed." Against the rules, the girls "would push their beds together. Our counselor was an Indian. He understood us."[26] The understanding gave comfort, a contrast to what had so often been felt in these distant places.

Two hundred and ninety Native American students of the Wind River area attended BIA and mission schools in South Dakota, Kansas, Oklahoma, Oregon, California, and Montana in 1970. Up to 300 students remained and attended school in Lander and Riverton. The Lander newspaper editor estimated that there were 200 in the Lander high school in 1971. A Lander student gave attorney Gross a count of 158 in 1970. Estimates varied widely for those not enrolled, from 60 to "perhaps a couple of hundred."[27]

Counting students was an inexact science. Students might never return once they went home for a funeral and days of grieving, or an illness, or a holiday. Alfred Redman remembers that if they came home prematurely from boarding schools they might not re-enroll in the local schools: "They came back and had no place to go." He and William C'Hair remember them as the "push-outs."[28]

Graduation rates were low among those Indian students who began and stayed at Lander Valley High School (so named on July 1, 1969). However, the Wyoming Department of Education's definition of dropout left room for interpretation, according to a WSJ editorial by editor Bill Sniffin. The editorial reported that "dropout" was defined as "a student who is removed from school either by his or her own action or by the school's action . . . [and] does not re-enter that school or any other school that school year."[29] Apparently administrators failed to count those students who did not return after summer vacation as dropouts. This failure would inflate assumptions about the numbers continuing— making a difference where federal funding was concerned.

Don Wolcott and Bruce Campbell of the Lander Valley Guidance Department reported a Native American student dropout rate of 7.5

percent (up to 32 percent if deaths and transfers were included), according to Sniffin's editorial. Native Americans insisted that it was as high as 60 percent. A count of Native Americans pictured in the *Journal* of the LVHS graduating class of 1970 found only eight and in 1971 only twelve. The State of Wyoming did not keep enrollment figures for Native American students before 1990, a key failure that would allow suspect computation of the graduation rate and misuse of Native Americans funds. To examine the numbers that we do have, if 158 Native American students were enrolled in the Lander school in the fall of 1970, without any "dropouts" (or other leave takings) approximately 40 would have been in the 1970 senior class. But the number of pictures of graduating students suggests that only 20 percent to 30 percent of these hypothetical 40 Native American students graduated in 1970. This percentage would likely be lower if we knew how many students were initially enrolled; *some* probably left and went to boarding schools. In any event, more than *70 to 80 percent of the Native American students appear to have left the Lander high school among those who would otherwise have been in the 1970 and 1971 graduations.*[30]

By way of comparison, estimates of dropout rates in the general population at the time ranged from 29 to 37 percent. National studies revealed that Indian students dropped out of high school at a 50 percent rate, with the exception of one study. That study reviewed the reports of numerous tribes (including the Shoshones and Arapahos) where the dropout rates in 1976 were 70 to 80 percent, just as approximated for the Lander Valley High School. The Brewton Berry Research Foundation called even the 50 percent figure "shockingly high."[31]

Wolcott and Campbell found that few of the 116 dropouts of their study voiced any complaints, and "with only a few exceptions," the students gave "no constructive suggestions." The exact statements made in the complaints voiced by the few were not reported. Wolcott and Campbell's conclusion was that "the schools on and around the reservation are doing all they can in terms of facility, finance, and faculty to keep and hold Indian students *short of showing favoritism*" (emphasis added).[32] Those who held power presented as fact their interpretations and statistics that Native Americans did not believe. They had too many decades of experience with non-Indians to have faith in the non-Indian judgments when money was at stake. They decided to seek legal help. Dennis Sun Rhodes, an Arapaho architecture student at Montana State University, found a professor, Jim Goetz, who knew of an attorney who might aid the Wind River group. Attorney Michael Gross recalled:

> Dennis Sun Rhodes called me and asked me to come to Wyoming to discuss Indian school reform issues. He told me there was a group of Shoshone and Arapahoe parents who had begun meeting with an Episcopalian minister-missionary, Father David Duncombe. . . . The main emphasis or concern was high schools . . . I learned that Wind River Indian kids suffered discrimination at Lander and Riverton High Schools, were called names, were ridiculed by non-Indian teachers, in other words were suffering from most of the ills described by the Senate Subcommittee Report. There were no Indians on either school board.

Other indications of prejudice came to light around the time that the Wind River people sought a lawyer. The first involved two Lander students, Bob Spoonhunter (later the sculptor for the Wyoming Indian High School insignia), and his sister, Agnes, "always at his side," who found an interoffice memo that was demeaning to blacks and Native Americans alike. They brought it home to their parents and soon many in the tribal community were incensed by its contents. Shoshone Barbara Sage said the memo stated that Indian students "used [pause with hand gesture to the hair] on their hair to keep from showing black blood." In other words, as Alfred Redman (b. 1936) of the Arapahos remembered, "to straighten it out." The writer called the substance "dippity-do-da."[33]

Edward ("Ted") Duncombe (b. 1956), son of the reservation's Episcopal priest, wrote a letter to Gross shortly after his time at the Lander school that recounted additional incidents. He began by describing his first days as a freshman in January 1970, when he noticed "sharply divided" groups, the "Indians," the "Cowboys," "Hippies," and "Soashes." Ted was considered a "Hippy" by some because of his long hair and a

"Soash" by others because he was "an Anglo, in a band, and a member of the newspaper staff." A few times he was called an "Indian lover," which he took as a compliment. The Cowboys appeared to be the most hostile; they taunted other white boys with names such as "fag" and called the Indian boys "bucks." Duncombe wrote that Assistant Principal Eugene Patch called from 40 to 100 students in to visit his office in the morning disciplinary ritual, usually for tardiness and missing days for punishments for previous tardiness.[34]

One day Ted observed a "Jock," as he called him, loudly baiting Indian boys about whites being prohibited from hunting on reservation land, a treaty right that whites had been able to usurp for many decades. In extended taunting of the "bucks," he (the "Jock") failed to get a noticeable reaction. Then near the end of the first semester of the 1970–71 school year Ted noticed several "Cowboys" chasing the Native American boys all the way out of the building, "where the Indians turned around and started hitting the Cowboys as they came out the door." The fight on school premises culminated in defeat for the "Cowboys," who then challenged the victors to a fight at Sinks Canyon, about fifteen miles from Lander. At Sinks Canyon both sides sought "reinforcements": "About 150 Indians and 50 Cowboys assembled with several yards between them. There were knives, chains and iron pipes visible in both groups. The Indians started moving up on their opponents. Then a car pulled up between the two groups and three students, Anglos, jumped out with guns. Everyone decided they didn't really want to see anyone killed, so they dispersed."[35]

As a result of the Sinks Canyon incident Ted Duncombe's mother, Patricia Duncombe, director of the St. Michael's Youth Residence, initiated a meeting with the Lander Valley high school board. She was accompanied on February 10, 1971, by her husband, Dave, and Ted, and a few others, including Darwin and Sandra St. Clair. The situation was powerfully intense; the younger Duncombe wrote about this meeting in the preface to his master's thesis ten years later: "Before a hostile board . . . and most of the school's faculty, (they) addressed the question of prejudice." Patricia later remembered being steered not to a quiet board room but to the gymnasium. There someone had set up a large number of chairs. Patricia found it necessary throughout the meeting to try to deflect defensive reactions in the crowd, "murmurs of 'not true,' 'nonsense' and so forth." A "loud protest" arose when she described the different entrance doors used by the Indians and various non-Indian groups.[36]

The Ethete group made several requests, including for funding for after school activities and busing. They reminded the board of the Indian students' special federal monies coming to the Lander schools. All the same, they were told no: "If we do it for you we have to do it for Hudson and everybody out in the country."[37]

When I interviewed Patricia by telephone in 2003, she described how at least people listened and sought solutions. However, she said that later they called Indian students into an office and demanded to know what they did not like at the high school. "Of course, no one spoke."[38]

The Duncombes wrote a letter after the school board meeting to describe their "severe disappointment" about their concerns being "turned into a 'public hearing.'" They also pointed out that the summary by Lander Valley High School superintendent Dr. Reng did not mention the specifics of prejudice that were brought out in the meeting.[39]

The Duncombes' letter proposed programs for increased sensitivity and awareness of the importance of faculty leadership and "equal access," asking that Native Americans be involved in working out the solutions and that prejudice not be ignored: "We must meet it with love and understanding and hope and work for a better tomorrow."[40]

The "Teacher's [sic] *Reply to Reverend Duncombe*" included mention of individual teachers' responses to "charges made" and ended as follows: "A motion was made . . . (and seconded) that after hearing the complaints made by the Reverend and Mrs. Duncombe concerning incidents of alleged discrimination against Indian students and, after having the matter investigated by the administration and hearing reports from the teachers involved, the board finds no evidence of discrimination and feels that no action is warranted by the board at this time. Motion carried."[41]

Thus it was clear that the Wind River tribal people would be able to achieve their main objectives—to curb problems of discrimination and lower the dropout rate—only through an Indian school.[42] Dealing with encroachments upon their resources would have to wait for another day. But the environment did not encourage the beginnings of an educational project. Non-Indians had already suppressed the basis for Indian identity; their history, culture, and language were nonexistent in their formal education and nearly lost. The tribal community had little access to reservation income or Indian education money for schools, and so racism and group alienation were the norms. The civil rights movement and American Indian outrage over the depths to which the dominant society had buried justice for tribal people were all that kept the situation from being entirely hopeless.

•

4

False Promises

Mid-1971

The Wind River tribal people decided to appeal to Congress for their school at Ethete. They felt that their chances for success were greater with Congress than with the Lander school board. The "old enemies" organized easily.[1] They had formed alliances long before in marriages, employment in one another's schools, and memberships in the Fort Washakie and Ethete Episcopal churches. There *were* Shoshones who brought up the past and tried to create a picture of tribal antagonism. The aim of this chapter is to describe how Wind River people and a coalition of Plains Indians organized for schools that expressed their culture and worldview, and to portray their clash with adversarial Nixon policy.

As a first step the reservation group needed to find a name and incorporate themselves. Their first choice, in early 1970, was the Organization for the Establishment of a Unified Reservation School. They then chose Wind River Wyoming Indian Leadership Council. The mid-March 1971 Articles of Incorporation show that they found the Wind River Shoshone and Arapaho Education Association (WRSAEA) to be an improvement, and that name lasted for about a year during important political activity. By June 1972 they settled on the Wind River Indian Education Association (WRIEA), the name that would last.[2] The officers were Allison Sage, president; Alfred Redman, vice-president; Alberta Friday, secretary, all Arapaho. Treasurer Sandra St. Clair was of the Pawnee tribe, married into the Shoshone. The board included St. Stephen's Arapahoe, Ethete

Arapaho, and Fort Washakie's Darwin St. Clair of the Shoshone. Membership included the Duncombes. Their attorney, Michael Gross, whose experience included incorporation of the Ramah Navajo school board, guided them through the process.

There was a school project similar to Ethete's in the reservation's St. Stephen's area (near Arapahoe). St. Stephen's had never closed its elementary school and was then, as now, centered at its historic and picturesque Catholic mission. There intricate Arapaho geometric designs decorated stucco walls, and inside, at each Station of the Cross, paintings depicted water birds hovering as halos for the saints. Some of Arapahoe's wood frame "stick houses," with their tiny additions and dilapidated parts, are clustered around the nearby clinic and social services buildings while many are scattered over the surrounding plains.[3]

The St. Stephen's Indian School Educational Association initiated the work to establish their high school in 1966. A curvy and sometimes deadly two-lane road approximately twenty miles long separates St. Stephen's from Ethete. High school classes at St. Stephen's had closed in 1966, as noted in chapter 1. The nearby Arapahoe school did not have high school classes; the only other nearby option was the high school in Riverton. Circumstances at St. Stephen's (except for lack of a land tax-base) ran parallel to Ethete's.[4] An overview of the establishment of their school is given in chapter 9.

The Arapahoe people did not favor the Ethete school at first, saying that its proponents were overly youthful. Their community had already lost ground to Ethete, as described in chapter 3, and perhaps did not want to lose more. But no large-scale political divisiveness developed. Loretta Fowler, in *Arapahoe Politics*, points out that the Arapahos had long structured their political system to prevent schisms; each Arapaho Council member is elected to serve the entire tribe. When the non-Indian and Shoshone opposition to the school became apparent, the Arapahos took a protective stance.[5]

The Wind River Wyoming Indian Leadership Council acquired a grant (before incorporation) from the Edward Elliott Foundation that helped pay for a trip to Washington DC in early 1971. Ben Friday Jr. believed that Reverend Duncombe wrote the grant application to the foundation to help reach their goals: to create "a reservation high school controlled by Indians—which provides (the students) with the tools they need to get along in the non-Indian world without losing their heritage and identity." Sun Rhodes, a young Arapaho studying to be an architect, went directly to John B. Elliott in his New York City office to follow up on the request. A letter from Elliott to attorney Gross expressed his delight at Sun Rhodes's "Indian sense of time—completely unrelated to any reference to a clock," and gave a promise for anything they needed in the budget request beyond what they could raise themselves. Leadership Council members planned to meet with BIA officials and the commissioner of Indian Affairs, Louis R. Bruce. Bruce was Native American (Mohawk-Sioux).[6]

Later they made many trips from the Wind River Reservation to Washington to lobby for their high school. These all required additional fundraising endeavors. Alberta Friday credits Michael Gross for his help in making the connections. Gulf Oil, the Kennedy Foundation, the Ford Foundation, and even a concert by Buffy Sainte-Marie helped pay for their school and for travel expenses. Barbara Sage and Alfred Redman joked: "In those days there were so many trips to Washington that you could just go to the Denver airport and have an Indian meeting! Nowdays they ask, 'Do you have your casino yet?' Then it was, 'Do you have your school?'"[7]

The WRSAEA "discussed their proposal with the BIA and members of Congress" within a week after incorporation (March 18, 1971). There were two positive outcomes. Commissioner Bruce committed "$25,000 in planning money plus the assurance that if the BIA has money available, as it believes it has, a contract for operation of a high school beginning next school year will be signed." Bruce was "confident" that he would be able to find "at least $250,000 for school operation."[8]

The WSJ reported that Mill Creek school board chairman Allison Sage Sr. said he was "tickled to death" by the promised funding. The board planned to begin the school in rented Quonset huts in the fall of 1971; they would bring their children home from boarding schools, which "will cost the BIA a lot less."[9]

But as previously noted, some reservation students were not in boarding schools. The Lander high school principal, Jack King, was reported to have said that "the attendance of some 120 Indian students" would be affected as well as that of "several Caucasian students" from the reservation. Riverton was reported to have thirty to fifty reservation students.[10] Each Indian student represented a guaranteed federal government payment.

WRSAEA had the support of Wyoming U.S. senators Gale McGee (D) and Clifford Hansen (R), along with Representative Teno Roncalio (D), after the association's March 1971 visit to Washington DC. Also, a few days after the visits, the *Riverton (WY) Ranger* reported that the chairman of the Senate Interior Committee, Senator Henry M. Jackson, said he favored the management of federal schools by "local Indian school boards" under a National Board of Regents for Indian Education. The intention was that the board would "include 'a substantial number' of Native Americans, as well as professional educators." The support of Senator McGee is remembered by one school advocate as being particularly important: "Sen. Gale McGee was on the Sen. Appropriations Committee and also on the Foreign Affairs Committee. Without his help we would never have got off the ground."[11]

The Wind River people lobbied effectively. Perhaps most important to their success were their own mediation skills; they were warm, confident, respectful, and observant while representing their case. However, their cause was not well accepted back in Fremont County. There would soon be behind the scenes interference and a setback to their progress.

The promise of funding from BIA reformer Louis Bruce was reminiscent of President Hayes's 1877 promise of the Sweetwater River country to Arapaho leader Black Coal—too good to be true. The check from the BIA never arrived. Barbara Sage described her disappointment: "The BIA made the promise—didn't follow up for one year and more."[12]

The *Wyoming State Journal* delivered high expectations and disappointment on the same front page in July 1971. The paper reported that "high BIA officials, U.S. Senators Hansen and McGee and state education officials" had met in Ethete to discuss the proposed reservation school; but a "Bulletin" next to the picture of the meeting's attendees announced a "delay for school." The bulletin "urged (Reservation students) to enroll in other high schools or boarding schools." A Shoshone parent spoke at the meeting, "Right now, my children attend boarding school—they are away from their family most of the year—and I would like to have them home."[13] The parent's plea was ignored. The students left once again in the fall of 1971.

Federal officials also blocked the Northern Cheyennes and the Oglala Sioux in their attempts to establish schools. The contracting delays, consistent with "old-liner" policy, according to Frye Gaillard in the *Race Relations Reporter*, were closely associated with the actions of "two obscure (BIA) bureaucrats," Elizabeth Skelly and Peter Campanelli. Gaillard described how they threw up "obstacle after obstacle" against the Shoshone and Arapaho. The obstacles "most seriously affected" the Wind River tribes since they had counted on the BIA contract soon to be in hand.[14]

Historian Jack D. Forbes documents in *Native Americans and Nixon* that even before Nixon's self-determination speech there was a "hard fight" in his administration between the "old-liners" and the reformers. But immediately after the speech, Native Americans seemed to have reason for optimism; the administration hired fifteen Native Americans to high-level positions to work under Commissioner Bruce defending their land and water rights. But what appeared to be Nixon's high-minded purposes had fallen apart by that fall. He then approved the purging of BIA reformers, beginning with the pro-conservationist Secretary of the Interior Walter Hickel. In his place Nixon appointed a new secretary, Rogers C. B. Morton, "ex-congressman and cattle-feed-lot operator," one of the "old-liners." He in turn hired those of similar mind.[15]

Forbes also reports that there were two powerful and "ultra-conservative" members of Congress, Wayne Aspinall of Colorado, chairman of the House Interior Committee, and James Haley of Florida, chairman of the House Indian Affairs Subcommittee, who sabotaged the policies of self-determination. Aspinall and Haley had energized the opposition as soon as the Miccosukee of the Florida Everglades proposed taking over all their BIA services. As described in chapter 2, the Miccosukee were successful in getting their contract that included a school in May 1971. BIA contracting official Alexander McNabb viewed the contract "as a model of Indian self-determination." The Nixon administration took away his authority over contracting and gave it to a member of the old guard in June. Powerful interests needed BIA officials who were willing to work with them.[16]

Bruce lost control of the BIA by June 1971. Morton appointed John O. Crow as deputy commissioner of Indian Affairs in July 1971 and gave him direct responsibility over BIA internal affairs. So the Nixon administration left the Wind River people in the lurch, along with the other tribal people who were seeking schools.[17]

Official efforts to block the establishment of Indian schools were a symptom of overall policy problems for American Indians; assimilation was once again at the forefront in attempts to take Indian water rights and other natural resources. As Forbes described it, Nixon's promises for Indian self-determination were hypocritical; there were huge conflicts of interest between his promises and his administration's "large-scale involvement with BIA-negotiated leases of Indian resources."[18]

Indian organizations fought back. AIM, along with the National Indian Youth Council, protested Crow's takeover and tried to place him under citizen's arrest at the BIA building in Washington DC on September 22, 1971. Crow was absent and instead Indians were arrested but released by a judge.[19]

The Episcopalians extended their support of the tribes for their school during the same time period that Native Americans were seeing things fall apart in Washington DC. The Episcopal Bishop's Committee at the Ethete Mission approved the reservation Episcopal land and buildings for high school use in April 1971. A building and land lease created an option, if eventually needed, to help overcome state legislator objections. The Episcopal Diocese of Wyoming gave final approval to the lease and added several mission buildings to it for one dollar per year. One was a dark and cavernous building built in the mid-1930s almost entirely of rock slabs that had been carried in wagons from the mountains by Arapaho men.[20] It was the gymnasium. Although the buildings would have been far below standard in Euro-American communities, interviewees did not comment on this comparison. The donation was the first real evidence that a high school could be possible.

The Episcopal Mission at Ethete had a long established educational purpose. When a woman at Fort Washakie told the Episcopal chancellor that the Shoshone people objected to the land and building being used for anything other than a church, the objection seems to have been ignored. Bishop David R. Thornberry wrote to the diocesan trustees that the lease helped further the cause of self-determination "so extremely important to minority peoples these days." The bishop also recognized in his letter that the church was "returning, at least for their use, a portion of their land which originally the Arapahoe people gave the Diocese of Wyoming for its school."[21]

The strong Episcopal emotional and physical support was not enough for survival. WRSAEA needed help. Not only had federal support gone into turmoil and collapsed by the summer of 1971—opposition in Wyoming was organized and active. Lessons learned in the Indian resistance of the previous decades became the underpinning for WRSAEA's defense; most important were the lessons from the Pacific Northwest tribal struggle for fishing rights in the 1950s and 1960s. There activists saw the advantages to be gained in collective action and in the use of the media. And so WRSAEA and their attorney, Michael Gross, met with a small group of tribal school board allies in early October 1971. They gathered "to shake up the BIA" at the Native American Rights Fund (NARF) offices in Boulder, Colorado. The Busby school board from the Northern Cheyenne Reservation in Montana, the Red Cloud school board from the Oglala Sioux Reservation in South Dakota, and the St. Francis school board from South Dakota came along with the WRSAEA Shoshones and Arapahos. These five school boards became the founding members of the Coalition of Indian Controlled School Boards (CICSB). They planned to seek the support of the Lone Man Day School of the

Sioux, the Ramah school board of the Navajos, that of the Miccosukees, and others.[22]

The idea of an Indian educational coalition originated at Pine Ridge, South Dakota. Birgil Kills Straight, chairman of the Holy Rosary school board at Pine Ridge, was the coalition's "driving force." The founding group planned that the CICSB would help the "farthest entity along" once it received funding and then help the next best developed project in line. According to Gross, this idea "really worked." As remembered by William C'Hair, "We knew how to use the media. We knew how to use pressure. We formed a Native cooperative network and a coalition throughout Indian country."[23]

Lander residents spoke out against a reservation district in October 1971. Just below their *Wyoming State Journal*'s front page pictures, a headline announced the tribal meeting at the NARF offices in Boulder, "Wind River Indians Will Attend Meeting in Colo." The article, apparently a news release from WRSAEA, stated that they and several other tribal representatives would elect officers and plan a visit to the BIA, Congress, and the Department of Interior in Washington DC:

Some 12 groups have formed Indian Community controlled school boards throughout the United States. [Indian schools] in New Mexico, Arizona, and Montana have demonstrated the ability of Indian people to manage their own programs, while the role of the BIA has been to foster these and similar projects. However, internal changes in Bureau operation appear to have caused delay recently in contracting for educational services on Reservations.

The alliance hopes to find ways to effectuate the administration's policy of increased Indian control.[24]

Episcopal land and buildings were important assets to WRSAEA when they sought to gain flagship status from the coalition. Gross described how the "CICSB put all its effort and weight behind Wind River—even though other groups were also trying to get funding. Wind River was the best prepared and farthest along. If Wind River succeeded, it would help everyone. This is exactly what happened."[25]

The twelve tribal school boards rapidly increased their membership and, according to Gross, "went around the country" assisting many Indian schools in their organizational efforts. Szasz wrote in *Education and the American Indian* that in "less than two years . . . the CICSB was serving 87 schools and organizations (with) technical assistance in all aspects of education" and providing legislative information. As described by Gross, the CICSB became "the leading national lobbying group for Indian educational reform during the next 10 years."[26]

One of the coalition's successes was in protecting a formative Indian school district on the soon to be Menominee (Restored) Reservation in Wisconsin. There internal opposition in Indian politics was similar to that found at Wind River. Gross said the opposition failed in its courtroom appeal against the district "largely because the Coalition showed up in force." Congress passed the Indian Self-Determination and Education Assistance Act after the Menominee won their legal battles, but no tribal group claimed credit.[27]

The CICSB brought times of near euphoria for Indian people; their collective activities and successes rose above whatever opposition might develop in Washington DC. They were gaining some control over their educational systems for the first time in their history.

AIM made an offer to support WRIEA (the Wind River Indian Education Association, their new name) in mid-1972. WRIEA refused AIM's offer. Barbara Sage noted diplomatically that AIM was better known for its success in working on the urban issues of relocated Native Americans. Later she added that WRIEA felt AIM would try to take the Wind River educational issue and use it in their fight against the BIA and federal government. WRIEA did not want to be taken over by a more powerful and militant tribal coalition—AIM's militancy was well-known regionally subsequent to its protest at Mount Rushmore in the fall of 1970. Given its identification with city issues, the militant group could be the death knell for any political hopes in conservative Wyoming. WRIEA kept their distance from AIM.[28]

Others on the Wind River Reservation (not needing non-Indian support) seem to have been more comfortable with AIM. A Wind River AIM chapter was formed in late October 1972. They stated that AIM's goal was "primarily a spiritual rebirth" with hopes of rejuvenating native religions. They defended AIM, saying that it "did not encourage militancy, but rather believed that Indian people should use firmness in solving those problems which face them."[29]

The local chapter emphasized the Wind River peoples' need for employment and for improvement in the condition of housing on the reservation. These Arapahos, members of a tribe that had long sought peace, couched their cause in terms of these everyday struggles, terms not speaking of the deeper anger of many who saw overt rebellion as the only way to be heard.[30]

WRIEA's fear of AIM's reputation was soon to prove well founded. Leaders of the eight American Indian organizers of AIM's October–November 1972 "Trail of Broken Treaties" planned a peaceful demonstration in Washington DC to make known a broad range of grievances. Approximately 80 percent of the caravan demonstrators came from reservations. They were confronted with what the national newspaper *Wassaja* described as Nixon administration betrayals and provocations. The promised housing "was a rat ridden church in Washington's ghetto"—there was no food or water, let alone bathing facilities. When they went to the bureau building in the hope of meeting with officials some were beaten by the guards, and police action was ordered against them. As a result they barricaded themselves inside the BIA building, where in the confusion and the pain of defeat, they destroyed files and records. Nixon fired Louis Bruce on December 2, 1972, to keep "powerful economic interests" happy. AIM was a convenient scapegoat.[31]

Nixon, the "law and order candidate," was no doubt disturbed by the 1972 violence. His slogan did not bode well for any minority group; conservative congressional lawmakers had explicitly used "law and order" against civil rights legislation from the mid-1950s to the late 1960s. Yet Nixon needed to preserve his façade as conciliator in interactions with minorities. Hence rather than prosecute, he paid the caravan members' way home at a cost of $66,650, according to Russell Means.[32]

This concession did not solve any of the problems that threatened and oppressed tribal people, nor did it quell the anger.

Some Native Americans were still afraid of AIM and its conflict with the government. They felt that the Euro-American reaction could include an increased distrust of American Indians as a group. Congress might then eliminate the BIA administrative function and re-establish a policy of termination, declaring any of the remaining treaty agreements null and void.[33] Wind River Indian opponents to WRIEA expressed shame over the confrontations shortly after the "Trail of Broken Treaties." Officers of the organization Parents Interested in Education (PIE)— Ivora Ray, Eva McAdam, Harlene Sorrels, and Audrey Ward—had this to say in a letter to the *Wyoming State Journal*: "These people who circulated these letters [against PIE candidates in a Wind River Indian Reservation election] evidently supported with pride the Indians who were on nationwide TV representing ALL Indians. Most Indians felt a deep shame and still do. Years and years ago these kind of Indians were called renegades and sent back to their reservations and became outcasts. Now they are called 'militant Indians.'"[34]

The views expressed in the *Journal* letter were likely a minority view among Native Americans. But non-Indians prevailed. From mid-1971 forward no meaningful BIA policy improvements were made under Nixon unless he was being publicly challenged on one of his hypocrisies or cover-ups (as described in chapter 7).[35] The president's professed policies could not withstand the antagonism of those who coveted reservation land for grazing, water, timber, and mining where Indians still resisted assimilation, holding firm against being scattered to the wind.

The U.S. Civil Rights Commission's evidence for Pine Ridge election fraud perhaps best explains the severity of its problems. AIM's rage at the BIA-backed president of Pine Ridge, Dick Wilson, his "goon squads," and other allies led to violent militancy and loss of life in the occupation of Wounded Knee in early 1973. Nixon's obstruction of progress toward self-determination had not just been passive; his administration channeled money through the "Law Enforcement Assistance Administration" to Wilson and local police agencies that, with "tanks and other heavy weapons," according to Forbes, "moved rapidly to prevent dissent by systematically dismembering AIM." Russell Means likened Wilson's means of control to that found in third world countries and branded Wilson himself a "tin-pot" dictator. The National Council of Churches stepped in to mediate an end to the violence. However, violence and killings did not end there; former U.S. attorney general Ramsey Clark reported in his preface to *Prison Writings* by Leonard Peltier that more than sixty Indians "died violent and unexplained deaths" as the FBI greatly increased its presence on Pine Ridge over the next two years. Forbes states that "several hundred" were killed and dozens incarcerated between 1973 and 1976. Peltier was accused of the June 1975 killing of two FBI agents on the Pine Ridge Reservation and was still in prison at the time of writing. Clark, counsel to Peltier, makes a strong case for Peltier's innocence.[36]

The purpose of AIM's activities—to actualize treaty and land rights, among other human rights—had received sympathetic national and even worldwide attention since the eighteen-month-long demonstration on Alcatraz Island starting in 1969. Prucha wrote that the outbreaks at Pine Ridge led to a greater awareness in the larger society and the continuation of American Indian progress: "The reality of the miserable conditions of many Indians and the deep desire of Indians to have a larger say in their own destiny were driven home to American society. The move for self-determination continued—with a new urgency."[37] The CICSB's organized efforts were ongoing during the Pine Ridge tragedy and turmoil. And there were other changes in the country as a whole that would have a strong impact on events in Wyoming.

5

The Non-Indian Fight over Indian Resources
Fluid Minerals and Hard Feelings, 1969–72

Many rural towns looked deserted in 1960. Midwest farmers had left to find work in industrial areas even before the Dust Bowl years of the Great Depression. Blacks were migrating out of the South to escape Jim Crow laws and practices in this same time period. The leave taking of blacks and whites reached its height in the decade between 1948 and 1958; more than 185,000 one-room schools decreased to about 52,000 by 1960 in rural areas (that is, those areas with fewer than 2,500 persons or unincorporated). The changes swept into sparsely populated Wyoming rather late, coinciding with and shaping the American Indian struggle for a school.[1]

This chapter exposes and best exemplifies the political, social, and economic injustices for Native Americans, showing the power whites held and how they took advantage of it. But unique aspects in this story also expose the fissures created from decades-old conflicts among the self-serving in this western region. We begin with aspects of a new Wyoming law that broke apart the old system.

Educators expected larger schools with a wider range of curriculum offerings to improve efficiency (cost effectiveness) and quality of education when they began their revamp of the system. However, those improvements were not without difficulties; they needed new laws to redistribute the wealth in larger districts. Wyoming's legislature passed the 1969 Wyoming Education Code in response to the state and national trends. The code called for "generally" enlarged districts and equalization of K–12 money within the geographic space *of each county* (or more *if* they chose to combine); a county committee had the duty to create equalization when it organized its districts, a duty high on the scale of human ideals.[2] As might be expected, the high sounding aspiration did not lower the influence of greed.

The most intractable problems surfaced within Fremont County, the county that encircled the Wind River Reservation. There the reorganization law peeled back and opened for view layer upon layer of discriminatory practices. But the law itself had its problems. The legislators found justice difficult to achieve, particularly in relation to Native Americans.

The code required all "unified districts" to include a high school— except the Indian reservation districts. There the reservation districts would be "supporting a high school" in the local towns.[3] Apparently the legislature gave little or no thought to Native American wants or needs; it was as if they had none. Farmers and business people who were struggling for prestige and success were the focus. The legislature had difficulty in aspiring to a broad view of just outcomes.

A troublesome problem for the Fremont County Reorganization Committee (FCRC) was the most basic: the requirement for larger districts. The Lander superintendent labeled centralized administrations as authoritarian, socialistic, undemocratic, and "un-American," his beginning salvo into the aspirational goals. Redistribution was not a popular idea. But the state associated local control in remote areas with more expense. These control and redistribution issues were major sticking points within the FCRC even when the reservation districts were not involved.[4] Those with vested interests in each of the newly shaped districts did not want to lose anything and in fact hoped to make gains.

The Wyoming Code placed a State Committee that included the State Board of Education at the top of the legal structure. The State Committee would have to give approval for any county plan to go into effect. However, the State Committee faced an array of strong-minded interests—the largest towns held banking institutions and published the newspapers; Wyoming's remote and rural areas held independence as a central value.[5] They were highly motivated to do so; these thinly populated areas had rich pockets of resources scattered among them. There were intense county squabbles before decisions ever reached the State Committee.

The approximately 55 by 70–mile, 2.2 million–acre Indian reservation dominates Fremont County. The county is about 90 by 110 miles at its longest, with highly irregular boundaries. The reservation's southern side is just south of the county's midpoint, while its northern boundary partially overlaps into Hot Springs County. Fremont County contains dramatic elevation changes, from 4,500 feet where most people live to over 11,000 feet in the mountains. Arid western flora cover the plains, while shrubs and pines grow up the mountain slopes until snow, ice, and glaciers take over.[6]

The residents of each settlement area felt pride in their western landscape and unique history, some of the latter important to the nation as a whole. The "Oregon trail," which led not only to Oregon but to California and Utah as well, passes through the southern portion of the county. There it runs near Split Rock, a landmark rock outcropping about ten miles east of a uranium-mining town, Jeffrey City, into a gorgeous stretch of grassland country following the Sweetwater River. President Hayes promised this country to the Arapahos in 1877. Earlier, before the completion of the transcontinental railroad, the trail had guided lumbering wagons to South Pass of the Wind River Range. From there it branched out into the various trails as it crossed the Rocky Mountains.[7]

Jeffrey City in the southeast corner of Fremont County was a "company town" of Western Nuclear, which sold to Phelps-Dodge in the late 1960s, and in 1970 the town was on the verge of a boom. It contained 700 to 750 people, but by 1980 more than 4,000 people lived in this off-reservation town running businesses and working for the uranium mine. The company housed the miners and their families in trailers and plain two-story barracks.[8] A dirt road led north to bluffs where collectors searched for agates and arrowheads a few miles to the east. Jeffrey City with its coveted wealth and ability to build its own high school proved to be a thorn in the side of the other FCRC towns, especially Lander.

Tourists with distant destinations remember the state for the more desolate parts of Fremont County, north of the Oregon Trail. There loud, dust-stirring trucks carry asphaltic sour crude oil from the reservation through Riverton on its main street. The Susquehanna-Western uranium mill supplied employment there to Arapaho men until it was abandoned in 1963—the EPA reported contamination of the area from its tailings as late as 1973. Mostly non-Indian people populate Riverton and Lander (see chapters 1 and 3). Twenty-five miles of winding highway separated the towns' populations of 7,995 and 7,125 respectively in 1970, the largest towns in the county.[9]

The smallest settlements were off-reservation, Hudson, ten miles from Lander, and Moneta and Lysite, near one another east of the reservation. European immigrants moved near Hudson in the early 1900s to mine its coal; at their peak Hudson's mining camps contained as many as ten thousand men. Only their patchwork housing remained in the 1970s under huge cottonwood trees rooted in the Little Popo Agie River sand. Fort Washakie boarding school boys once made midwinter wagon trips from 3:00 to 6:00 a.m. to shovel and haul Hudson's coal for their three-story stone buildings. They cut barrels lengthwise, mounted them beneath the wagon's bench, and filled them with hot stones for warmth during the trip, which was twenty miles each way. Still, the boys became so cold that they had to make a halfway stop to build a fire for warmth.[10]

Lysite (no population found for 1970) and Moneta (10 in 1970) together had one vote on the FCRC. Lysite ranchers raised sheep, but beneath the green grasses there were huge pockets of natural gas. The gas gave the Lysite-Moneta area a tax base that the FCRC had to redistribute— its per pupil valuation was an incredible $331,500. In December 1969 it consolidated with (and merged its income with that of) the off-reservation border town of Shoshoni (population 562), twenty miles distant and with part of its school district on the reservation.[11] Only stray Yellowstone-bound summer travelers supplemented Shoshoni's arid, ranch country income before the merger. Afterward, with its newly swelled income perhaps in danger of redistribution, it joined in the reservation school legal battles.

Central to FCRC conflicts were the reservation's Reclamation Project settlements (see chapter 1): Pavillion (population 181), Morton (5), and Kinnear (population unknown in 1970), named after non-Indian Napoleon Bonaparte Kinnear. These communities sit on idyllic agricultural lands around large Ocean Lake. Napoleon was a civil engineer where irrigation was vital—his half Shoshone wife, Isabelle, first purchased Wind River land in 1888. She and her relatives eventually bought up nearly one thousand acres in the Kinnear area. Oil and gas fields are scattered just to the west and north. The surface land, if it continues to belong to non-Indians is usually in a "split-estate" arrangement, discussed later in this chapter.[12]

Crowheart, near the Reclamation area, is visible only by some beehives, a post office, and an old white stucco store. It officially had a population of ten in 1970 but served many ranchers some twenty-five miles northeast of Fort Washakie. They raised cattle on sparse grasses and in the icy mud of Rocky Mountain springtimes.[13]

Crowheart has its unforgettable history too; its namesake, Crowheart Butte, prominent on the northeastern horizon, is where a terrible battle between Crows and Shoshones took place in the summer of 1856. The Shoshone chief Washakie met and killed the Crow leader "in solitary combat" after the loss of 150 lives, mostly Crows, in order to stop the bloodshed.[14]

Fort Washakie is still the government town where the Shoshones reside. Some remnants of the ranching and farming introduced by Rev. John Roberts remained in 1970. Pumpjacks methodically pumped oil from beneath a rise in the earth called Winkleman Dome, north of town. A large area of sagebrush-covered land typical of much of the reservation lay a few miles east of the area, its underground contents not of much interest. This is where many Arapahos settled on allotments and named their new home Ethete.[15] It seemed an unlikely place for conflict to erupt over a school.

The Wyoming State Constitution had long required a "uniform system of public instruction." But "uniform" did not necessarily translate to mean fair and equal, as the new code required.[16] It was the district's problem if the number of students in a district was high and the income relatively low.

A second irritant (for some) is that the land value on the reservation cannot be taxed. However, natural resources on the Wind River Reservation had been leased by the tribal people to corporations, as is common in nearly every western state. Those who lived on the surface of the land's underground resources (in a "split estate") *could claim the corporate "annual value of production" and equipment as a tax base.*[17] And so, since districts did not share incomes with one another, those districts on the surface of oil- or gas-rich land had tax base incomes that were disproportionately large.

Morton, Kinnear, Pavillion, and Crowheart, consolidated as School District 6 in May 1969 and populated mainly by whites, were *on the reservation* and claimed one of its two richest oil and gas tax bases (based on cumulative data through 1978). Fort Washakie's School District 21 claimed the other, explaining economic reasons for the often reported, although only partially true, political "split" between the tribes. District 6's paucity of students meant that their per-student valuation, or what it would receive for each student from taxes paid in the district, was indeed astronomical.[18]

Lander, the strongest opponent to a reservation district, had a per-student valuation that was over four times that of the Ethete district, where poverty was apparent. A crossroads divided a store from "Easter Egg Village," fifty or so faded-pastel government houses set among clusters of tumbleweeds and broken-down cars. Only the stone and wood remains of St. Michael's Mission, set apart on the southwest corner, saved Ethete's dignity. Lander, as described in chapter 3, was a relatively prosperous agricultural center in 1970. It had tax bases in Jeffrey City and unincorporated Atlantic City, where miners lived and mined iron ore for U.S. Steel.[19] Lander's opposition to a reservation district seemed to be motivated by the oil and gas wealth of the Fort Washakie area and the federal dollars that the Indian students brought with them. Native Americans knew they could not change that motivation; they remembered how "crazy" white men went at the sight of gold. They would have to deal instead with the towns' relationship dynamics in order to make gains toward self-determination.

A "one town one vote" expectation for the FCRC was actually more complicated than that and not so democratic. The *Wyoming State Journal* reported that three Lander representatives, Jim Duran, James M. Graham, and the outspoken S. J. Starrett, were at the April 1969 Lander meeting, when representatives from twelve districts first met. District 27's Hudson added one more vote since it sent its high school students to Lander, and Jeffrey City sixty miles distant potentially added one more vote, as its tenth and eleventh graders boarded in Lander, where they attended school. The committee chose Ivan Sackman of Riverton as chairman (Riverton's one vote) and the Jeffrey City representative as vice-chairman. The three representatives of the three Native American elementary districts were all non-Indian, although steadfastly allied with the Indian cause.[20]

Wyoming's 1969 law contained the usual requirement that territory defined as a district be contiguous. That was contrary to an *off-reservation* town's use of a non-contiguous *reservation oil and gas field* that lay in the middle of District 6, for its tax base. Dubois (District 2) was approximately thirty miles northwest of Crowheart and had a population of 898 in 1970. Its "any part Indian" population was 1.7 percent by the year 2000. It, like Shoshoni, would have had little other than a small Yellowstone-bound tourist business for a tax base to support its schools—except for its district's exceptional boundaries.[21]

Dubois had fought for its tax base claim with District 6 over a decade earlier. The response of the representative of the District 6 Circle Ridge oil field area to Dubois was, as the committee's secretary put it, "it is not feasible—it's impossible and everything else." Apparently Dubois had plans for a rather large expansion, so that even Crowheart and Morton felt they were being "taken in." "The gist of the whole meeting was, the Districts to be absorbed . . . were very bitterly opposed to the plan and the District absorbing equally anxious to take them in."[22]

Dubois for the better part won. By 1959 it claimed most of the Bar Gee area; that is, the Maverick Springs and Circle Ridge oil fields. This area was surrounded on three sides by District 6 in May 1969 (the fourth side being Hot Springs County). Hence the first proposal made in a full county committee meeting in October 1969 sought to resolve the Dubois conflict with the law. Jim Duran of the "Redistricting (Sub-) Committee" proposed that additional District 6 land be given to Dubois "to make the Districts contiguous"; Dubois needed to add a long strip of District 6 land for a connection to its oil fields (from a historical perspective, rightfully belonging to the reservation's Native Americans). District 6 did not give Dubois the land. The committee was still reminding District 6 and Dubois eight months later to get down to business and solve their differences or face consolidation.[23]

Jim Duran (of Lander) exposed other conflicts among the non-Indian towns in a second redistricting proposal in the October meeting. His proposal favored the larger towns (Riverton and Lander) at the expense of Jeffrey City, merging Jeffrey City's oil field, Beaver Creek, with Riverton and unifying the remainder of Jeffrey City and its uranium-rich area with Lander. Riverton and Lander had long warred over possession of Beaver Creek, but Duran's offer helped equalize funding. No record of representatives' votes was kept, but most of the smaller communities and the reservation must have sided together against the Lander proposals, which were voted down.[24] This may have been the beginning of an alliance between the small town and Indian districts.

The first FCRC proposals were more generous to the Native American districts than those to follow. One called for a *reservation-wide* district, in which *all* of the school district proportion of the tax base would have been shared across the reservation. In this option, Dubois would have been cut off from its oil and gas tax base.[25] The author of this proposal, not identified in the minutes, may have been one of the Indian district's representatives or just someone who was making an effort to comply with the equalization requirements of the 1969 Education Code. The committee may have been uncertain as to whether they had jurisdiction over the reservation.

The idea that the reservation might be unified as one school district, where its tax income and federal money would be kept, generated tremendous opposition. As Caroline Goggles said, "That had them screaming. They would have been very poor. They were used to getting all the funding. They were getting buildings from our money." Sandra St. Clair with her husband Darwin made the same point. Dubois used "big oil wells on the reservation supporting their district." The Riverton Reclamation area also separated its tax base income out from the Indian districts. William C'Hair stated, "When we said we want a reservation-wide district, the surrounding communities panicked."[26]

Ethete's representative, Silas Lyman, a strong supporter of the hopes for an Indian high school, saw that compromise was necessary; he went back to an October plan that combined the Indian elementary districts of the reservation. He planned that Fort Washakie would share tax base income from Winkleman Dome with Mill Creek and Arapahoe and divided the county's other districts according to tax base.[27] Lyman's compromise apparently did not offer enough to the largest towns.

Next Riverton made a proposal, which did benefit the largest towns but proved to be a waste of time. Riverton placed itself with Lysite and Shoshoni while it placed Lander with Jeffrey City, the reservation, and Hudson. Areas that did not want to be with a larger town probably defeated the plan. Districts 2 and 6 were placed together (sending the plan to certain defeat). No motions followed the presentation of this plan.[28]

A December 1969 report gave the FCRC an explanation about how the Dubois district came to be "gerrymandered" onto the reservation oil fields. The report was not reviewed in the minutes. The committee decided it needed an attorney. Jack Nicholas of Lander was selected.[29]

Harvey Woolery of District 6 made five different proposals on behalf of his subcommittee in the January and February 1970 meetings—all were defeated. All would have combined District 6 with Dubois, resulting in a per student valuation of $19,000 for them. Perhaps that was too high for everyone else, unless it was that Dubois, in spite of the money, still did not want to join with District 6. Several motions were made for various combinations of districts within the committee as a whole and defeated. District votes were not recorded. Woolery "saw no need [for his subcommittee] to meet further on this" after the rejection of his subcommittee efforts. Later attorney Nicholas pointed out that his committee's work had been largely guesswork anyway; they did not have enough information on location of resources to be able to set boundaries that would be equitable.[30]

Four of the Woolery proposals combined the Arapahoe district with Riverton's. The combination of the Riverton district with the Arapahoe district, 94 percent Arapahoe and having over two hundred students, would have helped equalize Indian federal money between the two largest towns and given Riverton administrative control over Arapahoe.[31]

At this point the smaller town mistrust of the larger towns became apparent even in the selectively revealing minutes. A proposal made by Lander's Starrett for a "study" of a one-district county seems to have precipitated their anger. He excluded reservation districts 14 and 21, ignoring Arapahoe as an Indian district, where until 1927 only white children had attended (although dominated by Indian student numbers in the 1970s). Lander, with its several votes, and Riverton would likely maintain school board control should such a one-district county materialize. Burke Johnson of Dubois and Woolery of District 6 joined (in spite of their historic animosity) to exclude their districts from the Lander study. A vote was not taken. Lander's *Wyoming State Journal* (*WSJ*) reported that Districts 14 and 21 had been given "special treatment by the 1969 legislation." They apparently believed that the reservation had escaped the code's requirements. But Nicholas clarified to the committee that they did have the prerogative to include reservation districts in their plan. He *did not* say that the committee could merge them with off-reservation districts.[32]

The committee went through a short period in April 1970 of acceptance of reservation control over a reservation school district "unification plan." But it wanted to be sure that there would be no unusual expense associated with the reservation's decisions; "extensive and expansive valuation location research would not be feasible." Proponents of unification of the three reservation districts, perhaps seeing that they had been given an opening, let it be known that they wanted a high school, and the majority of the FCRC gave approval for them to develop their plan—with two opposed. Lander and Riverton would have the most to lose, but again a record of votes was not kept. That proposal seems to have fractured any civility between those advocating for an Indian district and those opposed; "A discussion followed on the feasibility of continuing the meetings."[33]

The County Committee "dispensed with" the next (June) meeting; the FCRC attorney said that they would keep their responsibilities. They did so, but Districts 2 and 6 awaited their June school board elections to decide what to do about the committee's recommendation that they consolidate.[34] Consolidation of Dubois and District 6 *did not* follow the elections.

The reservation gave little attention to FCRC plans during this time of its confusion and dilemmas. Over a year after President Nixon's summer of 1970 self-determination speech, leaders began traveling more frequently to Washington DC. There, according to one anonymous traveler, they stayed in "flea bitten hotels" where among other things they were met with threadbare sheets: "One was ripped down the middle and no towels except small."[35]

The anonymous source chuckled at experiences of some thirty years past—"first time I was around people of color." And sometimes it seemed to be the first experience of Washington DC residents with Native Americans; on the basement floor of the Senate a black woman became fascinated with this Arapaho's long black braid and asked to touch it. He noted, "Black like yours," and allowed her to do so in return for touching her hair as well. Each must have felt hesitant to ask and yet asked anyway, much as did a five-year-old black boy who quietly asked to touch President Obama's hair in 2012. So hesitant and quiet was he in asking that the president had to ask him to repeat his question and then tell him, "Touch it dude!"[36]

Nixon's self-determination message to Congress distracted the Fremont County Committee from itself. Several members thought of asking the reservation residents what they would like to do about their schools, but both motions for reservation votes failed, 6–5.[37] Mill Creek and Arapahoe decided on their own to have a referendum vote.

A "Patron and Tax Payer" of Mill Creek's District 14 objected as soon as it gave notice of an election. His letter to the WSJ editor, asked: "Are you interested in how tax-paying property owners would vote as opposed to a cut and dried patron vote?" Not only did his Native American neighbors not pay taxes on their property and oil and gas income (the latter was paid by the extraction industries), but they were more numerous than those who did. The *Journal* assured readers that the vote would not be binding.[38] Those proponents for a reservation high school had both internal and external enemies.

Mill Creek, in a "large turnout" that included its non-Indian population, voted overwhelmingly for a reservation high school (175 for the proposal and 72 against) in late September 1970. The WSJ said that results were to be "used as a guide in recommendations to the County Reorganization and Boundary Boards." A few days later, the Arapahoe School District voted 126 for joining a reservation district and 40 against—to stay with Riverton. The *Journal* quoted the Fort Washakie superintendent, Leon Lanoy, saying that a "house-to-house poll" had been taken the previous year, which showed that most favored having a reservation district. Silas Lyman stated that if the unification were approved, a "new board would undoubtedly begin immediately to draw up plans for buildings," taking two or three years to be completed.[39]

The WSJ reported that results of the previous Native American vote were "at abeyance" two weeks after Lyman's optimistic speculation. They were, as far as the border and on-reservation non-Indian towns were concerned. One of the representatives presented a plan in the next FCRC meeting to split the reservation among the surrounding towns. Whose plan this was is not known; the FCRC kept ballots secret, and the minutes (October 1970) were the last found at the state archives until those of 1977. Secrecy can happen for many reasons, but when it succeeds, it keeps unlawful and or unfair action from being seen by the larger community. Hidden, the lawlessness of prejudice has no consequence of the sort that will assure justice. The WSJ of Lander reported that the committee sought an opinion from the state attorney general's office as to the legalities of a reservation school district. Children had attended reservation elementary schools since boarding school days, but after the vote for a reservation high school, FCRC members wondered if "segregation" might be a problem.[40]

The FCRC representative's plan to split up the reservation districts could have been related to the reservation's activism (as in voting). Also, recall that soon after Nixon's July 1970 speech there was renewed entrenchment against Indian self-determination by ultra-conservative members of Congress and BIA staff (see chapter 4). It may not be inaccurate to speculate that politically involved local people communicated with their congressmen.

Silas Lyman proposed a five-district plan in late October 1970, which again combined the three Native American districts. In the same meeting Stanleigh Starrett made two strange one-district proposals; one excluded the reservation districts altogether (by appearances not to Lander's advantage), and one included only "the assessed valuation" of a reservation district. The minutes did not say exactly where that assessed valuation was to be included. A motion was made that postponed the vote until the next meeting.[41] Apparently, Starrett needed to do quite a bit of talking to explain his motions.

The (excluded) reservation in Starrett's one-district plan separated the northwestern corner of the district from the southern and eastern sides. But the factor that probably caused the most difficulty was that Lander and Riverton were in one district, sharing funding and power. Their conflicts were apparently to the advantage of Native American hopes. The committee soon went back to Lyman's plan, even though its best "talking point" among non-Indians was only that it created greater autonomy for each of the five districts; it did not meet state equity requirements. The WSJ reported that the committee had "*given permission* to the Wind River Reservation to set up a vocational high school on reservation land" (emphasis added). The newspaper also reminded its readers that reorganization was "necessary under 1969 school law."[42] Mr. Starrett's motions had failed and the whole circumstance was very uncomfortable.

Lyman's five-district plan gave the Indian schools equity among themselves and independence, perhaps the best they could hope for. However, the proposal's failure to achieve equity among the totality of districts was extreme. Lander-Hudson's per student valuation was approximately $15,700 before the plan combined them with Jeffrey City with a valuation of over $37,000 per pupil; Riverton had $12,000 per pupil from its businesses and its southeastern reservation gas fields; the combined Indian school district's per pupil valuation was $9,000, the lowest among the districts and $10,000 less than Districts 2 and 6 (in spite of the $22,990 per pupil wealth in the Fort Washakie district).[43]

WRSAEA's mission was to protect their children's cultural continuance in the schools, not to make money. They also did not believe that whites would seek redemption by making things right with Indians at this late date. Fighting whites about money would result in getting nowhere with their mission (in spite of the aspirational goals regarding equity in state law). And so WRSAEA was fully behind Lyman's plan.

Certainly Lander did not want to settle for less territory and less income than it might be able to gain. Superintendent Reng opposed the reservation district, saying that it would "have the effect of promoting a segregated system and thereby *endanger federal funds*" (emphasis added)—a rare public admission of fear of loss of federal money. Dubois voted for the plan at first but nearly a year later, when things had not been settled, opposed it. They gave reasons that included their belief that "some arrangement could be made to connect our original district with the Bar Gee area (and) gain a greater tax base."[44] Dubois did not seem to mind repeating its oft rejected desires.

The Lander newspaper continued in 1971 to discuss the financing of the reservation high school and the resulting losses to the local towns. The FCRC held by one vote to their decision all the same, to propose five public school districts, one on the reservation. One notable speaker against the reservation school was Don Wolcott, LVHS staff member and lead author of the study that claimed an Indian student dropout rate of only 7.5 percent.[45]

Lander wanted to mitigate the damage. A vocational high school with limited curriculum would do just that. Starrett wrote a letter to the state committee opposing a reservation district unless it was a "good vocational installation." A high school (presumably a regular one), he said, would result in "isolation of the reservation" when the Indian people "want to be a part of America." But Native Americans understood the rhetoric and resented the proposal. The Lander push for a vocational school, according to Barbara Sage, confirmed what many in the tribal communities believed—that Lander residents regarded most of their children as "retarded."[46]

As reported in chapter 3, the *Wyoming State Journal* printed pictures of the annual One-Shot Antelope Hunt celebrations with prominent white men dressed as "squaws" in the fall of the year. One front page "Squaw Dance" photograph in 1971 was displayed directly above an extensive article titled "What the Five-District System Looks Like," with the proposed district maps.[47]

There were two public hearings on reorganization in October 1971, the first in Riverton attended by two hundred people, some from the reservation. There were many questions, but not much controversy arose over the board's five-district plan in the first meeting. Lander's John Reng spoke in favor of a taxation plan to equalize funding on a per student basis. A man from sparsely populated Kinnear pointed out the difficulties this would pose for small schools. The *Journal* noted in response to the idea of starting over with Reng's "brand new" concept that the county was under time constraints—the plan would need to be approved by the state committee and in place by January 1, 1973. Tom Shakespeare, author of *The Sky People* (a 1971 written record of the oral history of the Arapahos), spoke for the children at this first meeting: "As I sit here listening to the statements tonight, I haven't heard anything about the children; it's all been about money, how much we're going to lose, how much someone else is going to gain. When are we going to start talking about the real factors involved?"[48]

Attendees expressed strong opposition to a reservation district at the second October meeting, held in Lander. Four hundred people attended, and twenty petitions opposing the five-district plan were submitted, some from those with official positions in the schools. Some petitioners represented groups such as Property Owners on the Reservation. An administrator of Western Nuclear traveled from Jeffrey City to present his petition. But the FCRC voted, seven to five, to send their five-district plan forward to the State Committee for its approval.[49]

As usual the committee did not make the votes known. Among the seven would be the Indian districts' votes and four small towns. It may be safe to say that Lander's two votes plus Riverton's one, and their allied towns, Hudson and Jeffrey City, made the five. Perhaps the reservation and other rural people held in common the desire for freedom from the age-old control by larger bureaucracies. The *Journal*'s editor, Bill Sniffin, noted that the committee was certainly "brave" in going against their constituents but wondered if they were simply tired. He expected the State Committee to reject the plan.[50]

As editor Sniffin predicted, the Wyoming State Committee immediately rejected the first plan offered by the Fremont County Reorganization Committee.[51] From the state's perspective, this was the best offer that they would receive from this county. The five-school-district proposal provided relatively more equitable state public school funding among its reservation students and reconciled boundary conflicts with relatively few districts being formed. However, a unified reservation district necessitated that the state build a reservation high school, an expense that they could not, or would not, justify.

The State Committee ruled that five districts would not be an efficient use of money (too many districts), and did not provide for "equal educational opportunities." Additionally, there was no high school in the Indian reservation area (of course the state had not built one) and therefore there was no unified district by the law's requirements. The committee secured that opinion by saying that it did not see evidence of "adequate financial commitment" by the reservation community to construct and maintain a high school, although it recognized the reservation's support of other districts in these efforts.[52]

The State Committee held "much discussion . . . on the effectiveness of Lander and Riverton high schools in promoting good interracial relations," trying to make adjustments for the educational inequity of an area that had no high school. They believed that a district centered in a Eurocentric community could, with proper attention, adequately educate and communicate with its Native American students. They asked for "special emphasis" in the future on "the educational needs and opportunities of those children residing in the Indian Reservation districts now known as districts 14, 21 and 38."[53]

It may be that a certain amount of ethnocentrism got in the way as the State Committee tried to make egalitarian requirements. They apparently did not understand the importance of identity and self-determination to American Indians or see that ethnocentrism and prejudice were strong influences in the surrounding areas. And they seemed oblivious to the economic and cultural benefits that a school district could bring to a reservation community. The all-encompassing problem was that prejudice was embedded in expectations for assimilation. Native Americans lived on an island and were too different for understanding.

The State Committee argued for and recommended consideration of a *two*-school-district county.[54] Had this recommendation been followed, the reservation would likely have been split between the two largest towns. The state left that decision to the County Committee.

A simple mathematical formula seems to have determined the state administration's viewpoint; perhaps new information could change their minds. But economics probably determined the viewpoint of the farmers whose lives would be affected. That too is to be described by this story.

6

Reservation Organizations Oppose the School

Early 1970s

Indian self-determination in education instigated organized opposition. Three reservation organizations opposed a Native American area high school. The first was Property Owners on the Reservation (POOR), non-Indians who had acquired property on the reservation. John Wunder, the Mill Creek school board member who lost the election to Ben Friday Jr. (see chapter 3), was a proud member of POOR and, along with POOR, was against the school. He had other complaints as well; he introduced POOR to Lander's high school board as the "real property owners on the reservation" (seeming to imply that Indians had not paid a price for their ownership).[1] His representation of POOR came at a time when chances for an Indian school seemed good, in April 1971; Commissioner Louis Bruce had just announced his promise for financial support for a reservation high school, and the County Committee favored an Indian district (although many constituents did not).

Wunder's arguments focused on "segregation." The formation of a reservation high school, he said, "could result in such ethnic imbalance as to isolate the Indian [school children] in direct opposition to policies of the United States Government on segregation." However, he tangled the web of his argument by saying that children from Riverton and Lander "would in all probability" be bused "to attend the Reservation high school," not favored by POOR. There were 125 Wind River Indian Reservation students "segregated" in all-Indian boarding schools at the time.[2]

POOR's concern, then, was not about Indian segregation but quite the reverse: Anglo children might be bused to the Ethete high school. And an Indian majority would likely elect an Indian-controlled school board.[3]

The arguments spun by Wunder did not mislead tribal people. Merle Haas, director of the Northern Arapaho Tribe's Sky People Higher Education, explained the Indians' historical view by way of an analogy:

> The tribal people were around observing the settlers, the pioneers. They may not have known it but they were around. . . . The tribal people saw that they built fences around their property and used fire differently like for lanterns. The tribal people thought, "These people must be like the trickster spider." . . . Spider had a web that looked like the fence. So in actuality the Nih'oo3oo stories [*Arapaho Traditions*] are about spider but because white man exhibited characteristics the same as spider [he] has a place in the spider stories and was given the name Nih'oo3oo.[4]

In the case of a mass exodus of white students to a local town's high school the remaining Native students, by Wunder's definition, would be "segregated." The Supreme Court denied the substance to that claim a year later in *Lawlor v. Board of Education of City of Chicago* (1972); although African American school board "policies and practices" had increased the black student percentage and whites had fled the district, this did not constitute segregation.[5]

Bob Spoonhunter, in a *Casper Star-Tribune* interview, responded to the 1971 POOR "segregation" argument, as did Dennis Sun Rhodes, the Montana State University architectural student, by then appointed consultant to the Culture Department of the Native American Center for the Living Arts in New York City. In a letter to the editor of the Lander paper, Sun Rhodes noted the hypocrisy in segregation arguments when there seemed to be no concern about a 45–50 percent dropout rate at the Lander high school. He suggested that POOR's real concern might be about the "fear they will reduce their dominating role over the Indians." Spoonhunter stated that "the school would be open to all students" and that in fact many non-Indian students were expected. Reservation resident Bruce Chavez also sent a letter to the local paper. He noted that the school was not to be segregated but was simply one that "happens to be located within a predominantly Indian populated area." It *only continued the elementary education already established there,* and no one had ever called that segregation.[6]

A keeper of POOR's minutes recorded remarks about the possibility of a reservation school in a POOR meeting in September 1971. WRSAEA members were "not allowed to attend," according to Alberta Friday. She believed that it was Mill Creek superintendent Lyman who was able to obtain the minutes (which she brought to our interview). Recorded as present were "19 non-Indian property owners who reside on Wind River Indian Reservation and 5 members of the Shoshone and Arapahoe tribes." Chairman Wunder read the "Resolution" that spoke to ownership of reservation land and "illegal" segregation. Several people gave their opinions. One anti-reservation-school opinion was that "isolation of Indians in their own neighborhood won't do them any good." One attendee did not believe that jobs and education would help reservation residents: "What would the Indians do . . . spend more money for gas and in the bars? Anyway, they won't know nothing [sic] when they graduate."

The state's coordinator of Indian education, Larry Murray, spoke at the meeting, along with the then Lander School superintendent, Dr. Reng. Reng contributed that "all busing would cease on the reservation" if there were to be a reservation district. Murray, who left early, reportedly offered to "help us get $17,000."[7]

POOR tried to appear to side with the 1954 *Brown v. Topeka Board of Education*'s opposition to segregation. Yet they did not acknowledge the degradation of the Native American children in border town schools or their culture's diminishment, if not invisibility. POOR resented the collectively held American Indian lands and resources; this was its political strength. The "pressure of the land-hungry western settlers" had not ended.[8]

Schools, as centers of Native American community life, most likely seemed to fortify what remained of Indian holdings. And an Indian high school threatened the sense of entitlement held by many in the local communities. Education historian Margaret Connell Szasz summed it up: "Many frontiersmen were inveterate Indian haters, and as the frontier shrank in physical size this attitude seemed to intensify."[9] POOR's use of the concept of segregation as a weapon to work against Indian controlled schooling was asserted with dark, ironic humor; these "rugged individualists" otherwise would resent so much "to do" about the protection of American Indian rights.

POOR soon disbanded and joined with a similar organization, "Parents Interested in Education" (PIE), a Fort Washakie group, which they believed had more money and "many Shoshone members," in a better position to help them politically. Barbara Sage, a Shoshone/Caucasian rancher near Crowheart, explained that PIE was a Shoshone/Caucasian rancher group that provided the most active opposition to a reservation high school. Caroline Goggles explained, "They did not want an Indian controlled board. They knew they wouldn't be elected. We didn't intend it that way but we needed it."[10]

Shoshone Business Council member Alfred Ward confirmed Caroline's belief in courtroom testimony early in 1974. He objected to a reservation unified school district in part because a vote could lead to an Arapaho-dominated school board. Ward also testified that he was a member of PIE and the Fort Washakie District 21 school board. The latter, he had to admit, favored creation of a reservation district.[11] Conflict over a reservation school district existed only between *some* of the Shoshone population and the Arapahos—the split in opinion was largely *within* the Shoshone group.

Conflict should be expected in areas of necessary and close contact among groups with different histories and identifications. Many complex processes exist side by side, exert social pressure, and intermingle in the "contact zone," as Mary Louise Pratt explained. These processes are often found "in contexts of highly asymmetrical relations of power, such as colonialism, slavery, or their aftermaths."[12] The "aftermaths" on the Wind River included blending of tribes and non-Indians in families that had different rules of inheritance and degrees of transculturation.

The centuries-old differences that exerted their influence in the 1970s were mainly in the individualistic attitudes of the Shoshones in Sun Dance rituals and in external social affiliations versus the Arapahos' strong "ethos of tribal unity and harmony." There the authority held by middle-aged and older individuals (originally by formal age-grade), and by those in certain Sun Dance ceremonial roles, continued to facilitate consensus building. Arapaho families were usually not split by white-dominated political arguments; marriage to outsiders was relatively rare. The Shoshones, with a more flexible social structure, were vulnerable to factionalism, sometimes literally influenced by "relations of power."[13]

One of the first and most important concepts of Wind River Reservation social and political life, according to Barbara Sage, is "out-marriage," meaning marriage outside the tribe. A descendent can still inherit reservation land when the tribally recognized proportion of Indian blood or "blood quantum" falls below one-quarter, although the land will forever after be considered ordinary "fee-patent" land, no longer held in trust and subject to taxing authority. Out-marriage has the gradual effect of increasing non-Indian ownership of the reservation as well as facilitating cultural change.[14]

The Dawes Act first used the blood quantum terminology to limit the number of Native Americans eligible for land assignment—at least one-half Indian ancestry was a requirement. The federal government sold unassigned land as if it were excess land. The tribes have to some extent circumvented strict blood quantum interpretations. Members' adherence to behavioral standards can determine membership in tribal rolls more than actual ancestry. But the Arapahos have sought to limit higher percentages of "mixed-blood" membership because of the effect on per capita payments and land diminishment with generational expansion of the population. There was a tribal use for this dominant culture concept, and so it was absorbed. And in general the indigenous people have "internalized" the blood quantum concept, as Circe Sturm suggests in *Blood Politics*, simply as a result of the repeated and powerful governmental use of the concept.[15]

Economic standing of Native Americans and their descendants tends to be improved by marriage to whites, setting the stage for conflict. Tribal people in general are more interested in cultural identity than race and do not regard being "mixed-blood" as unusual, although sometimes the descendants' shift in cultural habits and attitudes is a disappointment to traditional tribal members. Native writer Wendy Rose had this to add: "Half-breed is not just a biological thing. It's not just a matter of having one parent from one race and the other parent from another race, or culture, or religion, or anything of that nature. But rather it's a condition of history, a condition of context, a condition of circumstance. It's a political fact."[16]

Fowler points out that some of the "estrangement of the two tribes" was "complicated" by the "significant 'mixed-blood'" membership in the Shoshone community. Shoshone marriages far more often than Arapaho marriages were with Anglos, since the early 1900s. At a low point in the populations of each group (in 1914), Fowler found "767 full-blood and 107 mixed-blood Arapahos compared with 498 full-blood and 342 mixed-blood Shoshone." Proportional discrepancies continued in the generations to come.[17]

Cultural differences may have encouraged the differential in out-marriage, but economic motivations were probably central for Euro-American ranchers. The Shoshones lived in ranching country.[18] The best solution for men who owned cattle but lacked property was to marry into the tribe, since for the most part the land could not be purchased. However, the tribes did have some rules that these ranchers had to contend with, namely that the Shoshone member (the wife) would "own the brand, own the land," as told by Crowheart rancher Barbara Sage: "Husbands could not be on the brand, could not own allotments, could not get range or graze cattle. Brands are registered but must belong to an enrolled tribal member to graze on the reservation. The man could be hired by the tribal member woman but she was the owner of the brand and allotment. Her white husband would be called a 'herdsman.' He had no land."

Some Shoshone women, enriched with cattle, gained status and gained for their children a chance for advanced education. As college graduate Barbara Sage said, "That's how the breeds got here—because of our grandmothers."[19]

Sage believed that her grandfather, a white man, married her grand-mother, about half Shoshone, for the ranching property and way of life it gave him. Sage, having grown up with her grandmother, identified with her culture and was considered a part of the tribe. The mixed-blood Shoshones were economically "much better off" than the other tribal members, according to Fowler, and often "had fairly sizeable herds of cattle or sheep." They tended to live "at Burris on the Wind River and on the South Fork of the Little Wind," areas on the northern and western sides of the reservation where ranching was dominant.[20] The PIE organization was centered in the ranching country of the north-western area of the reservation and its members were often known to be mixed-blood; a faction politically in concert with whites (see Ward testimony later in this chapter).

Internal group conflicts are to the advantage of a common enemy—when outsiders cannot easily identify splintered factions, the enemy uses the confusion. The Shoshones might not identify those members with some white ancestry as "mixed-blood," although according to Fowler they did so identify "a portion" with "alternate lifestyles," particularly in the Burris area north of Crowheart.[21]

Front page headlines reinforced simplistic non-Indian assumptions about tribal differences: "Tribes Differ on Reservation: Shoshones Show No Support for School" or "Shoshones Protest: 'Don't Include Us.'"[22] It appeared that there was a clear split in viewpoints between the two tribes. Euro-Americans gave much attention to supposed divisions between the tribes.

Chris Goggle described the struggle with PIE as "a continued fight all the way through. It was real dirty and political." Alberta Friday said those opposed to the reservation district, "turned me in to the school board as anti-white" and had "people threatening to beat me up." But Friday had the support of her school superintendent, Silas Lyman; "He was our biggest supporter. . . . When the farmers were accusing me of discrimination, he said, 'Prove it,' and they never did. Students were questioned. He just stood up for me all around." Friday pointed out that there were "individual Shoshone who were supportive but didn't want to fight with their own group. PIE was a small 'elite' group."[23]

However, they were able to mobilize "a great many people" from their district to attend meetings in opposition to a reservation district, according to Alfred Ward's 1974 testimony. Ward also testified that the Shoshone General Council, consisting of the Shoshone general membership, had voted against an Indian high school and that a referendum vote taken in Fort Washakie District 21, which included non-Indian votes, found 105 against the proposed reservation district and 78 for it (see Twitchell, later). On the other hand, Ward testified that the Shoshone General Council had voted *against* financially supporting the *Alfred Ward, et al.* lawsuit against the state for its four-district plan that included a reservation district.[24]

WRSAEA found the PIE group very difficult to deal with in part because of the activities of the coordinator of Indian education. As Barbara Sage said, "Murray was coordinator of Indian education on the reservation, a state job, yet, involved with PIE." A Lander resident and Shoshone, he was assigned to "assist eligible school districts in preparing applications for Johnson-O'Malley funds," a federal Indian education program, as was detailed in the Lander newspaper. The story pointed out that the Shoshone-Arapaho Joint Council, the State Department of Education, and the BIA had developed the annual plan. It did not mention the school boards of Mill Creek at Ethete, Fort Washakie, and Arapahoe as among those involved in the planning, possibly the coordinator's omissions.[25]

The state, apparently not anticipating conflict or favoritism, expected Murray to "act as liaison (to) the education department." He sponsored well-publicized meetings in Fort Washakie in 1970 and 1971. One two-day meeting was "at the request of a group" in that district. Discussion was organized around several questions concerning the "feasibility" of establishing a reservation school district.[26]

The PIE faction used the 1878 forced sharing of Shoshone treaty land, hard won by the venerable Shoshone Chief Washakie, in political rhetoric designed to stir up resentments. PIE blamed the Arapahos rather than Washington officials for the Shoshones having to share the land.

Yet WRSAEA members tried to avoid conflict with PIE. Loretta Fowler explained that historically the Arapahos "forbear to take advantage of Shoshone factionalism. . . . They sometimes compromise in order to maintain long-range cooperative relations, so that in conflicts with whites the two tribes' resentment of each other does not work against their joint interests."[27]

The federal government settled with the Shoshones in 1937 for the treaty lands upon which it had placed the Arapahos. It paid the Shoshones $4,408,444 in this, the "Tunison settlement," that came thirty-seven years after Washakie's death. The settlement added to the Shoshone economic advantage in royalty and severance tax incomes that, as mentioned in chapter 3, are split evenly between the unevenly populated tribes. In 1976 an individual Shoshone received $136 per month, whereas an Arapaho received only $90. The effect of financial discrepancies on health and material well-being may have played a part in some of the Shoshone resistance to the mutuality of democratic control of the schools. One Shoshone petitioner to the FCRC had this to say: "The Shoshone people as a whole don't want the reservation school. . . . It would set us back 50 years, and it's time we were progressing."[28]

Yet a third organized group argued against a reservation school district. This was a long-standing organization, the Shoshone Business Council. It was a small group elected by all enrolled members, the "mixed-blood" Shoshones of District 6 north of Crowheart as well as those of the Fort Washakie School District 21, and it had the responsibility to "conduct normal business," according to Alfred Ward. The "buying of land" or major jurisdictional issues were the responsibility of the General Council.[29]

The Business Council minutes from October 20, 1971, suggest that Murray helped strengthen opposition to a reservation school; he moved to "rescind our earlier actions supporting the idea (the 1969 vote), concept of a Reservation High School because, the development since in support of this idea that have [sic] created a great opposition among the Shoshone people." Among those present was Murray's sister, Ivora Ray of Fort Washakie, a member of the PIE group. She favored a more recent referendum taken on June 22, 1970, that was opposed to the reservation school, when the vote of a "cross section" of voters was taken.[30]

Starr Weed, a member of the District 21 school board, resisted what he could see was planned—he refused to vote on Murray's motion. He said he resented how his grandchildren had been treated in the Lander schools and wanted them to have their own schools where "they would feel more comfortable and at home." He felt that the Indians were not adequately represented on the council because of the mixed-blood and white culture influence: "The Fort (Washakie) council members were related to people in Lander." Furthermore, he believed the issue should not be dealt with by the council, "because I knew what the Business Council was up to and didn't feel it was their business."[31]

Weed defended the reservation school in its defeat in the June 22, 1970, referendum—saying that the American Indians had not come out to vote. Perhaps he hoped to engender a little levity and reduce some of the tension, although at the Indians' expense: "Well, you know how our Indian people are . . . they don't stop, and look, and listen to anything." He still refused to vote at the end of the meeting: "That's what way I'm going to stick. Because the referendum vote down here, that was mostly white people. That's the reason why I'm going to stick with the treaty rights, my Indians' rights, that's the one I'm going to stick with."[32]

The Shoshone Business Council meeting had another conflict. This concerned what rancher Louis Twitchell had told the members of the FCRC about the vote taken by the Joint Shoshone-Arapaho Business Council. Twitchell, as noted, represented District 21 on the County Committee. No one at the Business Council meeting disagreed that the Joint Council had in fact passed a resolution favoring the establishment of a new school, but there was fear about how Twitchell had communicated that to the FCRC. Did he leave the impression that the Joint Council vote was a powerful influence with reservation people? A member asked Twitchell if he thought the resolution represented "the feelings of School District 21," and in response, he who had helped in taking the referendum asked if he could tell them what he thought.[33] The following interaction ensued:

CHAIRMAN: Yeah, go ahead.

LOUIS TWITCHELL: When this law (1969) was first passed by the State Legislature the members . . . of the Board of School District 21 did not know what people thought. We instructed the Principal to contact each household . . . in School District 21 and asked them what they wanted. After this was done we reviewed the results and 76 percent of the people contacted wanted a High School on the Reservation.

Here Twitchell was interrupted but then allowed by the chair to continue.

LOUIS TWITCHELL: After this, a few months or a year or so after this we been keeping for two and a half years on this Reorganization. A vote was taken during the regular school election and the vote was 105 against and 78 for, I may be a little off on those figures. . . . *We felt that you take the white vote out of this and the Indian people still wanted a High School on the Reservation* [emphasis added]. After this there was a petition presented to the Planning Committee bearing 847 signatures favoring a formation of a high school on the Reservation. And these signatures came from the three districts that would be affected. Of these 141 signatures were enrolled Shoshones and in my opinion the majority of the Shoshone people want the High School on the Reservation. This is my opinion.[34]

Twitchell's opinion was important on this point—it potentially countered any Euro-American community beliefs that the two tribes were split on the issue. However, Alfred Ward was also present at the meeting and strongly objected to Twitchell's opinion, since the Indians did not identify themselves as Indian in writing. Furthermore, he objected to their separate identifications in the first place: "And then separate the non-Indian from the Indian, what do you do with the poor—of the breed . . . an Indian on rolls which I happen to be and whether you need, divide me in half."

The Shoshone Business Council voted in the October meeting to rescind their previous support of the reservation school. The vote was

6. Starr Weed, 2009. Photograph by author.

taken early in the meeting when apparently, with five members present, the chairman not voting, and Starr Weed refusing his vote, there were three votes. The chairman pointed out at the end of the meeting that while they had rescinded their previous support of the reservation district concept, the council was also "affirming that *the school problem is within School district 21 and is not under the jurisdiction of the Business Council*" (emphasis added). He closed the meeting saying that he would have "School District 21 and the State Board of Education plus the Planning committee," informed of their vote.[35] This would evolve into another half-truth for WRSAEA to fight.

Starr, in his slow and measured fashion, showed dark emotion as he described his reaction to the Shoshone Business Council's withdrawal of support for a reservation school: "That really bothered me and hurt my feelings and they were not even asking for their school."[36] Starr still kept the minutes from this meeting in the trunk of his car after thirty years. The reservation people who desired self-determination faced strong opposition. But their emotional determination to see the survival of their identity and culture was at the core of their being.

Ivora Ray immediately put the results of the Shoshone Business Council meeting to use. She represented "a reservation parents' organization," according to the WSJ, at the November 1971 meeting of the State Committee (see chapter 5). There she testified that the Shoshone Business Council had "rescinded the five-district proposal because it was not the wish of the people of District 21." The newspaper concurred, stating that Mrs. Ray was "referring to a referendum in which a proposed reservation high school was voted down by that district." Ray said they did not oppose the school so long as it was not imposed on "the reservation as a whole." Darwin St. Clair, a Shoshone and activist for the school, ran for the Business Council and won although, it must be said, the Shoshone people had many reasons to elect him.[37]

This chapter has shown the intense on-reservation and border town opposition and controversy that swirled around the subject of Indian-controlled education. Wind River advocates saw defeat coming if they confined their political activity to the local area.

7

Indian School Opens

1971–72

The Wind River Shoshone and Arapaho Education Association members got "on their cars" (as they would say, and as some of their German immigrant boarding school teachers would have said) to travel to the Denver airport some 350 miles away. There was a plane that flew out of Riverton, but they usually went to Denver by car. (The noisy little Riverton plane was unsteady, besides being too expensive; thoughtfully, the airline kept paper bags at the seat backs.) So they got on their cars for the first leg of the journey to Washington DC—as with the Lander school board (see chapter 3), it would be easier to work with Congress than it had been with the Shoshone Business Council. Sandra and Darwin St. Clair, Alberta "Tiny" Friday, Ben Friday Jr., Tom Shakespeare, Dennis Sun Rhodes, and Michael Gross made this trip in early November 1971.[1] This was Wind River's renewed surge of effort at the national level for educational self-determination after being let down by the Nixon administration earlier that year (see chapter 4).

The WRSAEA group was able to acquire funding for the trip from the American Association on Indian Affairs and the Native American Rights Fund. The newly formed Coalition of Indian Controlled School Boards (CICSB; see chapter 4) sent a representative. The support of these organizations was important to morale even though funding was limited; Alberta Friday remembered that they had to stay in the Presidential Hotel—one that did not live up to its prestigious name.[2]

Language barriers as well as a low budget played a part in their experience in the city. Members of the Wind River coalition usually walked or took a taxi together. Alberta described how on the way to one meeting, there were too many to fit into one taxi, and they took two: "Well, we made it to the BIA and they didn't. They couldn't communicate with that Chinese driver." Sun Rhodes solved the problem, "Dennis Sun Rhodes, who was studying to be an architect, drew that building." Unfortunately for the driver, "he had a wreck just as he got them there and so they paid him and got out of there."[3]

Sandra St. Clair performed secretarial duties, typing last minute documents for attorney Gross well into the night. Reverend Duncombe continued to call politicians from Wyoming. Sandra remembered, "It felt like he was feeling the way we were,—Why can't they just let us do this? Why were they putting things in our way? Without Fr. Dave, he had a lot of backbone, without him we would not have made it."[4]

Gross orchestrated the roles of the group in Washington. They had to have "somebody to go in and sit down at the BIA office, somebody to call, and somebody to say what needed to be said." Sandra was the one appointed to speak up and point out that the local town schools "were using our money when we needed it."[5]

However, receptionists told them that the officials were out and not coming back. As Sandra St. Clair put it: "They were wanting us to leave." Gross too remembers that at the BIA, "The intransigence was palpable. 'Who do these Indians think they are? They're not even tribal council delegates.'" All the same, St. Clair, a former Miss Indian America, took on her assigned role, "But we want to know something *now*!" They did not leave.[6]

Starr Weed, then a District 21 school board member, said that Wyoming's U.S. senator Gale McGee telephoned him around the time of the delegation's visit to Washington. McGee called to inquire about the imminent visits of "Ward and [the] McAdams." He asked Weed, "What are they coming here for?" Starr said he explained that it was about the school, and McGee told him, "Well, I've already made up my mind." The delegation learned that U.S. senator Clifford Hansen (then past Republican governor of Wyoming) and Democratic Senator McGee (a former University of Wyoming history professor) put pressure on the BIA to meet with them. Also, WRSAEA members found that Edward "Ted" Kennedy was very supportive when they visited him; his aides "did a lot to open doors." Still the answers were disappointing. Ben Friday Jr. described how Commissioner Louis Bruce told them there was no money, and he could promise them nothing.[7] As described in chapter 4, John O. Crow, who favored "old-liner" policies, was in charge of BIA internal affairs by the fall of 1971. Gross called an old law school friend who knew an up and coming *Washington Post* writer, William Greider, to change the way things were going.

On Sunday, November 7, 1971, the *Washington Post* published a full-page Greider commentary titled "Indian Runaround: How the Bureaucracy Vetoes a Nixon Vow on Schools." Greider's portrayal of the high dropout rate among Wind River Reservation students and of BIA resistance to the Wind River Association's efforts to achieve their school was documented for the Nixon administration and the country to read. Greider pointed out that when children reached high school age on the Wind River Reservation, they were "scattered across the map." He wrote that there were 300 students in Lander and Riverton schools, about 150 or so in government boarding schools (not including those who were in out-of-state mission schools; see chapter 3), and some 200 who did not continue in school at all. He quoted the president of WRSAEA, Allison Sage Sr., as saying that people wanted their children back home, where they could "attack the drop-out problem, or rather the push-out problem." Greider's story added that the Wind River parents were trying to get "their own community high school which, after all, is not exactly a radical proposal."[8]

Greider exposed BIA roadblocks to the school by the innuendo in its own statements: BIA official Elizabeth Skelly was quoted as saying: "They like the idea, but they see all the problems they are getting into. They have a feeling they might get out on a limb by cutting off the bureau. There's much more reluctance than one might think. After all, this is a big step for these people to take."[9] BIA paternalism stood out even in word choice.

Skelly's suggestion that WRSAEA was "cutting off the bureau" intimated a threat akin to termination: "the problems they are getting into." According to Greider, Skelly also indicated more short-term difficulties— the BIA now required WRSAEA to show community support for its school proposals. WRSAEA would have to do a community survey all over again. Greider reported that the original surveys showed 900 parents and students in favor of the Wind River district and "fewer than 100, mainly Shoshones," against it. WRSAEA had planned to open the high school in the fall of 1971. With the "run around," the school had not opened, and "40 or 50 Indian children did not go back to boarding school," or any school, because the school they expected to open did not do so.[10] A new survey might not have shown such strong support.

Greider countered Skelly with what President Nixon had said a year earlier: "Consistent with our policy that the Indian community should have the right to take over the control and operation of federally funded programs, we believe every Indian community wishing to do so should be able to control its own Indian schools." The story also quoted a letter from Native American Commissioner Bruce supporting the financing of the Indian-controlled schools. Michael Gross observed, "The next day Vice President Spiro Agnew's office called the BIA to ask [in Gross's paraphrase]—'What the hell is going on there?'"[11]

Ben Friday Jr. recounted that Senator McGee took up the cause and told the group "not to worry" about where the money would come from. In fact, he told them, "Let me worry about it." Friday remembered that Senator Hanson's aide, Ted Williams, later with the Associated Press, was present in their meeting as well as McGee's aide, John Vinich of Hudson, Wyoming. Friday believed that both Wyoming senators helped "to get money lined up." A letter from these senators to Commissioner Louis Bruce in early November 1971 began as follows: "This is to request that you move expeditiously in drafting a letter of commitment for operating funds relative to the pending proposal of the Wind River Education Association."[12]

As Friday said, letters from senators have powerful effects; the BIA immediately made an offer of money for the schools. However, Gross had an "iron clad rule" that he had developed during his days as negotiator with government officials for the Ramah Navajo school board: "Never leave a meeting with a government official without getting a summary of the meeting signed by the official, or better yet an actual commitment or promise, in writing." The BIA officials said that they needed two days to put the contract in writing. "We offered to come back. In two days we did."[13]

The BIA put up one last bit of resistance; when they handed over the January to June 1972 contract, it was two inches thick. Gross asked to see a corresponding contract, "the State of Arizona's Johnson-O'Malley contract for that year." The official had the Arizona contract in his hand when he returned a few minutes later; "It was so thin you couldn't see it sideways." The WRSAEA's contract was full of "controls or detailed record keeping requirements," and amounted to much less than the several-million-dollar Arizona contract. "We got the Wind River contract chopped to 1 inch and signed. We went home."[14] It was good to have a lawyer during the time of BIA recalcitrance. And the *Washington Post* article ensured the happy outcome.

The BIA Division of Education acted immediately on WRSAEA's November 10 request. Allison Sage Sr. received the award of $100,000 for the Wyoming Indian School on November 11, 1971; the contract would begin on December 1 of that year.[15]

WRSAEA allowed only one compromise, possibly to protect the helpful Senators Hansen and McGee. The contract, according to the *Wyoming State Journal*, named the reservation school the "Education Resources Center." The senators' November letter of support for the school contained careful wording; WRSAEA's proposal was "for an educational program aimed at those Indian students currently not attending high school but otherwise qualified to do so."[16] Lander and Riverton could dismiss the school as a school for "drop-outs." However, the McGee and Hansen letter did not prevent any student from attending the new reservation school. It also did not prevent a name change in the near future.

Events with the contentious BIA mirrored the entire struggle that the Wind River Reservation people had for control of their lives and resources. The BIA was necessary to them all the same; the BIA would do what it could to protect its "subjects" from a complete takeover by the local states and community towns. It needed to keep its paternalistic role. And so Native Americans had a schizophrenic relationship with the BIA; they were thankful that their relationship had never been "terminated," but it was obvious that if they had not gotten some publicity for their predicament, Nixon's BIA officials would have ignored them (and the president) without fear of charges of insubordination. This was an important fact of history when the Wind River people later opted for a state public school rather than for one under the BIA.

It was not only the Native American push for a school that exposed the BIA's pattern of near autonomous rule. It had long failed to cooperate with the U.S. Department of Education "despite continuous urging by Indian people and concerned congressmen." Congress found it necessary to establish the American Indian Policy Review Commission in 1975 to investigate the government's mismanagement of Indian affairs. Columnist Jack Anderson reported in 1976 that a memo by the Review Commission's director indicated that the BIA was mishandling and neglecting its responsibilities to the people they were meant to serve. Anderson, according to an authoritative source, was the "most widely read columnist" in the country. Ted Duncombe, by then an intern at the *Anniston Star* in Alabama, followed up with his editorial, "Abuse: Anderson's BIA report won't surprise Indians of Wind River Reservation."[17]

There is a question as to why Nixon sought media attention for policy improvements for Native Americans in the first place—with his promises from 1970 undermined in the BIA, possibly with his approval. Several writers have suggested answers to this question: George P. Castile argued that the indigenous "small scattered populations," could be more easily managed and identified with less ambitious causes than were found in the huge rioting crowds of the late 1960s civil rights movement. Roxanne Dunbar Ortiz concluded much the same; support for some Indian control and other liberal causes was part of a "neocolonialist technique" meant to diffuse the more "explosive situations" such as the "anti-war and black liberation movements."[18]

Guy Senese pointed out in *Self-Determination and the Social Education of Native Americans* that it had long been argued that Indians should be given administrative responsibilities in their institutions (such as education) in order to quell resistance and harness their "active involvement in their own exploitation," a disturbing line of thought.[19]

Had the powers behind the BIA resistance to Indian-controlled schools and services trusted Nixon or understood his full intent, it may have given them pause—perhaps they had not heard of "neocolonialist strategies," or it could be that they did not want to see *any* concessions. "Self-determination" was dangerous territory to those with financial interests in Indian resources, and the threat of loss of this political base was dangerous for Nixon. Louis Bruce, according to Jack Forbes in *Native Americans and Nixon*, was not the only Indian advocate in the Nixon administration to lose his power shortly after Nixon's speech.[20]

The Ethete high school's contract that authorized their school to open was preemptory to the State of Wyoming and Fremont County decision-making processes. The American Indian school could for the time being survive as a trust responsibility (see chapter 2) under the accreditation and funding of the federal government's BIA. The Rosebud Reservation people established the Holy Rosary School, and in 1973 the Duckwater Reservation Shoshone on the west side of the Rocky Mountains opened their school "in the spirit of self-determination."[21]

The Wind River Reservation's high school opened in early January 1972. The tribal community knew that having a high school in place by any name—a "Resource Center" or an "interim solution"—was a victory that would be difficult for their opposition to reverse. And with a "special emphasis in American Indian studies," it held promise for renewed and strengthened identity; as Gross described it, the community "seized control of its destiny through education." The classes included Arapaho and Shoshone languages, art, history, and tribal government. A summer program prepared students to work at the Arapaho Ranch. According to Ben Friday Jr., the first graduation is remembered with humor and pleasure: "The first and only graduate was the Underwood boy, Pat, in

'72. Senator McGee came out and was speaker for graduation." Chairman of the Board Allison Sage also spoke, saying to the lone graduate: "May you have many happy reunions!"[22]

There were only thirty-two students, but Gross remembers the community's pride in its fledgling school. They wanted to be "on the map," and so the principal ran local radio notices of the lunch menus "just like Lander and Riverton did, 'chipped beef on toast, milk, and strawberry jello.' These menus were entirely made up. Though the kids got fed, nobody knew in advance what would be served each day!" William C'Hair described the experience: "I put a lot of work into it and you don't know how it'll feel until . . . you see a reality of it. . . . There's a reoccurrence in various times, something happens and then you say, 'Yeah, it was worth it.'"[23]

Insecurity plagued the new school from the beginning. The $100,000 from the BIA would not meet the school's needs for long, and the County Committee's struggle was far from settled. Even the name that WRSAEA planned for their school, "Wind River High School," had to be given up. District 6 claimed the name in a Monday board meeting prior to the Resource Center board's Thursday meeting. And so, as Alfred Redman remembers, "We had a contest. Bruce Chavez came up with the name, 'Wyoming Indian High School.'"[24]

The board hired Barbara Sage as director and Irene Mountain Sheep as bookkeeper when the school opened. Patrick Goggles (later the district's state representative), son of Chris and Caroline Goggles, served on the BIA high school board for ten years, six as its chairman.[25]

The school functioned as a contract school under the BIA for a total of twelve and a half years. The BIA sent a "letter of intent" each spring to provide funding beginning in the following fall, according to the high school's former home economics teacher, Marilyn Groesbeck (b. 1947). The teachers never knew the amount until fall arrived. They came back each year "on a good will basis," as was common in BIA schools. However, the existence of the school had an immediate impact on the economy across the reservation. Michael Gross said it was possible "to see first-hand the critical links between education, economic development, and political control." That was true even for those who had opposed the school; Alberta Friday told of the irony most enjoyed—two of the PIE activists "were the first in line to get jobs" (that is, Shoshones with the Fort Washakie organization Parents Interested in Education). Asked if they were hired, she responded, "Yes, they got the jobs. They [the Arapahos] are a lot gentler than my tribe."[26]

The school had to meet BIA standards for accreditation. All teachers had to have physicals each year and complete numerous federal forms. Groesbeck related that all the teachers she knew were certified with the exception of Arapaho/Shoshone language teachers, their subjects not being available in university training programs. Native language teachers simply had to show the ability to speak and understand their language before an Arapaho or Shoshone Language Commission. Later they received on location classroom methods training from the University of Wyoming, the University of Colorado, and Central Wyoming College. Native language teachers were required to have an associate degree after 2005.[27] The opponents of the new school continued to criticize it for not being accredited until it became a state school under North Central Standards. William C'Hair described the situation:

> And then they said, 'their school is not accredited.' It sounded impressive. It sounded like something that really matters. Now people don't understand accreditation, they don't know what it's all about, but the opponents of the school . . . they say you shouldn't send your kids over to that school. It's not accredited. . . . That became kind of a popular song. So then we went to North Central. We got accreditation through North Central. Then it was a surprise to find out only a small percent of the criteria was on academics. Most of it was physical plant. . . . You had to have certain kind of sinks in your kitchen, the codes, you know. . . . Everybody thought (with accreditation) your kid was gonna be so much smarter. So, as I say, . . . they really didn't know what they were talking about then but it sounded good.

The school had been open for less than a year when its newsletter, *Tribe Talk*, proudly reported that a representative of the North Central

Association (NCA) had stated that it was "well on its way to full accreditation . . . all teachers are fully certified, and the school offers a wide range of courses." The NCA representative went on to say that the graduates would be accepted "by any Junior College in the state as well as the University of Wyoming." Only the construction of a new classroom building, planned for completion in the spring of 1973, stood in the way of NCA accreditation.[28]

But employees still had to deal with other bureaucratic issues, such as government audits. Fortunately, the school had Irene Mountain Sheep, a Haskell Institute graduate and skilled bookkeeper. She was known in the community as "the power behind the throne," according to Barbara Sage. "Everything was recorded and the books balanced in that beautiful, legible handwriting of hers." Barbara remembers that just after the school opened, the BIA auditor made a surprise visit to their school office, "that little, bitty shack" (on the mission grounds). The audit only took a half day: "The BIA looked at the books and sent a letter. Everything was fine." Irene worked at the school for nearly two years and then for many years at the BIA.[29]

Sage related that many of the students, "the drop-outs, the push-outs," came to the new school to play basketball, recruited by future coach Alfred Redman. She said the school did not have uniforms for the players but this made little difference; the entire community was excited to see their rag-tag team compete. It was fortunate that the school started when it did. Just as the WSJ carried the story of the Wyoming Indian School's opening there was another story, the story of the closing of the Noble Hotel, the place where the Indian boys slept through the night after playing basketball games for Lander Valley High School.[30]

The Wyoming Indian High School (WIHS) organized a basketball tournament of American Indian high schools in the winter of 1972. One of the first students, George Groesbeck (b. 1952), relished remembering the all-Indian tournament, with players from Chinle, Arizona; Fort Hall, Idaho; Intermountain Indian School, Ogden, Utah; and Fort Duchesne, Utah, and Ramah, New Mexico. They and their coaches stayed at the homes of Wind River Reservation families. Groesbeck also told me about the choosing of the basketball team name and emblem. Someone at the school's Parish Hall cafeteria gave the choices: "'Wind River Braves,' no hands went up. 'Wind River Chiefs' and everybody put their hands up." He laughed as he told me: "Ain't no Braves—the Chiefs!" And so, in a self-description reminiscent of the non-Indian use of the Indian image as mascot, they took their image back. They *were* the leaders, not mascots.[31]

Alfred Redman, the high school's coach of many years, did not have a teaching certificate at first and so the board hired a coach from eastern Colorado. The community interest in the game was so intense that, according to Ben Friday Jr., the coach complained to the board. "He couldn't be coaching them with so many people telling him what to do. So that's when we [the board] had to tell some of the men not to sit down there with him 'cause *he* was getting paid to coach."[32] With Friday's encouragement, Alfred then went to school to become the Wyoming Indian High School coach. Many illustrious years of regional and state championships followed.

The school facilities were all antiquated. It held its classes in the old St. Michael's Mission buildings, and the school bus as described by Alberta Friday was only somewhat improved from the 1940s: "The first bus was like an old army van with broken windows." Alberta and other interviewees seemed to enjoy describing the oddities of that early makeshift environment. Their conditions were similar to those of most American Indian schools. Daniel M. Rosenfelt described the Indian school disparities of the 1970s: "The most conspicuous disparity cannot be hidden: The quality of school facilities serving Indian children will almost invariably compare unfavorably with facilities serving non-Indians."[33]

Students skirted sagebrush and crossed roads to get to classes scattered across about a quarter mile of terrain. One small building on the southwest corner, which students called "the bead shop," held the art classes. Teachers presented social studies and history in Parish Hall and English in the Balcome House, named for a turn of the century Episcopal warden who encouraged industrial and crafts training. They explained mathematics and additional English in an old log building that was to the north and some distance behind a fast food and sundries store and gas station. Students continued to play basketball in Faith Hall, known as "the old stone gymnasium." They used a nearly windowless cement block building, known as "Blue Sky Hall," for home economics. Today it is the place for many funerals and ceremonial giveaways, a centerpiece to plains tribal values.[34]

A prefabricated building replaced all the old buildings except the stone gymnasium in November 1972. The ceremonial "Four Old Men" honored the groundbreaking with ceremony, Nickerson "West" Shakespeare "taking the first ground up." Sandra C'Bearing remembers the prayer that gave thanks for the students' "opportunity to go to school and learn like anybody else. To go to the high school and get a job, and support your family, and go to college, and come back and do something for your people."[35]

Marilyn Groesbeck described how many students came to the high school after having "been out up to six years." Fully grown men and women hoped to regain self-worth after the demeaning failures. Perhaps given their ages, everyone accepted their smoking in the school. Ben Friday Jr. related that the staff furnished ashtrays. But there was an occasional problem; the BIA intended that the food be eaten only by students and staff. And so as told by Alberta Friday: "There was one boy who came to school just to eat, and they put him in jail. So the kids put out a cup in the dining room and they collected money to get him out of jail."[36]

BIA "contract school" regulations *permitted attendance of Indian children only*. This situation ended rhetoric that a reservation (Indian) school would be in conflict with federal policy. And for Native Americans, segregation had its benefits. "Segregation," with local control, gave a chance to recover what had been suppressed or ignored in the non-Indian schools.[37] But the new state law threatened Native American school board control in the reservation's elementary schools.

The BIA high school was not *unified* with its elementary and middle schools. The Wyoming Education Code of 1969 defined a unified school district as one under the control of one board of trustees and administered by one superintendent of schools.[38] Thus if WRSAEA lost the

7. Faith Hall, the stone gymnasium, at the Episcopal Mission at Ethete, Wyoming, 2009. Photograph by author.

boundary struggle battle, *the* BIA *school would be of no help in establishing a "unified district."* The reservation's *elementary and middle schools, which so far had had Indian control, would be required to affiliate with other districts in order to be part of a unified district where other boards would have control.*

The high school stood alone under the BIA. This was an insecure position—if the local towns won control, it would be convenient and advantageous to the BIA budget to abandon the Indian school to the non-Indian district affiliated with their elementary and middle schools. On the other hand, if WRSAEA won the struggle, they would be independent of the local towns and have state and probably federal construction funds *for a public high school and other schools as needed.*

The county was having its own problems. By the time the school had its federal contract, the County Committee was "bemoaning the rejection of (their) plan" by the State Committee. But then the state gave Fremont

County (the only county in the state that needed an extension) until January 1, 1973, to finalize reorganization of their districts. As always, a major roadblock to progress was the state's requirement to produce details as to equalization of per-pupil valuation. One FCRC member said, "Maybe we should fold this thing up and go home. Let's let the state figure this thing out, if they want to." But the Lander representative goaded the committee forward with its work—"We're acting like whipped pups."[39]

The FCRC discussed the November 1971 preference by the State Committee that they split the county into two districts. They considered two ways of doing it but defeated both ideas. The plan that would have pleased Riverton and Lander (by giving them the Indian districts), displeased others—Wind River (District 6) and Dubois would be placed together, and to add to the displeasure, with Riverton. The other plan, proposed by Silas Lyman, would have placed the Indian districts with other outlying districts, giving the Indian districts a more equitable distribution of county taxable resources. However, his plan was doomed in that it placed the competitive towns of Riverton and Lander together in the first district and Wind River and Dubois together (with the Indian schools) in the second.[40]

In a tactic of the stymied, the County Committee appointed a subcommittee. Its mission was to look at one- and two-district plans. It came back with several district plans, one from Lander's Starrett that achieved near equal per-student valuation but with unpopular combinations: Lander with the reservation and Dubois with District 6. After the committee voted down a two-district plan in January, it voted for a one-district plan proposed by Starrett and as a result was threatened with a lawsuit by attorney Gross.[41]

As it turned out, the Lander school board was not happy with Starrett's proposal either and voted the one-district idea down. Riverton, with its territorial problems with Lander, also opposed Starrett's proposal.[42]

Oddly, the Fremont County Administrators Association submitted a letter to the County Committee that asked them to put off the decision until July 3, 1973, more than six months after the deadline. The FCRC decisively rejected the suggestion. But by early 1972 no one could see a way out. The county's varied complexities presented insurmountable problems: the two main population centers mistrusted one another and did not want to give up Indian student federal money; one outlier town edged into non-Indian controlled reservation resources and wanted more; and the sparsely populated areas mistrusted the larger towns and were often fighting with one another. The entirely frustrated committee with no solutions voted 12 to 1 to adjourn 40 minutes early in their mid-February meeting, an "unheard of" move, according to their attorney.[43] The proposal by the county administrators was not so strange after all.

The towns and their solutions needed an intervention to attack their problem at its roots. Only the Indians were outside their squabbles.

8

Indian People Speak, Face Retaliation

1972–73

The County Committee replaced the January one-district plan with one that they liked better, a four-district plan that divided the Indian districts between the two largest towns. In the one-district plan not only would Lander and Riverton have had to share their oil and tax base incomes and Indian student federal money, but they would have had to work together: "boy, when Lander and Riverton had to get together under a one-district plan, that sure didn't last long!" chuckled one rural representative.[1]

Silas Lyman of Mill Creek tried to bring back the FCRC's strongly opposed five-district plan in May and again in June. Lyman's plan included a reservation district (see chapter 5); the four-district plan was "nothing more than a plan to get rid of unification on the reservation," he said. The Wind River Indian Education Association would need a unified district in order to replace the BIA school with a *public* high school. Each time Lyman's motion died for lack of a second. The committee's actions incensed the Native American community. Their desires for self-determination and expression of their cultures through their schools had long been the least of county considerations. But centuries-old oratory and negotiating skills would soon serve them well.[2]

Chester Armajo, one of the Arapaho youths who had once had to hitchhike home after Lander school activities and was now serving as a board member of AIM, spoke with passion at the June meeting of the FCRC. He spoke about the town's use of federal Indian money in the library where they were sitting and about its failure to address cultural issues for Indian children in its schools; Indian culture had no place: "it makes an Indian person feel lower than a white man." Local town control meant that Indian people "had no voice in their destiny. . . . You can see your system has failed. You're trying to make an Indian into a white man, which you can never do. Why don't you let us decide what road to follow?" He described the Indian people's breaking point: "We have had no real voice, just a few token positions. That's why Mr. Lyman was overridden here. Is that justice, that you can't even listen to a man on your own board? I don't see justice being created here. . . . I'm seeing white people taking the upper hand over Indian people. We can't put up with it any longer."[3]

One FCRC member was confused by Armajo's speech; he thought it was mostly Indian people who opposed a reservation district and said, "I don't understand this situation." "Mixed-blood" Shoshone had apparently been effective in their campaign against a school (see chapter 6). Ivora Ray was present and further confused the crowd, saying she wanted consideration for "the people of District 21" (the District 21 school board was *not* in opposition to the new school). Ray went on to add derogatory implications: "We want our children to get a qualified education, where they can compete with other people from other societies, where they will not always get a compensatory education." Barbara Sinclair (Sage) was there to point out: "There is now a high school on the reservation, one of the prerequisites of the State Organization Committee. The student population is there, the school has been established. Maybe just for once you can give the biggest consideration to the reservation rather than the more populous areas within Fremont County."[4]

Several other Native American people spoke in favor of a reservation high school. Lloyd Dewey's father, Scott Dewey, stated in response to a comment by Chairman Sackman that the four-district plan was settled, "We will oppose being ignored in our right to determine how our reservation will be run. . . . We're providing a place to educate our people in our own community, just like Lander and Riverton." Allison Sage spoke passionately: "If you can't hear those war drums, they're beating now. . . . We're not going to sit here and lie down like we've always done. We started that reservation high school with 30-plus students and ended up with over 80. But you're denying us the funds from the state."[5] His statement gave another reason to seek a unified district; financial security.

Tom Shakespeare, a member of the National Congress of American Indians, spoke: "I try to respect a man for what he says. Thinking back while listening to this, I remember Chief Joseph, who said, 'I'm tired. Let us put their heads and our hearts together so that they can do something better for our children.'" The committee stuck to its four-district plan; perhaps they had received too much criticism for their five-district plan. They awaited the State Committee's June 12 hearing.[6]

Eighty people from the Wind River Reservation traveled to Cheyenne to testify in the State Capitol Building before the State Committee in June. The out-of-state Wind River Indian Education Association supporters who arrived in Cheyenne included Birgil Kills Straight, Lakota chairman of the CICSB. Many people from Ethete's Easter Egg Village came as well. Some of them were elderly women with handkerchiefs in the pockets of their paisley dresses and draped in shawls—Lander's ridicule during the One-Shot Antelope Hunt had not changed their way of doing things. They rode a charter bus and spent the night in a motel near the Capitol. Alberta Friday remembered rumors that they would be arrested the next morning—they were "prepared to be arrested." Some of the fears of police came about because WRIEA had been connected with AIM.[7]

The Cheyenne police were indeed at the motel on their motorcycles the next morning but not to arrest them; merely to escort them to the Capitol. The Native Americans had the attention of the media: "Everyone knew we were going to speak." Later the Casper paper reported "Many dressed in colorful tribal regalia, danced and sang to the beat of drums on the State Capitol grounds—to the delight of the tourists."[8]

Fifteen Native Americans took the podium in the House Chamber to give testimony before the State School Organization Committee. Twelve were in support of the reservation high school. But Alfred McAdam, a Shoshone member of PIE, said they wanted their children to go to Lander and Riverton and that the Shoshone Business Council supported the four-district plan. Mrs. McAdam said she "resented" the Arapahos "coming down here and saying they represent the Reservation." She reminded the committee that there were two tribes on the reservation and said that there was "a split on the reservation and there always will be." The State Committee was disabused of the selectively chosen information: Chester Armajo interrupted to point out that twelve members of the WRIEA delegation that day were Shoshones; Robert Friday, a Mill Creek teacher, said that there was *not* a split reservation vote but "only [a split] within the Shoshone tribe."[9]

Armajo and Friday were no doubt disturbed by the double-bind that reminders of history put them in with their Shoshone allies, alliances that had come about in dealing with basic life conditions and exigencies and in mutual opposition to the Lander and Riverton enculturation of their children. The descendants of "traditional enemies" were now friends.[10]

Armajo testified that Lander and Riverton high school personnel "don't give a damn about the Indian student. . . . Lander and Riverton people don't like Indians. They don't know anything about Indian culture. . . . White men have never been able to relate to the Indian people and I don't think they ever will. They steal our water . . . now they want to steal our children. The only reason white people deal with us in areas like Lander and Riverton is for money." Armajo also did not hold back in responding to PIE. He charged that they had "no interest in the education of young Indian people. They are people, who in a sense hate others on the reservation. They are 'red apple' Indians—red on the outside, white on the inside. People like these are the ones who sold us out, sold our lands, so many years ago."[11]

Allison Sage pointed out that twenty of the eighty-three students at the Ethete high school were Shoshones. He also stated that although the school had opened six months earlier, "so far the State Education Department has not seen fit to visit our school," while they had made repeated visits to Cheyenne "for guidance and services." Kills Straight summed up the reason for their testimony as follows: "We want the right to control our own destiny and have our children respect Indian ways."[12] The testimony was a rare opportunity for Native Americans to describe their ongoing experiences for whites as well as the neglect and injustices of over a century.

The behaviors of some opponents of the WRIEA school concept were offensive. Attorney Gross described the circumstances: "We had expert witnesses and affidavits from all over. We submitted the Senate Subcommittee's report. At the hearing some opponents sat behind me. I later learned they were making rude comments and hand signals whenever I spoke. This backfired."

The chair of the State Committee, Jess Jessen complimented those who testified for "the orderly and intelligent way this testimony has been given." He added, "We on the committee will deliberate this plan in a conscientious manner, I assure you."[13]

Optimism and pride reigned. They had won respect in this, a modern day uprising for the ordinary right to educate their children. Alberta Friday remembers a celebration "feast" was held at the Cheyenne Park the afternoon of the testimony. "Everyone was in support of AIM, with food and money. [There was] one AIM song and someone said, 'Boy, that song really tastes good in my mouth.'" The AIM song was the theme song used for the reservation news and job ads radio program "and they [the rest of Wyoming] never knew. That was the closest people there had to participate in something radical."[14]

When the Native Americans rose up to win their right to a school the State Committee seemed to enjoy the opportunity to support their cause. But back home there were those who were threatened; the Riverton school board retaliated. They voted to withhold their acceptance of Johnson-O'Malley Act (JOM) federal funds that would otherwise pay for transportation for Indian students to and from after-school events. One board member said his protest was against the "war dance" on the State Capitol lawn. WRIEA chairman Allison Sage Sr. responded: "This is the type of discriminatory attitude we have been faced with so long in the local schools. . . . People in the state and on the State Committee for School District Organization must now realize that this situation exists here." His response was reported in the state-wide *Casper Star-Tribune* (CS-T).[15]

Mrs. Alfred Ward and Mr. and Mrs. Alfred McAdam wrote to the WSJ: "Members of P.I.E. uphold and approve the recent actions of the Riverton School Board." The guest editorial asserted that the "patrons" (that is, with inclusion of non-Indian voters) of District 21 had voted 105–78 against the unified school district concept on June 22, 1971 (reported by Ray to be June 22, 1970, in the October [1971] Shoshone Business Council meeting).[16] Twitchell and Weed believed that it was mainly whites who had voted against the school (see Ray, Weed, and Twitchell in chapter 6).

Mrs. Ward and the McAdams pointed out the kindness of the Shoshone Chief Washakie for taking in the Arapahos, followed with reiterations of the complaint that he did not really want them. The Arapahos were chided for their lack of gratitude, "Now why bite the hand that has been feeding you?" There was no mention of the Tunison settlement.[17]

Mrs. Alfred McAdam wrote another letter (June 1972) that blamed the reservation high school for causing "such a split among the people of our tribe" and urged attendance at a Shoshone General Council meeting where the issue would be discussed. She closed with "Let's ALL (by this, I mean those Shoshones who are for this drop-out center and those who oppose it) attend the General Council meeting." When a vote was taken among the 129 who self-selected to attend that meeting, 106 were opposed to a District 14 High School. The vote was reported in the Lander paper as a split *between the two tribes* with the headline, "Tribes Differ on Reservation High School, Shoshones Show No Support for School: Arapahoes [sic] Show Strong Support for School." The more distant *Casper Star-Tribune* stated that the Shoshones were "generally split" on the school issue. But Mr. Starrett used the Shoshone General Council vote to support his views in the following State Committee hearing. "Whites fed the discord to better swindle broken tribes," was said of such divides decades later in the Casper paper.[18]

All the discord wrought a positive outcome; Native Americans took over their rightful powers. The Arapaho General Council gave control of the dispersal of the JOM money to the Arapaho Business Council. Larry Murray had been in charge of the dispersal of these funds to the Indian and Lander Valley and Riverton schools. Immediately the Lander paper raised questions as to how the Arapaho takeover of dispersal of funds would affect Murray's office; what proportion of the JOM 1972 budget ($118,750) would be allocated to each school; and whether or not it could be used to help fund the District 14 Resource Center. The town(s) wanted to know what would happen to the Indian money that they were accustomed to using.[19]

The Lander newspaper published a front page four-district map that depicted the reservation divided up among the surrounding towns. There also was remarkable and monotonous testimony just before State Committee's decision was made known. The chairman of the FCRC, Ivan Sackman of Riverton, opposed his own committee's plans; he (like everyone else) saw the problems in trying to consolidate District 6 and Dubois and the failure of the committee to deal with "out of proportion" tax base differences. But most arguments emphasized supposed tribal differences; Starrett repeated the Shoshone Council vote, Ivora Ray repeated her June statements that she did not want "compensatory education" for her children; she wanted them to experience different lifestyles. The towns and reservation waited with tensions running high.[20]

The State Committee voted unanimously against the county's four-district proposal in late July 1972. They said the plan did not provide for "equal education opportunities" in general and that it did "not contain provisions which provide for the educational needs of Indian children on the Reservation." The State Committee's recognition of the County Committee's treatment of Indian student educational needs was a huge victory that prevented disaster. The committee's chairman denied that their vote had anything to do with "the discussed unified Reservation district," but now the FCRC would have to go back to work with greater consideration for the Indian districts if they wanted their plan to succeed. There can be little doubt that Native American testimony in Cheyenne had greatly influenced the state and raised respect for WRIEA. The local paper gave Gross's several explanations of "coercive assimilation" for public consideration.[21]

National attitudes and congressional action may also have influenced outcomes in Wyoming. Congress passed the Indian Education Act one month before the state educational administrators rejected the county's plan. It established "broad new programs . . . to meet the special educational needs of Indian students" in public schools and on or near reservation schools. The act also encouraged input from Indian parents as well as their "participation and approval of a committee" for assistance. However, its stipulations did not provide for Indian parent oversight, crucial to the development of programs for Native children in public schools. Parent oversight would have to wait for the Indian Self-Determination and Education Assistance Act of 1975, discussed in chapter 9.[22]

Still, the June 1972 act did improve funding. It mandated that "an amount deemed necessary for Indian student programs and projects" under Title I funds (allocated in 1965 for educationally deprived children, including Indian children) be exclusively designated for them. Additional amendments were made to the 1950 Impact Aid legislation so as to meet the needs of Indian children exclusively (as opposed to Indian and other children living on non-taxable land). JOM money was still being received by the states for the purpose of funding Indian education.[23] Potentially, the Wind River people were no longer without resources for a public high school and its operation.

The Indian Education Act and most likely the political actions taken by the Wind River people began another process, one of inquiry among high school teachers and Riverton's Central Wyoming College professors. They along with the LVHS Indian club soon offered a week-long program on Indian history, anthropology, and art. Also two new Native American studies courses were offered at LVHS that fall. These were funded by Title IV of the Indian Education Act. The WSJ made it clear that American Indian history had been taught "for years" in the history classes at LVHS. However, the grant writers and teachers said they hoped to educate white students about local Native Americans, whose "ways and wishes . . . they know very little about." It was hoped that the knowledge provided would help overcome the "gap in day-to-day relations between reservation residents and residents of the Lander community."[24] Clearly some in the border towns understood the race relations problems. Several members of each tribe were asked to give advice on course content.

County officials did not react so well to Native American political action or the Indian Education Act. There was some background to their reaction; they were already twisting anti-discrimination arguments against a different American Indian cause in February 1972. The Tribal Joint Business Council had asked that two Native Americans, one from each tribe, be on the five-member Hospital Board of Fremont County at that time. They told the commissioners that without representation they would withhold $280,000 that they had "earmarked" for contribution. A memo from Washington to the tribes supported withholding the funds. There was no vacancy at the time, so the hospital board offered two ex-officio (non-voting) Indian memberships, an offer rejected by the tribes. Apparently the tribes were correct in feeling that the board's "no vacancy" rationale was just an excuse. The hospital board elected a white man from Riverton to keep a balance *between the two towns* when a Riverton resignation took place in the following summer.[25]

Officers and members of the Arapaho Business Council wrote a letter to the editor of the WSJ inviting better relationships between Indians and whites. Commissioner J. M. Kail responded; the Indian "threat" of withholding of money had been "extremely disturbing" to him, "I as any devout American, respond adversely to threat." Kail then, in his front page letter, made what appeared to be his own threats, writing that questions had been raised "concerning the Commissioners [sic] jurisdiction in other areas of mutual interest such as access road construction, welfare, health services and law enforcement." He suggested that the Arapahos could have avoided "ill feelings" by giving a phone call. He stated with condescension that some "would be do-gooders . . . primarily whites," must have put the tribal council up to writing to the *Journal*. He argued against being "regulated by (ethnic) distinction." And so he did not advocate for seeing and hearing the minority group; he argued for their invisibility. Laughlin MacDonald of the ACLU Voting

Rights Project stated (in a 2006 Fremont County voting rights case) that the county's position in this hospital dispute was "A significant lack of responsiveness of elected officials to the particular needs of minorities."[26]

An Indian Health Service doctor immediately wrote a letter to the editor of the WSJ pointing out that 15 percent of the county population was Indian and that $280,000 would be a significant loss to medical care. The county commissioners stuck by their decision all the same and appointed a white man from Riverton to the Hospital Board. An editorial comment from William Sniffin chided the commissioners about the loss of Indian health care money to the community.[27]

The Hospital Board issue dominated the front pages of mid-July 1972, while the paper reported only once the news of the state's rejection of the County Committee's plan for its failure to take into account the needs of Indian students. An explicit argument to ignore their needs soon paralleled the argument for "non-distinction" used by Commissioner Kail.

The County Committee sent a one-district proposal to the state in September 1972. This plan recommended that policy place "special emphasis upon the special educational needs of Indian children in the county *as has been demonstrated in the past*" (emphasis added).[28] Thus the county presented the state with the most divisive and confusing plan found in the county or school history. It recommended the status quo. The committee might as well have flaunted its angry attitudes openly; they saw no way out of their conundrum. Plans with only a few districts ran into physical or political dead ends, while plans with several were in conflict with state law. And they either did not believe that special educational programs could make any difference or simply were defiant against any state law that made them let go of their control and income.

Lander and District 6 (Riverton Reclamation Project area) denied differences among ethnic groups in the one-district proposal, akin to Kail's earlier Hospital Board arguments. They said that they "categorically reject the principle of special recognition of ethnic differences or needs in favor of educational policies applicable to all students regardless of racial origin. Accordingly, it is extremely difficult for your Committee to single out programs specifically designed to meet the special educational needs of the county's Indian children." Since "special recognition" of Indian students would not be given, there would be no programs for the state to examine and *no way to know if their schools were doing anything to meet Indian student needs*. It is telling that Lander and District 6 joined one another in refusing to recognize "ethnic differences." Their alliance in this regard confirmed the theory put forth by Starr Weed; they were "related" in heredity and in the politics of Indian-white relations (see chapter 6). The defiant Lander-District 6 statement was juxtaposed with a contradiction: "Virtually all of the county school districts have applied and qualified for special funding . . . made available by the Federal Government," a large sum therein intended to meet the special needs of Indian students.[29] There were limits to how much they could flaunt their attitude. The county plan had to *avoid* making arguments against federal provisions for Indian student needs if they were to continue to receive federal money.

The committee used some edgy double talk; they had used financing from federal programs to benefit Indian students "not because of their race however." The benefit of federal funds depended on district of residence. Indian students in several districts, they said, had benefited "indirectly;" Riverton (where there had been an "Indian culture course") and the three Indian districts had benefited directly.[30]

The County Committee listed the reservation's District 6 as a "*non-reservation*" school district (emphasis added). Apparently some of its residents still wanted to claim this carryover from its "non-reserved" status in the early 1900s. Shoring up the "non-reservation" description of District 6, Indian school districts were referred to in the county's plan as being on the "*reserved portion*" (emphasis added) of the reservation.[31] In a sense, this terminology acknowledged that only this part of the reservation had been saved for the Indians.

Notably, Riverton held back from saying that it rejected "special recognition of ethnic differences." Like Lander, Riverton had a high number of Native American students and perhaps wanted to be more accommodating. Later they both opposed a one-district county. It is apparent that the various districts were in such unresolvable conflict that they stated and left standing all of the various policies without comment.[32] By their defiance and carelessness they seemed resigned to the state's rejection of the plan.

Of course, the citizens of Fremont County were not happy with the plan for a countywide district. Rumors were that the Riverton school board would take legal action if this plan were approved. They again reviewed old considerations; why not put a vocational school on the reservation—as first proposed by the committee in 1970 and by Starrett in 1971 (see chapter 5)?[33] The FCRC was stymied and going in circles. The timing was right for a modern day ambush.

Alfred Redman objected to the September FCRC plan from the Coalition of Indian Controlled School Boards' September 1972 meeting in Denver, Colorado. He was in a good position to be the WRIEA representative; the BIA school board had named him project director, and the Robert F. Kennedy Memorial had granted him a Kennedy Fellowship for his work in getting the school established. Redman stated that except for the BIA high school there was no high school "within the three reservation districts," an important distinction, since there was another high school on the reservation; it served the mainly white students of District 6, Morton, Kinnear, Pavillion, and Crowheart. Redman's point was that unless the State Committee ensured that the needs *of Indian children* were met, WRIEA would take them to court. The WSJ reported that Redman was "disturbed" that the new high school was still being referred to as the "Resource Center." Its proper name was now "Wyoming Indian High School."[34]

The United Press International and "many newspapers and radio stations" nationwide published Redman's statements. The power to name their school meant that they might also control the way things were done; the UPI quoted Barbara Sage from the CICSB meeting saying that until this time Indians had been "voiceless in the white man's approach to teaching."[35]

The *Denver Post* article on the CICSB meeting, "'Abysmal' Level Cited for Indians' Education," revealed how widespread the CICSB had become. It stated that "about 150 members of Indian school boards and other

organizations" were in attendance. Listed as present were represen-
tatives from Montana, Wyoming, New Mexico, South Dakota, North
Dakota, Iowa, Wisconsin, New York, Minnesota, Idaho, Arizona, Florida,
Colorado, and Pennsylvania.[36]

The *Denver Post* quoted Abe Plummer, then vice-president of the
coalition and director of the Ramah Navajo High School, as calling for
"a 'revolution of kindness' which would result in an Indian take-over of
Indian education." He stated that the white system of education was an
"alien system" that had "systematized our lives into a state of ennui."
Birgil Kills Straight, CICSB president from the Red Cloud Indian school
board at Pine Ridge, added that although the Indian Education Act held
"great promise," implementation had not taken place and funding was
not yet available, something he wanted legislators to know.[37]

The publicity gained by the coalition helped lay the groundwork for
nationwide change, but at the time each delegation had to return to deal
with the struggle back home. The PIE group in Wyoming had already
accused Redman of presuming to speak for them. Redman responded
that he spoke only for WRIEA.[38]

The County Committee deliberations continued into late 1972. The
State Committee would have decision-making power for the county if
they missed their January 1, 1973, deadline. In rare agreement, Lander,
Riverton, and WRIEA opposed the one-district plan. Attorney Gross
stated that "five constitutional rights of Indians were violated in the
one-district plan, one being the right to have a unified school district
on the reservation."[39]

Lander and Riverton seemed to be acclimated to power; they initiated a futile lawsuit against the State Committee for rejecting their
four-district plan. The state filed for a motion to dismiss the suit on the
grounds that the plaintiffs could speak only for Lander and Riverton
not "all other persons, citizens and taxpayers of Fremont County." As
hearings on the one-district plan drew to a close, Governor Hathaway,
Superintendent of Public Instruction Robert Schrader, and the state's
attorney Jerome Statkus said that they would "adjust the one-district
plan to assure proper representation of the Indian population." A woman

from District 6 complained about the "adjustment"; state officials' didn't understand tribal differences to the detriment of the Shoshones.[40]

The State Committee held a meeting with the County Committee in Teton County's Jackson, Wyoming, on its one-district plan (which they probably hoped would be final). Jackson is 150 miles northwest of Lander, and State Committee members may have taken a plane from Cheyenne, more than 400 miles away, in cold and snowy November. They found a holiday atmosphere with mountain trails and wildlife near Jackson but "no speakers in favor of the plan." Alfred Redman presented a resolution for a school district made up of Arapahoe and Mill Creek, but Lander was opposed to that; they wanted the court to decide on the Lander-Riverton lawsuit against the state for its July rejection of their four-district plan.[41] Things were rather awkward, and certainly no decision was to be made in the Jackson meeting.

One thing is clear. The twisted arguments from the planning committee did not work. That recalcitrant and insulting presentation combined with the summer testimony from the tribes and complete lack of support by constituents for the most recent plan led to one outcome: the State Committee rejected Fremont County's one-district plan. Instead the committee recommended a separate district on the reservation (Redman's earlier proposal) *one more time*, on the grounds that they had found "no provision was made for educational needs of the minority group." The school boards of Lander and Riverton dropped their lawsuits against the State Committee the next evening. At least the one-district plan was dead. There might still be hope for four or more districts combined to their benefit. They would wait and see what the Fremont County Committee would do next.[42]

The Fremont County Committee had time in December for one more meeting and *one more proposal*. They proposed a six-district plan, contrary to state recommendations but in agreement with the state when they placed Fort Washakie with Lander and the remaining two Indian elementary districts together. The state and the county also agreed when they separated Lander from Riverton. However only the County Committee understood the controversy between Dubois and District 6 and kept them apart. Constituents wrote to the local paper to express resentments against all the attention being paid to the "special educational needs" of the Indian children.[43]

The representatives gave in to compromises previously avoided. They planned that the district of residence pay tuition regardless of the high school chosen by the student; Dubois and District 6 agreed to shift their boundaries so that they traded reservation oil fields to help equalize revenues between the two districts (and never mind the Indian districts); Riverton and Shoshoni traded territory so that certain oil fields raised Riverton's per pupil valuation. The plan gave no method to equalize funding for the Arapahoe or Mill Creek districts with other districts. In fact District 6 (a non-Indian district on the reservation) had a per student valuation that was nearly five times more than in these Indian districts.[44] The concern for equity for Indian students was low or non-existent in Fremont County.

The Vietnam War was still dragging on in 1972–73. One sad *Riverton (WY) Ranger* drawing showed a man with his head bowed in his hands over the caption, "Our Own Severe Losses during the Renewed Bombing."[45] Fremont County citizens heard of and viewed the killings and trauma and questioned those in power, but that did not end their fight for self-interest. Only the State Committee could put an end to the squabbling. Or so it seemed.

The State Committee may have stalled proceedings deliberately while deadlines passed and so were empowered to take over, which they did. This was the fourth rejection by the State Committee of the county's plans. The six-district plan was inefficient and inequitable. Even non-Indian districts had gross inequities; Riverton would have had approximately $13,367 per pupil and Shoshoni and Lysite $21,999 per pupil.[46] The state did not comment on the issue of American Indian education since they gave Indian districts *de facto* control through their own governance.

Fremont County had waited weeks for the State Committee's decision while 96 inches of snow piled on top of them in "record-breaking cold."

But the snow was not to end in March any more than the school district boundary struggle was to end in 1973. The autonomy of Indian districts seems to have become a state priority after the Indian testimony in the summer of 1972. Yet opposition was entrenched. The county's first plan, the rejected 1971 five-district plan, remained the best that the county would offer to the state (see chapter 5).[47]

The State Committee laid out a plan for four districts in early March 1973, a close approximation to the county's first offer. It combined *the three reservation Indian school districts with income basically unchanged.* But playing into its own downfall, the state tried to solve a few non-Indian differences; they placed Riverton and Shoshoni together in one district to eliminate *their* per-student valuation discrepancy (which would prove to be a serious problem for Shoshoni) and split the Beaver Creek oil field between Lander and Riverton to solve their long-standing dispute. They placed conflicted Dubois and District 6 together as well as Lander, Jeffrey City, and Hudson. At least one entity was very unhappy in each of the planned districts.[48] Political activity became intense.

Superintendent Zerga described how the districts schemed to get what they wanted: "Each district was very wary about who were friends and who might not be friends. A lot of decisions were made behind the scenes. . . . PIE went all over the state, cookie sales and that sort of thing, to find anyone who would support them. . . . Kept a lot of us awake at night."[49]

Journal writer Jan Wilkinson sympathized with PIE's opposition to the reservation district: Fort Washakie parents would "be forced to pay tuition" under the state's plan and "Shoshone tribal members" had voted in the General Council "and a legal referendum" to have their children attend school in Lander. She did not mention the votes of the Joint Business Council and the District 21 school board (see chapter 6). Wilkinson presented the financial worry that Fort Washakie's and Mill Creek's bonded indebtedness to Lander's district would not be paid off under the State Committee's ruling. The state clarified that the reservation district was scheduled to pay off the bonds by 1979 with the help of other districts regardless of what boundaries were drawn, and as in the last county plan, tuition would be paid by the home district should a student attend a school in a different district.[50]

But the most basic financial worries remained. If Lander lost Fort Washakie, they would lose about "75–100 high school students," each worth "about $1,600 per student," and would suffer the loss of four classroom units. The Shoshone tribe hired an attorney by April 1973 to challenge the State Committee decision with allegations that the four-district plan: "1) enforces segregation; 2) [makes] questionable whether a valid high school exists on the reservation which meets Wyoming's statutory requirements; and 3) [forces] Fort Washakie . . . to pay for two school systems." Dubois (with Wind River) also contemplated a lawsuit against the state, they said, because of the distance from Riverton, making for "inefficient administrative unit(s)."[51] It should be noted that the town of Shoshoni, which had increased its tax base when it was combined with Lysite, would now *lose money* when combined with the much larger town of Riverton with its much lower per-student valuation.

A restraining order against the state was filed on April 18, 1973, by the town of Shoshoni, and, according to the *WSJ*, "members of the Shoshone tribe—who represent both themselves and the tribe," that is, the group known as PIE. Attorney Gross filed "a motion for intervention" to the restraining order and was allowed "to intervene on his client's behalf," but in a crucial decision *the State Committee was enjoined by the district court not to proceed.* Fremont County citizens had walked through corridors of snow for quarrelsome meetings all winter and spring. The snowfall reached a record breaking 16 feet, 3 inches by April 23, 1973. It seemed that there was little to do other than scheme and argue.[52]

Midsummer did not bring much improvement. State officials tried to force Fremont County to cooperate by blocking its taxation authority for operation of its schools. The Fremont County district judge ordered the county authorities to proceed in collecting these taxes. However, they were not operating under current law; their school district boundaries remained in limbo, and so the county was forced to collect the taxes under previous Wyoming statutes. They soon realized that they faced "grave budget problems" and could only hire teachers and order supplies based on past enrollments. The designated state funds would soon run out if enrollment from the reservation were low.[53]

Jeffrey City, still rich in uranium, added a crushing blow; it was trying to remove itself from the Lander district. The Jeffrey City separation would cost Lander "$7,443,541 in assessed valuation."[54]

Larry Murray and the state were ready to part ways after the state came to oppose PIE and the larger towns. It is likely also that the necessity for his position had declined after the Arapaho Business Council took over the dispersal of JOM funds. He and his family planned "to devote full time . . . to their ranch near Pavillion" in August 1973. He had managed Indian education funds in Fremont County for nearly four years.[55]

There were other turning points in the summer and autumn of 1973. Around 15,000 members of the "Rainbow Family of Living Light" planned to come to the reservation's mountains for a religious festival. The tribes asked Governor Hathaway to help in protecting their forest lands; he did, and the tribes turned them away. And Spiro T. Agnew resigned. The *Intermountain (ID) Observer* remarked regarding Agnew (although it suited Nixon as well): "It may be more than just an ironic twist of fate that the man who has come to epitomize the concept of stern justice for anyone who breaks any law should himself turn out to be a crook."[56] Richard Nixon (fearing impeachment) resigned the following year.

Fort Washakie completed the tribal office complex built from "native stone of the Sage Creek area," in the late summer. The governor came to the opening and gave his politically neutral position on school district reorganization: "I feel the Indian people have a right to determine where their children go to school, (and) to have more input in the schools." He soon ordered that Ethete's first traffic light be installed.[57] The shiny new fixture stood out against the pale shades of low-lying buttes attracting the attention of a high-flying hawk.

Native Americans had won equal opportunity battles against the county towns for their students. And the towns that were aligned against the state and WRIEA had reached a stalemate that only the courts could settle—or so it seemed.

9

Fights in the Wyoming and Federal Courts

1973–75

This chapter stands as a testament to the strength of Wind River and national Indian determination to establish control of their schools. The struggle took place in the courts and against the Nixon administration. Congress took notice and produced the most comprehensive Indian self-determination legislation yet.

Wind River people had long lived with interlopers longing for their lands and so knew the basics of legal proceedings. They believed that the courts *could* settle conflicts and secure their rights. And so, side by side with the state, they went to the district court to seek an order to dismiss the PIE and town of Shoshoni mid-April claims that blocked the state's four-district plan. Michael Gross went to work for WRIEA with enthusiasm; he developed abundant arguments against the notion that a reservation high school would be segregated. The existing Mill Creek School District was not segregated, and the state's plan would not affect enrollments. Furthermore, the Supreme Court had recognized in *Wright v. Council of City of Emporia* (June 22, 1972), "that neighborhood schools and local control are important, if not over-riding constitutional goals."[1]

Gross prepared to show that there would have to be some evidence of manipulation of enrollments to prove segregation as had been found in *Keyes v. Denver* (June 21, 1973). The State of Wyoming had done just the opposite by putting school district choice into their plan. Finally, lest it had been forgotten, Gross noted that it was federal law that had created the "Reservation entity (with its) undeniable physical and population characteristics." Why, since there was a "separate homeland" for the tribes, should school district boundaries not be drawn within that homeland?

Arguments based upon "Equal Protection and Free Speech" ran as follows:

1. *Brown v. Board of Education* stands for the principle that like treatment for different groups, when it produces harmful educational, psychological, and social effects, is a denial of equal protection of the laws. Integration (forcible) has produced disastrous effects on Indian children in Fremont County. If that is true, then it cannot but be affirmative state action to attempt to overcome the harmful effects of previous arrangements.

2. In similar fashion, *Gomillion v. Lightfoot* (1960) stands for the proposition that political restructurings necessarily depriving a known racial or ethnic group of political representation also deny equal protection of the laws. In this case, any other reorganization but one that provides for a reservation district will drown out Indian votes in a sea of Fremont county non-Indians, thus ending Indian control of the three elementary schools.

3. Finally, to the extent that coercive assimilation has had harmful religious or cultural effects on Shoshones and Arapahos, a *Wisconsin v. Yoder* situation is made out: State practice, uniformly administered upon all segments, tends in certain cases to deprive persons of their First Amendment rights because of the peculiar nature of their beliefs and customs.[2]

Courts in the United States have had difficulty recognizing the *Wisconsin v. Yoder* religious and cultural arguments as legally similar for Native Americans; Indian beliefs were foreign to Eurocentric thinking and integral to the Native way of life. Gross soon published an article in which he laid out the legal reasons not only to permit states to "create Indian-controlled school districts" but to *require* them to do so.[3]

The district court began to proceed in early October 1973 on the matter of whether the state's four-district plan should be instituted in spite of the PIE and town of Shoshoni claims (April 1973) in *Ward v. Schrader* and *Geraud v. Schrader* (Robert Schrader was state superintendent of public instruction). One of the more revealing pre-trial events was the deposition of Eugene G. Patch, assistant principal at Lander Valley High School. It seems that Patch's most prominent role, like that of most assistant principals in minority schools, was as disciplinarian.[4]

Gross began by questioning Patch's authority over attendance and discipline and many other details—he had been assistant principal for ten years and a coach before that. Gross played to Patch's apparent enjoyment of the extent of his experience, knowledge, and authority: "You are the man, then?" he asked, and the witness agreed, "I'm the man."[5]

Patch seemed confused by the difference between "treating all students alike," a non-discriminatory approach, versus doing things differently for Indian students under federally funded Indian programs. When asked about punctuality he said that his comment "probably shouldn't be for the record," a comment found in the record about the difference between "Mountain Standard, Jack King (the principal's name) and Indian time." He added, "there's an hour difference between [*sic*] all of them."[6]

Gross questioned Patch about possible racial strife; Patch said the Sinks Canyon incident had been instigated by resentment of interracial dating. "I got them together; we discussed the situation; everybody had a chance to blow off some steam. There was a meeting of the parties somewhere out of town. There was supposed to be a big fight, and so on and so forth. It never ensued." Patch did acknowledge that there was a "confrontation . . . between the Indians . . . (with their allies), the long-hairs, versus the cowboys." He pointed out that in the past this would simply have been called a "fight," but "since 1970 it has been a racial incident. Now, what the difference is, I don't know."[7]

Patch testified that to his knowledge there were "30 or 40 students" present, fewer than one fifth as many as estimated by observer Duncombe in his 1974 letter to Gross. Patch further stated that he was never able to "pin down" who started the fight, and so no one was ever disciplined. He said he had made phone calls to parents but never reached any Indian parents, in part because one of the girl's grandfathers was blind and deaf. Patch said he tried to reach them through the Indian home school coordinator.[8] It seems that Patch was a member of the dominant group that held unquestioned control and so perceived racial strife as minimal.

Patch's testimony suggested that there was no effect of community distance or dominant society on reservation parent involvement, "I think any community who chooses to be involved can be involved regardless of their remoteness to the attachment. . . . Those students and those parents who have chosen to become involved have been deeply involved. . . . Students participating in school activities—which, incidentally, as far as I'm concerned, is very, very poor—those Indian students who have chosen to participate have participated nicely, done excellently." He volunteered that students from Hudson "who were the heart and soul of our basketball teams . . . hitchhiked in the middle of the winter to be involved."[9] He did not mention the hitchhiking Indian students.

Gross interrogated him about political structure; did school board composition affect the school? The assistant principal testified that he was "unpolitical [sic] oriented" and that he could "see no way, shape or form that a boundary established by a political entity can affect the education. Now, the attitude of the individuals within that boundary might affect that educational structure." Thus, as Patch was forced to discuss it, he recognized that the boundaries within which individuals elect school boards can affect educational programs. The Lander Board had never, "to [his] knowledge, considered constructing a school facility on the Wind River Indian Reservation."[10]

Patch made clear that the Indian student dropout rate was quite complicated. While his definition of dropout agreed with that given by editor Sniffin in the *Wyoming State Journal*, Patch used a different term: "disenrolls." This might include only students who officially "disenrolled." The meaning of the term *dropout*, he testified, could be "very, very indefinite."[11] Terms could and would be manipulated so that actual completion rates were not acknowledged and nor were solutions to invisible problems sought.

Attorneys for the state and WRIEA attempted in a hearing a few weeks later to determine who their courtroom adversaries would be. They made the case that District 24 (the town of Shoshoni) lacked standing in Wyoming law to seek judicial review of the state plan—they were not Indians, the persons whom they claimed would be harmed. But the circumstances of mixed identity proved useful. The court could not dismiss—the state's coordinator of Indian education Larry Murray entered to help his allies once more by testifying that his blond, blue-eyed son was an enrolled Indian, eliciting humor in the courtroom. "'What Is an Indian?'" asked the local newspaper.[12]

There are many small domes of prehistoric design on the frozen clay and crusty snow of the reservation floor. Native Americans curve willow branches to form the shape and cover it with wool blankets and quilts. These structures are home to many spiritual gatherings. Well-worn paths through sagebrush lead to a bonfire at the time of ceremonies where boulders are placed in the flames. Older boys and men carry the boulders, red globes at their most intense degree of heat, on antlers or pitchforks to the inside pit of the lodge. A flap no more than a few feet high allows a crawling entrance. Inside, a spiritual leader acknowledges each prayer. Michael Gross attended a sweat lodge ceremony with about ten others on a bitter cold late January afternoon:

> I had no idea what would happen or how long it would take. When we all got seated someone closed the flap. Immediately we were trans-ported into another world—totally pitch black, no light whatsoever. [With water tossed onto the stones] the rocks started steaming and when the flap closed, the tent inside turned into an oven, fast. Chant-ing started. Sweating started. A voice told me to put my head down to keep it slightly cooler. I did so. I became claustrophobic. I nearly panicked. But I bit my tongue and endured the event, which, after all, was in my honor in a way, a blessing ceremony for the trial. The chanting rose in intensity. I heard my name and Father Dave's but could not understand anything else. My anguish endured. . . . Finally, after about 25 minutes the ceremony came to a halt. The flap opened.

The late day sun entered. We crawled out into the snow. We couldn't feel the cold at all. Our bodies were steaming.

After a "sweat," a few participants often serve a warm vegetable or beef soup. At leave taking, winter's dim sunlight is completely gone; only the Milky Way's cold glitter remains to give direction.

Gross was rejuvenated by the sweat lodge ceremony but soon had to face the state plan's uncertain fate in district court. There was testimony by members of the PIE organization and by WRIEA members in February 1974. University of Chicago professor of education Donald Erickson, who had led an Office of Economic Opportunity evaluation of the Rough Rock School in 1969, also testified. He spoke about the deplorable circumstances and outcomes of Indian education corresponding to findings of the 1969 Special Subcommittee on Indian Education. Alfred Ward's testimony revealed the mixed feelings of the Fort Washakie district. His concern, as it turned out, was "not a racial question at all"—that is, segregation—but instead was about a probable Arapaho-controlled school board.[13]

The judge upheld the State Committee's plan. He ruled that the State Committee decision "was in conformity with law" (thus overruling the segregation charges without speaking directly to them) and that the committee's "findings of fact were supported by substantial evidence." However, his orders handed over control of the final outcome to the State Supreme Court; he left the injunction that prevented the state from implementing its plan in the county "in effect pending further litigation."[14]

Lawrence Geraud with Alfred Ward, Alfred and Eva McAdam, and Ivora Ray followed up. They filed an appeal in July 1974 to the State Supreme Court "on behalf of the city of Shoshoni and the Shoshone Indians."[15]

The Wyoming State Supreme Court ruled on the State Organization Committee's four-district plan on February 7, 1975. It disappointed all who hoped for a final outcome. The justices ruled the case "a legislative function" that should only be "delegated to the county committee and the state committee" and *not to the courts*. The courts could only review the state plan to determine whether the state had acted in conformity with the law and not in an arbitrary or capricious manner. The court found arbitrariness and capriciousness; and while the state and county committees each stated that their plans met criteria of equity and efficiency, *they offered no evidence of such*. Even the State Committee set boundaries that were not explained: "There may be a good explanation, but we do not know what it is." The court in fact noted a discrepancy in valuation of over $5,000 per student between two of the districts proposed by the state.[16]

Although the court seemed informed about the new law, it did not seem informed about recent deliberations in Fremont County; it said that the benefits of equity and efficiency would be more easily accomplished in a one-district plan. True, but the comment could not have created more frustration. Was the court aware of the many one-district difficulties encountered by the local county committee?[17]

The court gave commentary on key points; it acknowledged Indian objections to "coercive assimilation" in the border town schools and noted WRIEA's alternative "Indian control, directed to the ways of Indians." But it gave a mixed and rather contradictory review on these issues: "There has been no convincing argument made why a board of trustees should not be made up of Indians, if that is the political complexion in the expanse of the district," *but* it was not "satisfied from the record that the headquarters must be located on the reservation and must be dominated entirely by Indians without regard to the high standards and controlling statutes by which Wyoming schools are governed."[18]

Perhaps arguments for "Indian control" had gone too far. The court had no objection to a school on the reservation except that it saw no necessity for it, and such a school, "dominated entirely by Indians," might not meet Wyoming educational standards. It seems the justices were not convinced that prejudice was hurting people in Fremont County and were not aware that certain prejudices had infiltrated their own judicial perceptions of Indians.

PIE argued that since the reservation did not have a public high school, the plan for a reservation district was unacceptable. The justices of the court disagreed. That was something that could be in the planning stage. Also, the justices did *not* say that a school on the reservation would be "segregation." They stated that Wyoming law did not allow public schools to be established so as to make a "distinction . . . on account of sex, race or color." The name of the school, "Wyoming Indian High School," had perhaps too strongly suggested Indian control and segregation. It is apparent that Wyoming law was intended to prevent discrimination but, used from a Eurocentric viewpoint, could defeat that purpose. The omnipresence of "distinctive schools" for Euro-Americans, often named after their heroes, went unrecognized—the Wyoming court only stated, "No distinctive school may be established for Indians." But the Montana state legislature allowed boundaries to be drawn coterminous with those of the reservation, and a desegregation plan in a federal district court in Milwaukee, Wisconsin, allowed Indian students to be assigned to schools that met their needs in 1977.[19]

The harmful effects of assimilation, argued by Gross to result in inequality, did not seem to be given much weight in Wyoming. And so the court did not deal with pedagogic issues relevant to Native American student success. Research that would have been helpful on these points surfaced in the 1990s and 2000. The court rebuffed the State Department of Education Committee for what it intuited at the time: "It is not enough that the state committee falls back on the answer that its plan must be accepted because of its expertise in education."[20]

The Wyoming court may also have needed more knowledge about the invasions and land takings on the northeastern half of the reservation; it did not understand why WRIEA and the state excluded the northern part of the reservation from their plan. As described in chapter 5, the northern part of the reservation had found a reservation-wide district to be completely unacceptable.[21] And so a point of view that WRIEA originally favored helped defeat their cause in the Wyoming court.

The Kennedy Senate Subcommittee Report had made clear the injustices and disastrous outcomes of white-dominated Indian education more than fifteen years earlier. But since the court saw its purpose as only to determine whether the state and county had followed Wyoming law, Gross's arguments had little effect (however, see epilogue). The State Supreme Court sent the "mass of factual data, expressions from so many people at the county hearing, plus testimony (10 volumes plus 10 depositions and, when stacked, [measuring] about two feet in height)" back to the weary Fremont County Committee.[22] The court could not rule directly on the rights of Indians to control their community's schools.

In 2002 Michael Gross still had painful memories of the 1975 State Supreme Court ruling: "I tried to cheer the troops, telling them this was just a bump in the road and we would eventually prevail. The troops, though, saw it otherwise. They thought this fledgling lawyer had failed and they would be better off without him. They may have been correct for the next year (March 7, 1977) the group managed to reverse the court ruling."

WRIEA appealed the case to the U.S. Supreme Court. The Wyoming Department of Education joined WRIEA in that appeal. The U.S. Supreme Court reviewed the case, refused to hear it, and sent it back to the FCRC by October 1975. The county had until April 1977 to submit a plan.[23]

Court actions in Fremont County (and the AIM uprisings) coincided with President Nixon's abrogation of many congressional actions as well as his own pronouncements. Any trust that may have remained in his 1970 expressed concern for self-determination ended by early 1973. He had failed to allot contract authority through excessive "impoundments" (withholding of funds otherwise designated for programs by Congress), $18 billion in all. Part of what led to investigations as to whether these impoundments were grounds for impeachment were $18 million for Indian education.[24]

A 1973 letter from Senators Edward M. Kennedy and Walter F. Mondale stated that the Nixon administration's "attitude . . . toward providing quality education for American Indians, has been negative from the start." Nixon's policy statements that favored Native American self-ruled programs were nothing but shallow words; they were left without funding for the education needed to protect and carry out self-rule. Nixon's defense was that he was providing "prudent management of federal spending." At the same time, he was bombing Cambodia and making use of government funds to improve his private properties at San Clemente and Key Biscayne.[25]

The Coalition of Indian Controlled School Boards (CICSB), under Executive Director Gerald Clifford, prepared to fight the administration's takeover of allocated funds by hiring five attorneys: Steven L. Engelberg of Washington DC; John G. Ghostbear, Kirke Kickingbird, and Ralph F. Keen of Oklahoma; and Vine Deloria Jr. (the son of the Native American author by the same name) of Colorado. Kickingbird was an active advisor, being director of the Institute for the Development of Indian Law, Inc., a non-profit organization that he and Vine Deloria Jr. had started. To give it standing in the court the lawsuit needed not only the Indian school districts and Indian educational organizations but "an appropriate plaintiff," a child injured by the withholding of the schooling funds. The coalition chose Alfred Redman's six-year-old son John, enrolled at the reservation's Mill Creek District 14 School in Fremont County. Jerry Reynolds, Washington correspondent for *Indian Country Today*, remembered that "the Coalition, attorneys and everyone else were delighted to have a case brought by a 'Redman' and represented by an attorney of record named Ghostbear."[26]

Kickingbird related that to get the funds "un-impounded" they had to "apply for funds, get turned down (as would be the case since the money would not be released), then file the lawsuit," all in a short time. "If the money was not used it would go right back into the Treasury and would no longer be available. And we were under a time-line and so were sweating it out." Thus they petitioned for "injunctive relief." The administration argued that harm *would not* be done by refusing the injunction. Judge June Green made the funds available under injunctive relief after the *Redman v. Ottina* (John R. Ottina, then acting United States commissioner of education) lawsuit was filed in conjunction with a similar case involving the Minnesota Chippewa tribe. The administration then dropped its opposition and rushed to take the actions required by Congress to grant these federal funds—to develop regulations for implementing programs, publish rules for administration of programs,

8. John C. Redman (b. April 1, 1966) at approximately eight years old. Photograph by Mike McClure. Courtesy of Alfred and Mary Alice Redman.

and appoint the National Advisory Council on Indian Education. To avoid "an adverse decision on the record," just prior to Judge Green's decision an affidavit was sent by the commissioner of the Office of Education, Department of Health, Education, and Welfare, vowing that the office was "now determined that it will promptly take all appropriate steps . . . to implement the programs . . . of the Act." The affidavit made the case moot and avoided the "adverse decision on the record" for the Nixon administration. The administration saved face for the moment. Justice was restored, and as readers know, Nixon resigned in 1974 with impeachment and conviction probable.[27]

The CICSB connected American Indian people across the country, building power and confidence in the assertion of their rights. One of its most remarkable accomplishments was the saving of American Indian programs from the Nixon administration impoundments—had these programs been lost, it is impossible to say whether federal support could have been regained. Native treaty rights were at stake, and the loss of federal programs would have threatened tribal structure itself. Certainly educational self-determination needed the continuation of federal programs.

The CICSB also succeeded in lobbying Congress for the Indian Self-Determination and Education Assistance Act (known by Wind River Native Americans by the last three digits of its congressional number, "PL 638"). Congress passed this law in January 1975, just one month before the Wyoming Supreme Court made its ruling known. It was powerful legislation that gave Native Americans more control in shaping their federal programs. Michael Gross remembered that "many Indian communities and tribes" were able to get contracts that allowed acquisition of sites and construction and renovation of facilities for classrooms. Most important, it gave American Indians "maximum . . . participation in the direction of educational as well as other Federal services." Indian parents could elect committees that had "authority to approve or disapprove (federal) programs" when a local school board was "not composed of a majority of Indians." The law also required that local schools prorate federal money for Indian student needs, a requirement long seen as needed by Wind River parents. Finally, the act allowed for "preferences and opportunities for training and employment." Federal programs could now prepare Native Americans and their organizations to take over the administration of the contracts and grants provided in the law. Guy Senese noted that the legislation gave the BIA "a high degree of discretion" in the details of oversight. However, that was counterbalanced by what David Wilkins saw as Native Americans' "renewed sense of the importance of their sovereignty."[28]

St. Stephen's Indian School Education Association acquired BIA funding for its high school at the old St. Stephen's Mission on March 26, 1975, almost immediately after passage of PL 638. The St. Stephen's School still remains a Bureau of Indian Education K–12 school because it does not have a land base (and so has no base for state taxation). The Catholics no longer fund it, but the community keeps the name as a part of their historical identity, creating some confusion for outsiders. Also, St. Stephen's did not merge with the nearby Arapahoe public school because of differences in history and services. That school was originally established for non-Indians and now has a charter school. The state provides funding to St. Stephen's today because new state law requires that funding for reservation students be equal with funding for other students across the state.[29] The school also benefits from Indian student federal money, something Riverton residents may sometimes want.

As we have seen, the establishment of the high school at Ethete was made difficult by its competition with some of the surrounding non-Indians for federal money. The state's aspirations for equality were almost forgotten. But the successes in federal court and in Congress, outlined in this chapter, were to last. The next chapter tells how it all circled back to Ethete.

10

Control of Their Destiny

1975–80s

The Fremont County Reorganization Committee had no choice but to resurface and reconstitute once the Wyoming Supreme Court sent the case back to them. Silas Lyman of Mill Creek had retired to California; the committee replaced him with its first Native American, Alfred Redman. Stanleigh Starrett had died; Jim Duran represented Lander Valley High School. Jim Eager now represented Arapahoe, and Louis Twitchell continued for Fort Washakie. Several chose not to serve again. The committee hired the Riverton school attorney, Dick Leedy, for legal representation. He immediately questioned what would happen to the reservation districts' "bonded indebtedness" if there were to be a full-scale reservation "federally-run school system." Reservation districts had used hundreds of thousands of dollars to build their public schools.[1]

The Arapaho General Council, with Ben Friday Jr., as chairman, voted unanimously for Leedy's removal as the FCRC attorney. Friday was known among the Arapaho as a "gentleman," meaning that he was "a gorilla" when it came to politics.[2] The FCRC ignored Native American Indian wishes; Leedy continued to serve the County Committee. This would not be the last that they would hear of Friday. Native Americans would take over in the county to make self-determination and cultural preservation possible through their schools.

The Wyoming Supreme Court's declaration of its limited role and the U.S. Supreme Court's refusal to hear their case had left the gate wide open.

The subjects of the court's rulings felt free to make their own "common sense" decisions. But even so, the 1969 law did not make it easy. Only a one-district solution would meet its requirements. Otherwise they would be "trying to put together a jig-saw puzzle with parts that do not fit," as the Wyoming court had observed.[3] Perhaps the farmers would rather have cultivated a field invaded by Prickly Pear cactus.

But new members and some distance on past bitterness gave renewed hope. Alfred Redman was influential, even inspiring as a friendly and magnanimous Native American crossing cultural boundaries. His old experience as a Lander high school "play-maker and team player" could not have hurt his efforts on the County Committee.[4] And the towns could no longer ignore the Mill Creek district's long holdout for an Indian school. Little or nothing was heard about "segregation" again. The concept had no use as applied to the reservation school except as propaganda. At any rate, they probably did not want to bring it up again; the State Supreme Court preference for a one-district county would do away with local control.

The unstable extraction industry income was the primary ongoing factor (other than human greed) that made the 1969 law unrealistic. The Lander school board approved $500,000 for construction of high school classrooms at Jeffrey City early in 1976—as it happened just four years before it was hit with drastic population losses in the uranium boom and bust cycle. It would soon have met the state's requirement for at least five hundred students per district if its population had held up. The standards as of early 1976 also required that the districts' differential in "assessed valuation per student should not exceed $3,500." But the county's differentials were enormous and shifting—in 1976 there was a $31,297 *average assessed valuation per pupil differential* between Riverton and Lander, with Riverton on the low end.[5]

By March 1976 the committee was once again ready to quit and turn the planning over to the state. The attorneys for the state and county boards recommended against it, and so they went to the State Committee to ask for concessions. They got important ones; the state would not hold the per-student valuation and number enrolled per district

9. Alfred Redman Sr. at school retirement, 2005. Photograph by author.

as requirements but rather as "guidelines." There were already seven counties in the state that had districts composed of fewer than five hundred students. And Wind River (District 6), Dubois, and Shoshoni districts found it difficult to argue against reservation districts based on size; they each had fewer than five hundred.[6] Reverend Duncombe must have been pleased to hear that the requirement for a student body of five hundred had been dropped—an important sign of Indian school progress. Mundane life activities often take place with no thoughts of death until tranquility is shattered.

Death intruded, breaking human ties, disrupting social progress, and destroying youthful hopes. Rev. David Duncombe was murdered on April 24, 1976. His death represented a common experience on the reservation—death too soon, death by homicide, death to hopes for tomorrow, death ruled by the insanity of alcohol.

Prosecutors and defense attorneys raised questions in the courtroom as to whether it was the sixteen-year-old accused, Billy Tillman, or his brother Frank, or both who had stabbed Reverend Duncombe multiple times, and as to why. John Yellow Plume (1954–2008) answered the questions perhaps as well as we need to know: "He was just a drunken kid."[7]

A federal grand jury charged both Billy and Frank with "first-degree homicide and aiding and abetting each other in commission of the crime." Later testimony by Frank's wife, Rose, and that of the Tillmans' mother, led to Billy alone being found guilty of second degree murder. Frank was over eighteen years old and so would have been eligible for a longer sentence.[8]

Reporters asked the prosecutor, U.S. attorney Charles E. Graves, if he thought Rose was a believable witness. He responded: "I'm going to live with the fact that I think the jury believed her and I think she was sincere on the witness stand. I think she was afraid and she was living with what she had to do." Billy, out on bail pending sentencing, was a passenger in a 1:00 a.m. high speed rollover vehicle accident. He was thrown from the car and killed.[9]

As reported earlier, Sandra St. Clair remembered in her interview for this book that Reverend Duncombe had the "backbone" to give his well-respected support to their struggle for the school; he made calls when they were in Washington DC and intervened to get church material help. Without his encouragement, she said, the school might not have come to be. Michael Gross remembered the tribal community's sorrow surrounding his death:

> Father Dave's funeral remains the most moving funeral I have ever attended. In that beautiful little sanctuary overlooking the snow covered Wind Rivers, dignitaries of the Episcopal Church assembled in majestic white robes, not only from Wyoming and the West but from all over the country. Dave's entire family was there. And hundreds of Arapahoes and Shoshones. Later there was potlatch in the high school gym which lasted for hours. I was shaken. Dave had been a mentor as well as a friend, a man who unhesitatingly hopped on roofs to fix leaks or gave his own money to help buy a plane ticket for someone. I have never known anyone else like him.

A young man in 1976, Ted Duncombe also remembered the funeral as profoundly moving. He wrote that his father was "given a full Arapahoe funeral, in conjunction with the Episcopal ceremony. The things that were said at the funeral left me with a singular understanding of the significance of his work there."[10] Ted shared what Dennis Sun Rhodes, "my brother in the Indian way," said in his eulogy:

> Many, many Non-Indians, "Whitemen" pass through Indian Country to help Indian People. It is very rare for a Non-Indian person to have the qualities in relating to Indian People the way David Duncombe did.
> David was a Man who loved Life, loved his Work, and he developed a *Precious Fatal Love* for the *Indian People, Past* and *Present* [emphasis by Sun Rhodes].
> There was one concept that David really truly believed—Pertaining to his relationship to Indian People. He believed in turning the *Decision making process over to the Indian People*. He was against the Paternalistic Attitude that some Past Missionaries developed towards Indian People.

All the things He stood for in His work here is a testament to this belief. The Farm, Rebuilding the Mission Complex, the Museum, the Renovation of the interior of OUR FATHER'S HOUSE, and His work directly and behind the scenes to get the Wyoming Indian High School established.

I would like to ask all the People left behind who have charge over the things he helped to start, stand strong and make sure these things grow to help the Indian People Control their own Destiny.

Sun Rhodes understood what Reverend Duncombe had known, the essence of the purpose in the Arapaho struggle for a school. They needed once again to take "control of their own destiny" after the decimating defeat and subjugation in the wars and reservation placement that were meant to take away all pride. He had become of the same mind with them and received the name Yellow Cloud. Ted found the message, "Our personal happiness is not the key to how we must use our lives," in his father's writings. However, Reverend Duncombe's death dealt a nearly fatal blow to the Arapaho-Episcopal relationship; according to Alvena Friday (b. 1931), "The bishop (of Wyoming) sent someone to get the typewriters and copy machines. We were just left on our own."[11] The church had little or no support. Alvena is a continuing member of the Ethete Episcopal Mission Church.

The Episcopal stone buildings in their circle remain essentially unchanged; worn by sand, snow, and winds, they are bleak in winter's sun. The Episcopalians had sent the reservation their best, and he was no longer with them. The sacrifice was too much. But the Arapahos know how to hold in their hearts the spirit of one long gone and are never completely done with anything anyway; the old buildings have not been abandoned. Projects, an agency, a museum, a post office, and a parish hall, sometimes used for Arapaho celebrations and "Cedaring," an individual blessing ceremony, keep the insides alive and warm. Only the old stone gym is dark, empty, and cavernous. Donations, though well intentioned, lie in messy rows across the floor. The high shadowy walls are cool in summer and as cold in winter as Wyoming winters get.

The Fremont County Committee did not meet again for months. Perhaps they understood and respected the Arapaho abstention from socializing after a death. When they finally did meet, they continued to flounder in trying to fit disjointed pieces together.[12] They were distraught and discouraged. Eventually most members accepted plans presented by Alfred Redman and other reservation representatives. It could be that the sudden death of a priest who lived among Indians suggested thoughts of redemption. But at first only Indian representatives saw that they could quit worrying about State Committee opinions. The County Committee had a new position of power.

Fort Washakie superintendent Severt Rist and principal John H. Williams wrote to the committee in August: "Why not ask for an eight or nine-district plan and keep everyone happy?" Redman followed up with a motion for eight districts. Lander, Hudson, Riverton, and Dubois were among those who struck it down—the Fremont County school districts looked forward to a total of $142,358 in grants arising from the Indian Education Act of 1972.[13] More districts would mean a smaller share of the money for them.

Redman remembers being pressured from all sides to give something up and, on top of that, having to endure jealous bickering, "Whenever I had a committee appointment, someone from the Shoshone group would demand to be on it." However, the chances for a reservation district were the best they had been in years. Lysite and Jeffrey City (with their own revenue sources) were voting with the reservation districts, and Dubois was still eyeing Morton-Pavillion reservation oil and vacillated in their vote; if they could get the land to gerrymander, a vote for more districts was a vote for their independence.[14] One thing was certain; no one wanted to go back to the Wyoming Supreme Court.

Redman's August motion seems to assume that Hudson would join with Lander (which it did, not long afterward). He left Arapahoe with Riverton, and Fort Washakie and Mill Creek to stand on their own as elementary districts. Fort Washakie could then decide which district they would join for their "unified district." The motion died in a close or tied vote.[15]

The Lander representative proposed a two-district plan that *no one* voted for in the September meeting. Instead, the committee unified behind Redman's eight-district plan, "a multi-district reorganization (that) would best meet the educational needs of the large and diverse county."[16] By so stating they turned their fate over to the Native Americans. They were otherwise defeated by their conflicts or by interests that were far too self-serving. At least they would let the Native Americans suffer defeat this time.

Yet one adjustment remained to be made. Arapahoe wanted to have its own district. Jim Eager of Arapahoe motioned for a nine-district plan with the "rationale of local control and motivation." The committee reviewed the state's past reasons for rejecting plans, such reasons suggesting that this one would be rejected too, and went forward with Eager's proposal.

No one among the sixty or so persons who attended the following hearing spoke against the nine-district plan. A proposal to use federal Indian school money in the equations evaluating an area's qualifications to be a district smoothed the way. A statement by Scott Dewey, Arapaho grandson of Chief Sharp Nose, summed up their feelings: "Our position is unique. The whole Fremont County is unique. It is so big and has the diverse resources. Indians should have the prerogative to determine what they want. We want children educated for self-determination in a few years, not 35 or 40 years from now."[17]

Wyoming's "wide-open spaces" created the feeling of a special identity among the surrounding communities as well. They were ready to sit it out and do what they wanted without too much concern about the remote State Committee for School District Organization.

The State Committee rejected the county's nine-district plan—it obviously failed to meet "the criteria of the 1969 school code." The Lander and Riverton representatives took advantage of the disorganization that routinely followed such rejections; they filed a bill in the State House of Representatives to accomplish their long-standing goals—to take over the Indian and Jeffrey City schools. Their bill did not decide the fate of Wyoming Indian High School. They thought it was likely to "remain as a Bureau of Indian Affairs School." The bill died. Jeffrey City, with its own high school since 1974, *again* let it be known that they wanted to be a separate district.[18]

Now everyone was ready for the most drastic solution yet; Jim Eager and George Zerga went to the legislature with proposed amendments to the 1969 law that gave the County Committee final say for reorganization. The Wyoming legislature passed the revisions in March 1977. Zerga had his perspective on how this became possible: "Other counties had to close their schools and so (some were) more than happy to punish that board [the State Committee]. . . . In a lot of senses everybody was angry with everybody else and there were a lot of hard feelings at the time. . . . We didn't want our names on things because you couldn't afford to have more enemies than you already had." He remembered that Representative John Vinich, a Democrat whose life was spent in the Lander allied town of Hudson, played a helpful role:

John Vinich was a lot of help but behind the scenes—in the minority party. He could steer you to legislators.–Very, very helpful in pointing out the legislative process and . . . which legislator had the most influence in a particular committee and what they like or disliked as far as school districts were concerned so that we did not inadvertently stir up a hornet's nest.

This was in Cheyenne and we didn't know all the people . . . (Vinich was) on the side of the smaller districts. But like a lot of people, he could not come out and say it. . . . It was an interesting time but I'm glad it is over. It makes the old Chinese proverb, "may your life be interesting," make a lot of sense.[19]

The State Committee was left in existence but impotent to contest county decisions. Bluntly, the new law stated: "The state committee shall approve the (county) plan of organization as submitted and shall enter an order establishing the districts in accordance with the plan." The law continued to require equalization of per pupil expenditures as nearly as was practicable, but now it would be up to the County Committee to decide exactly what that meant. The law did not require a minimum enrollment, and a district could vote to affiliate with some other unified county district. The County Committee could now end the hopes for takeover by the larger towns. Lander's newspaper reported that they found the new law confusing and inconsistent.[20]

Native Americans and their representatives had worked their way into the now up-side-down power structure. Ben Friday Jr. replaced Alfred Redman when Redman left the committee. They each worked to prevent factionalism and promote unity, quickly earning the respect of the other representatives, who were often divided. They were fully comfortable with democratic processes as practiced in the monthly General Council meetings.[21] And paradoxically strengthening tribal powers, the small town representatives rarely lost sight of their own self-interest—they needed the three reservation representatives' votes. Separate Indian districts would be a small price to pay in order to continue with highly discrepant revenues (in, say, District 6's favor) as well as for freedom from oversight by Riverton or Lander.

Opposed political beliefs and feelings remained strong during the time of Indian successes in Fremont County. Lee Catterall of the *Wyoming State Journal* called an American Indian Policy Review Commission report that favored sovereignty a "radical report." Wyoming representative Teno Roncalio criticized the idea that "American Indians should have the right" to control "all affairs within their boundaries" as impractical and even "dreamy."[22] Yet in this border town area of frontiersmen, American Indian leadership had gained power and respect.

The new 1977 statute contained a provision that the County Committee consider a *Boundary Board* plan of organization. Thus a frustrating rehash of the past several years of county struggle took place just before the reorganization law was signed by the governor—school district superintendents each wrote their requests to the Boundary Board, including Lander which wanted Mill Creek, Jeffrey City, Fort Washakie, and Hudson in their district. It is little wonder then that the board replied that it would only review the final plan; it was the County Committee that would decide the boundaries.[23]

The March 1977 bill was signed into law by Governor Ed Herschler.

It gave a new deadline, June 1, 1978, for the county to present its plan. Perhaps amazingly—but perhaps not, given the new dimensions and standards that they gave themselves—the County Committee completed the task well ahead of time, on November 18, 1977. According to Zerga, not everyone was in on the plan before the meeting, but Ben Friday Jr. was: "The Riverton lawyer said there was no plan, at which point Ben Friday Jr. said, 'Oh yes, there is a plan, and here it is.' And so things turned out differently that night than was expected. Riverton . . . voted for it, but they saw the handwriting on the wall."[24]

Thus it was Ben Friday Jr.—as his wife, Alvena, noted, a "traditional man" and a pillar of the Ethete Episcopal Mission—who presented the fully detailed and amended motion for a nine-district county.[25] His "gentlemanly" demeanor, long-term political leadership on the reservation school issue, and most centrally, his humility and trustworthiness made him an ideal representative to make the presentation. His many roles and his actions here signified the defeat of county arguments for invisibility of the Indian people.

The 1977 statute provided that elementary districts could unify or affiliate with a surrounding district that had a high school, or they could fully join with a surrounding district. The reservation's Indian areas chose affiliation—Fort Washakie with Lander, Arapahoe with Riverton, and interestingly, Ethete's Mill Creek school board voted to affiliate with Wind River's District 6 in preference to Lander. Even this was not without its controversy—ninety-eight Mill Creek people (ethnic group not identified) wanted to remain affiliated with Lander. The tiny Hudson district had joined with Lander. Jeffrey City, already having a high school, did not need to unify with Lander. It became a unified district. Lander registered the only negative vote.[26] They alone stubbornly continued to vote for their control of the Indian schools.

There was one final issue to resolve after the nearly ten years of struggle: the Dubois–Wind River boundary. The FCRC had left these two districts "to resolve their differences" in May 1970. But it seems that Dubois did not want to trade their land to District 6 to get access to District 6 tax base land. District 6, the long-term claimants to the reservation's Circle Ridge oil fields, apparently felt that they should get something (District 2 land) out of the deal themselves. Dubois added to the difficulty by being internally conflicted about using a one-mile strip of the northern boundary of District 6. They argued that a one-mile strip suggested a gerrymandering process and "might be open to lawsuits at a later period." In any event Dubois did not want to be required "to trade any land, as the disparity in valuation between District 6 and District 2 (was) already excessive."[27]

The board was unable to reach a decision on the "several plans to make District No. 2 contiguous." But Jim Eager helped negotiate a land trade in mid-December 1977 wherein Dubois gave land to District 6 in return for the necessary one-mile wide, and approximately twenty-mile-long strip from the reservation's District 6. Some eighty years earlier the Arapahos, under threat of eviction, had accepted the allotment of their land, which made it saleable to non-Indians. If heartbreak over his people's defeat in this matter was felt, it did not show. Ben Friday Jr., motioned for approval, and the reservation land arrangement was voted in by the County Committee.[28]

The per-student valuation for District 2 was $23,035.36, and for District 6 it was $32,902.09 at the conclusion of the gerrymandering. Per-pupil valuation for Ethete's District 14 was $9,497.02, while it was $38,269.59 for Fort Washakie. Araphoe's District 38 was $2,972.37. Justifying the extreme discrepancy for Arapahoe, the County Board pointed out that although it had the lowest per-pupil expenditure in the county, it had "one of the highest" in the state. Given that Arapahoe qualified for additional federal funding, the Arapahoe school board was expected to "operate a quality educational program."[29] Control over enculturation was more important to the tribal communities than money. In fact, Native American motivations reveal a clear contrast to that of the non-Indian communities; while the latter competed for territory and income, Native Americans were mainly interested in maintaining their cultures and determining their destinies.

The State Committee questioned the legality of the county plan in a resolution on February 28, 1978. Perhaps they wanted things to turn out better for the financial interests of the Native Americans. Or it could be that the State Committee's collective ego came first. At any rate, the State Committee's legality question helped settle things. Judge Robert B. Ranck of the Ninth Judicial District of Fremont County ordered the State Committee to give its approval.[30]

Nine Fremont County school boards took administrative control in their districts on January 1, 1979, after over ten years of deliberations and struggle. The nine districts are in place to this day, with one exception. The uranium market fell due to environmental and nuclear power concerns, and mining ended in the Jeffrey City area in the early 1980s. The author of *Yellowcake Towns* described how the trailers were "carted off," and weeds grew through the streets. Only a few employees stayed to prevent the 8 million tons of waste that remained from contaminating the Wyoming winds. The school laid off eleven of the Jeffrey City teachers in 1981—by 1986 only eighty-eight students remained of the more than five hundred in attendance in 1977. But Jeffrey City held out for nearly a decade. According to then Lander board member Michelle Hoffman, Lander incorporated the Jeffrey City school district once again in the mid-1990s.[31]

Arapahoe's District 38 and Fort Washakie's District 21 remained K–8 districts in 2009, the only two such districts in the state (for further developments see epilogue). Central to our story, the reservation elementary district, Mill Creek, became the foundation for a unified public school district. After tribal canvassers urged everyone to register to vote, the district voted three to one for the BIA Wyoming Indian High School to become a public school. The vote consolidated the high school with the Mill Creek elementary and middle schools, making for a unified district in 1983. It is not segregated; Fremont County has an open enrollment policy.[32]

The reasons for the tribal choice to become a state public school rather than to remain with the BIA were many and powerful; as discussed in chapter 7, there was a recent history of excessive paternalism by the BIA, and the BIA seemed to have autonomous rule, both factors greatly resented. It was a distant administration that did not demonstrate accessibility or understanding of circumstances, such as late confirmation of payments for teachers. Admittedly, there was no experience with the state with which to compare the BIA, but the district, as shown above, did have some resource income with which to proceed. An amendment to the State Constitution in 1978 required "equitable allocation" of state income "among all districts in the state," although Native Americans may have taken a "wait and see" approach to that; apparently that amendment was not adequately implemented (see lawsuits later in this chapter). At any rate, federal funds would continue for each student. They were financially in a position to build a much needed, large and beautiful high school complex, something the BIA had never provided. But perhaps one of the most important reasons to choose the state was not expected; there was some leverage there. Local newspapers were quick to publish stories and take sides with the local districts when they had problems with the state. There was a strong sense of empowerment. One participant commented that it was "the time when things changed—the turning point away from accepting white dominance."[33]

One problem did remain. The reservation land for the high school was not theirs. The Episcopalians had purchased some of it from tribal people (Yellow Calf and Seth Willow) for their mission farm in 1913 and 1919, but the tribes had given them much of it as a gift. The two forty-acre parcels that could be documented had been sold to the Episcopalians for twenty-five dollars per acre during the time of Indian starvation.[34]

Allison Sage negotiated with the church to sell the land back to the school district in 1985. The school board told Sage to "get it done," according to a member at the time. As a result, the Indian School District gave a "donation" of $93,000 in exchange for the land, according to Dan Hudson, the Wyoming Indian School District's finance officer (1985–2010). The "donation" went to the diocese in Laramie, Wyoming, not to the local mission. The paperwork, however, shows a sale of the approximately 140 acres for a total of ten dollars.[35]

Some Arapahos involved were surprised to learn that the land was exchanged for a significant sum or did not believe that it was. The school board wanted at least some of the donation to be returned to the Ethete Mission, according to one who knew of the transaction. When none was, bad feelings remained. "We felt on several occasions he [Bishop Jones, president of the Episcopal Diocese Corporation] spoke with forked tongue." As described in chapter 4, the same Episcopal church had leased this land to the Arapahos in the 1970s for one dollar per year in acknowledgment that it was tribal land, given to the church in the first place. Agricultural land values from 1986 could not be found by Fremont County officials in 2012.[36] But this story does not end here (see epilogue for a better moral to the story).

Reservation people saw district revenue bonds placed on the market on October 19, 1987, a day otherwise known as "Black Monday"—the day the stock market crashed in an unprecedented drop felt around the world. The "bond market resurfaced" two weeks later, and the bonds were sold by 10:30 that morning. As Hudson put it, "away it went." The high school building was completed and the doors opened to high school students in the 1989–90 school year. The following year, seventh and eighth graders moved in with the high school students while their building was remodeled. Rep. Patrick Goggles was elected to serve on the district's public school board after serving ten years on the high school's BIA board (see chapter 7). He served twelve more years, eleven as chairman.[37]

A lawsuit changed the entire basis for equalization of funding across the State of Wyoming in 1980, just a year after the County Committee was able to establish district boundaries. No longer would district boundaries determine the wealth of a school. *Washakie Co. Sch. Dist. No. One v. Herschler* asserted that under such method, equitable education for each child (as required by the State Constitution) had never been accomplished. The *Washakie* ruling required that state revenues arising from the various state taxes be used in its "foundation program" to equalize the amount available for each "classroom unit" within each district. The classroom unit formula took into account the number of classrooms needed in spite of a small student body and thus allowed small schools to survive. The Campbell County School District sued the state three times after 1980 to change the funding equation, each court action giving increasingly greater weight to the number of students rather than to classroom units. Yet the state of Wyoming has not "equalized funding sufficiently," and so federal rules permit the Indian schools to receive Impact Aid in addition to the state formula funds. The schools also receive additional federal grants that provide a relatively small and unstable bonus for the education of low-income, Limited English Proficiency children.[38]

The Wyoming legislature considered consolidation of school boundaries again in 2003. They quickly dropped the proposal when House Minority Leader Chris Boswell (D), apparently aware of history, reminded everyone that this was not a good idea: "School consolidation stirs up 'enormous emotion.'" Boswell also "warned the House members they would need plenty of courage to face their constituents at home if they voted for the amendment." Only two members spoke in favor of the consolidation amendment in spite of the state's overall $5 million education deficit. A state senator proposed that Wyoming drop its constitutional requirement for equality, and that also failed. Wyomingites continue to find ways to share the wealth despite past claims that the efforts were "socialistic" or un-American.[39]

Schools shape lives; they maintain and change cultures. We question things and learn much about what is of value in schools. The federal government, with the churches, attempted to use the schools to wipe out Native Americans' culture and, with it, their identity—but Native Americans intended to take it back, through the schools. They intended to prepare students to deal with the Euro-American world in every aspect. When the tribes turned away from the BIA school form of education and requested state-run public schools, they were looking for better quality education and equal treatment with cultural presence.[40] They accomplished these goals in most ways but then had a different set of problems: state control over the funding that their resources would help provide and over the content as well.

The tribes welcomed most of the external world content, but the requirements associated with state testing, to be covered in the next chapter, have edged out much of what might have been done to maintain the tribal languages and, to some extent, culture. The Arapahos and Shoshones were never able to institute system-wide Native language, as in Indian schools of the Southwest. There and in Hawaii, and among the Maori of New Zealand, recovery of the native languages in hundreds of schools is associated with improved self-esteem, successful school achievement, and adult success in life.[41]

Teachers have attempted to establish language immersion ("immersion" meaning that nearly all instruction is given in the native language) at Wyoming Indian Schools among preschool children but so far have not succeeded. However, anthropologist Stephen (Neyooxet) Greymorning has worked with language teachers beginning in 1993 in order to slow ongoing language loss. Children and a few adults in addition to the Elders are capable of using the Arapaho or the Shoshone languages; they have not become extinct, in part as a result of the work by Greymorning and several teachers (Pios Moss, Alonzo Moss, Richard Moss, Tom Shakespeare, William C'Hair, Alvena Friday, Stanford Diviney, and Ula Tyler).[42]

Wyoming American Indians enjoy something other than getting an education within their own cultural environment—"games" where the Indians win with unsurpassed skill and motivation. Athletic skills are not new for Native Americans. According to an Elder voice in the award-winning documentary *Chiefs*: "There once were young men known as messengers who ran so fast it appeared their feet did not touch the ground."[43]

Basketball games are among the greatest joys on the reservation. The Elders, midlife officials, gossiping moms, and babies are all there. When games are away, "Last one off the reservation, turn out the lights!" Alfred Redman became a certified teacher and coach in the mid-1980s (see chapter 7), after which the Wyoming Indian High School Chiefs had a fifty-game winning streak. That broke a previous state record, it so happened, of another Wind River Reservation school, St. Stephen's.[44] Redman credits some of their success to prejudice. He told of several

examples, one involving a situation where men drove up in a truck behind the bus he was driving, to throw bottles at the bus:

> I almost put the brakes on but someone would have got hurt. So they passed and kept throwing bottles. Once they put a dead deer in the bus (chuckle)—at Meteetsee. Once we drove up to a gas station and they said, "Oh, f—, here come those Indians again." Once they [non-Indians] stood outside the gym with big beer bottles holding them out for the students to smell. The photographer in the Junge documentary [*Chiefs*] caught people yelling [racial slurs] at us but he couldn't use it because you have to get permission to use people's photographs.

After the pre-game incidents Redman always asked the boys, "Did you see or hear what happened out there?" They would have seen it. 'Well, then (holding his arms out), get after them.' That's why we ran the score up so much. That's why we won. Sometimes our average was more than a hundred points. But I never told them about it, they saw it." One player, Myron Chavez, was known as "The Magician" and was twice named the State 2-A Player of the Year. "If some coach decides to run with the Chiefs, he'd better buy a good horse," said one editorial.[45]

The "County Shootout," where teams from towns of all sizes play one another, is probably the most impressive. The WIHS boys beat Lander, 105–92 in 2003, while the girls won the tournament in 2006 and 2009 under Coach Aleta Moss and Assistant Coach Alfred C'Bearing. The girls' teams have been equal to the boys' teams in their wins in the years for which I kept records (2001–9). They were conference winners in eight of nine years and state champions in 2003 and 2004. They could not help but win in 2004 when, in a "Showstopper," Diana SoundingSides hit 14 *three-pointers* against Big Piney, tying the national all-time high school record, as featured in *Sports Illustrated*.[46]

10. "The magician," Myron Chavez, approximately seventeen years old, mid-1980s. Photograph by Mike McClure. Courtesy of Barbara Sage.

11. Mylan Glenmore and Melvin Villa of WIHS hold their first place state trophy, 2009. Photograph by Randy Tucker.

Local editorials invited people to attend the Shootout games in the WIHS gymnasium (its capacity being 3,100), where it was said one would hear not the national anthem but the pounding of drums and "the haunting cries of tribal voices." Perhaps the visitors would root for the Indians. Still, opposing teams continued to commit racial insults in 2004. "Wyoming's Native American High School Athletes Play through Persistent Racism" read one *Casper Star-Tribune* headline.[47]

Redman could not say if the cruel words got to the boys. He himself did not take the language personally: "Discrimination will always be out there. It starts around middle high school and goes to around age 55 is what I see." Redman was named to the Wyoming high schools' Coaches' Hall of Fame in 2002 and to the National Athletic High School Coaches' Hall of Fame in 2008.[48]

The influence of Native American leadership brought the resolution of nearly impossible district boundary conflicts between the reservation Native Americans and the towns and even among the towns themselves. And as to the goal of the entire struggle, the Indian schools, a centerpiece to their community, have helped save tribal culture and history. They are a place where there is opportunity for student personality development along the lines of their forebears; the schools are a home outside of the home, where essential tribal values, bearing, and identity can be commonly shared. These ways of being for thousands of years enabled survival and expressed humanity—today tribal identity and self-determined life connect a people and strengthen all of their endeavors.

11

As Seen from the Sun Dance Grounds

A Public School

A curving two-lane road leads reservation travelers through sage and grass covered hills toward low plateaus on the northern horizon. The travelers pass many pastel houses and trailer homes, some with dirt and gravel driveways that swerve around potholes and have teepee poles lying to the side. Horse pastures surround the homes and include the reservation's most outstanding structure, Wyoming Indian High School. With its modern lines and Arapaho geometric motif, it sits just above the Sundance Grounds (chosen for a view of the rising and setting sun). Those who choose to enter the school breathe deeply in a cool and shadowy, high ceilinged entryway with large oil murals painted by Arapaho artists. Teachers have placed posters of Native art in each hallway, and Indian women often sell bead work at lunch tables or the reception counter. One hears songs and greetings each day in Arapaho and sometimes Shoshone.

Dark paintings of Arapaho Elders in wooded mountains decorate the shadowy foyer. Utility lunch tables come next in the large open area. The mix of tribal history and contemporary life is what the schools are all about; the mission statement includes both the intention to teach tribal culture and the objective of giving competence in dealing with the external world. The Arapahos, strong on symbolism, chose a bridge between two cultures, Arapaho translator Cleaver Warden, as their icon. Respectful communication is an essential in Arapaho life and politics. The school medallion depicts the wings of the water bird in a halo-like semi-circle above the icon, a reminder of spirituality, oneness with nature, and the importance of cultural continuance. The tribal leaders followed through as well as they possibly could on their promise for the expression of Indian identity and self-determination through the schools. There were limitations and some disappointments.

The Wyoming Indian Schools enroll approximately 650 students each year, 99 percent of whom are Native American. The students descend mostly from Plains Indian nations: Arapaho, Shoshone, Cheyenne, Black-feet, Apache, and Flathead.[1] Extracurricular activities play a central role in sustaining their cultures. Most high school students belong to the Traditional Club, which sponsors activities designed to recapture the life experiences of the ancient tribal communities. One yearly activity involves the killing of a buffalo and preparation of the meat and hide. A wintertime activity involves listening to the traditional stories presented by parent, auntie, and grandparent teachers. The school conducts graduations in Arapaho ceremonial style and dress.

One of my earliest experiences at the high school was a funeral. It was December, and the large gymnasium was filled to capacity. I was squeezed in between strong, leather-clad shoulders and preoccupied with what people wore, including the dresses and scarves of elderly women. Young children running up and down bleacher stairs filled the place with noise. Then the large side doors opened to dense, fog-laden arctic air where Arapaho men slowly entered, bearing the weight of a casket draped with an Indian blanket. With the casket came a sense of doom; we knew that soon we would all see the pale and motionless man in his prime. But first there was a light jingling sound, and I saw a long line of tiny, delicate girls come dancing in and up the aisle, their colorful dresses with small jingle bells sewn over every inch.

The school gymnasium is the place of many funerals. All are heart rending and lengthy. Young men drum and sing plaintively in Arapaho (not to be translated to outsiders), with the oversight of Arapaho women. The casket, too often holding a youth, is elaborately surrounded by Indian blankets and flowers. At such times the entire school community is an extended family. Prominent members of the tribes speak in both languages for each gathering. And everyone stands in line, encircling the gym floor, to have a chance to speak with and give lengthy hugs to grieving family members. Then Arapaho women serve an enormous selection of food, including warm fry bread, commodity soup and choke-cherry sauce, traditional sweet sauce made from the chokecherry tree's small purple fruit.

Family members gather at the grave site by mid- to late afternoon, when a pickup truck arrives carrying the deceased. They lower the casket and packed personal belongings into the grave and scatter some sandy soil by hand before young men begin to shovel it in. Small groups gradually walk away through the sparse and dry prairie grasses.

The school provides counseling and make-up work for students who are absent for days during times of family loss—it gives closely related staff members five days paid leave. Tribal Elders sometimes perform the Cedaring blessing ceremony after funerals. Elders lead ceremonies of appreciation and thanks on other occasions, such as a Christmas visit by an alumnus in the military. Adults, often teachers, present items to honorees in generous giveaways at the nearby Blue Sky Hall during an evening of singing in the Arapaho language, drumming, and dance.

The Elders' cultural practices in the schools are healing ceremonies, part of a holistic way of life. Episcopal or Catholic churches hold their religious ceremonies on Sundays nearby. But legal decisions hold con-tradictions about the practice of integrated Indian spirituality in the schools.

Students from more than two cultures accomplish schooling together in spite of personal differences. Eber Hampton of the Chickasaw Nation experienced it this way:

> I value aspects of my Anglo education and respect its necessity and power in this society, but my deepest values and my view of the world were formed within an Indian culture. . . . The juxtaposition of the two words *Indian* and *education* has almost always been prob-lematic in spite of the fact that American Indian parents and Anglo

policy makers agree on the importance of education for Indians. Part of the problem lies in the fact that Indian education is inherently a bicultural enterprise that has been directed at two sometimes competing and sometimes complementary goals; assimilation and self-determination.[2]

The tribal cultures have remained a presence in the Wyoming Indian Schools in no small part because of their teachers. The principals may or may not be particularly interested in or knowledgeable about Native American ways, but about one-third of the teachers grew up on the reservation and act as a counter to this often foreign leadership. They model tribal values, helping to revitalize the culture.

Teachers tell history from the local and nationwide Indian perspective. Ancestors of some of the students played key roles, and although often tragic, their stories transmit integrity and dignity about which to feel proud. The civics class, "Tribal Government, Law and Order Code of the Wind River Reservation," prepares students for their lives on the reservation.[3]

From elementary school forward the teachers center activities, art classes, and the content of reading in Native American experience. They integrate the tribal community's attitude into the teaching process, as in Sunday tutoring, presence of food at nearly all events, the ease in sharing personal donations and parent-like directives. The students give a particularly respectful quiet to the more obvious enculturation efforts, such as classroom visits and talks given by Elders.

Educators design programs and classes to create attitudes, values, and cognitive orientations and even to model the control of impulses. Most tribal teachers are aware of carrying forward the Native American practice of placing education of children at the center of community life.[4] Their presence provides role models for the students and hope for the entire community. Without American Indian schools these individuals might leave the reservations—a great loss to this and future generations.

Non-Indian teachers can provide a bridge between cultures and add new "healing capacities" for those students who are struggling with loss.

The best of these teachers find a transcultural sense of belonging that facilitates effective teaching through examination of their own backgrounds. Many of them have leadership roles in the schools.[5] Several have spent nearly two decades in the schools and know the widespread family networks from grandparents to newborns. Some have married into or been adopted into tribal families.

There is not just one unified dominant culture among the teachers in the Indian schools. There are persons of African American origin, white persons from southern states, and several of various European ethnic groups from Wyoming rural towns where loyalties run strong. Their diversity probably helps students feel that they are part of a well-rounded world but also may create assumptions by students and administrators that are inaccurate.[6]

Non-Indian teachers in many Native American schools, unaware of their ethnocentricity, may confuse and alienate their students. The discontinuities have led to negative feelings toward the students, student feelings of being rejected, teacher discouragement, high turnover, and high dropout rates.[7]

Student-teacher relationships between Indians and non-Indians are central to any predominantly Indian school—white students were found to drop out at twice the rate of the Indian students in a college program in an Indian area when the teacher was Indian. Usually the problem is for the Indian student, where the teacher can be seen "as enemy" and education becomes a "critical filter . . . filtering out hope and self-esteem."[8]

Native American students generally have well-developed listening skills, something teachers at the Indian schools may misperceive. These Plains Indian children, raised with the oral traditions, give little eye contact and have a delayed response, termed "wait times," that better facilitate self-reflection and the absorption of information. Silence, as Donald Fixico states in *The American Indian Mind in a Linear World*, seems to help secure the Indian child's thoughts and confirm beliefs.[9]

One dimension that has posed cultural conflict has been the Indian students' expectation for autonomy. Their habits can clash with the

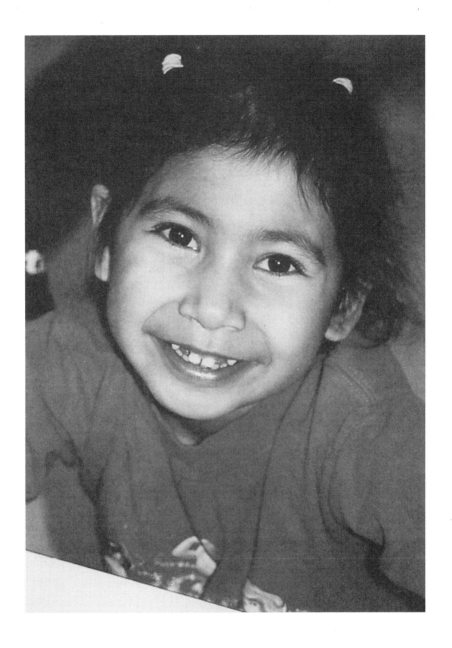

12. Phyllis Gardner, 2003, grandchild of Mildred Goggles, a non-Indian who came to WIHS in 1973 to teach business and marketing, and stayed. Photograph by author.

teacher's expectation to be able to guide and maintain control. At the Wyoming Indian High School this is not always the case; teachers allow students great leeway as to where they sit (as on a window sill) or whether they sleep or listen (who can tell which it is?). If the teacher makes an issue of the student's behavior this can pose a threat to the student's dignity and result in teacher-student conflicts. Teachers may "fall back on" their formal authority as teachers, and the reticent Native American student may shut the teacher out with a ball cap visor or sweatshirt hood. Students sometimes become apathetic, a state that is strongly related to dropping out of school.[10]

Native teachers in general ignore harsh discipline practices of non-Indian teachers. They tend to "look the other way" from culturally unacceptable loud and demanding tones, perhaps due to the low availability of teachers for the reservation area. Alternatively, they may accept the behaviors as a cultural difference, given experiences in nineteenth- and twentieth-century Native American boarding and day schools.[11] Such behaviors seem to cause some (as in other schools) to feel offended—Native teachers usually do not fraternize with particularly judgmental and punitive staff.

Rosemary Christenson, an Ojibwe professor of American Indian studies at the University of Wisconsin, summed up the problem this way, "It's all tied up with identity and cultural dissonance." One review of studies of Indian youth of several tribes found that "one third cited conflict with teachers (as the problem) that led to their decision to leave school." Students are likely to experience loss of self-efficacy when the school environment threatens their ethnic "belonging and . . . historical continuity." Teachers often perceive loss of self-efficacy as resistance or a failure to cooperate. These perceptions often begin anew the cycle of teacher-student conflict. Observations of successful Indian teachers show that a caring teacher who gives attention to individual students and helps with their work is most important in preventing students from dropping out.[12] But the drastic option to drop out is often preceded by a more common problem: absenteeism.

The Arapaho and other Indian cultures highly value relationship connectedness, compassion, and responsibility, as seen in the traditional stories and often in today's way of life. Anthropologist Franz Boas first made clear that cultural traits are a product of "the relationship between the organic and inorganic, above all the relation between the life of a people and their physical environment." When ancestral land is available, it provides a base for descendants who then can live out their lives in family groups. Today these descendants of those who provided for one another as hunters in yearly migrations across the prairie still share with and support any one of their members who is in need. This usually means giving money needed for monthly bills or helping with a funeral; it may mean leaving work or school to be with an ill or grieving relative, even as far away as are the Arapaho in Oklahoma.[13]

There are many losses. Warm and caring school personnel can help bereaved students reconnect.[14] The Wyoming Indian school board has hired Elders from the community as "grandparents" to be available to provide tutoring and counseling. These are vital personnel for the students. One or two are nearly always present in the grandparents' room.

Often past events directly traumatize students and their families. As William Faulkner lamented: "If there were only some painless way to efface the memory—that . . . immortal memory awareness which exists forever still ten thousand years afterward in ten thousand recollections of injustice and suffering." Past intentional efforts to destroy Native American cultures and existence continue to contaminate their communities today.[15] Depression, violence, accidents, disease, and tragedies related to addictions are omnipresent concerns. Anxious parents and tribal officials cooperate with reservation police and federal agents to investigate teenage misconduct. Yet sudden losses, often exacerbated by violence, dominate local newspaper stories and influence staffing for security in the schools.

The statistics to be presented in the following paragraphs concerning the deaths of Native Americans in Fremont County may seem to belie the effectiveness of tribal attempts at creating order and safety, or to raise doubts about their culture as a healthy environment. However,

Posttraumatic Stress Disorder (PTSD) has long been known for its devastating effects, including intergenerational outcomes—in other words, among the children of parents with PTSD.[16]

The high rates of unemployment, divorce, addiction, homelessness, mental illness, and suicide among veterans are well known. The relationship of victimization to substance abuse has also been established. But we rarely speak of the mental health problems of indigenous peoples as being related to government policies, mistreatment by local government authorities, and generations of posttraumatic stress.[17]

Historians and anthropologists generally underemphasize Native American mental health problems, perhaps out of respect for their privacy. Certainly, there is a great deal to say for those who have recovered or who by protective community characteristics were never affected. These are a magnanimous people, compassionate and inclusive. Bonds within the family are powerful—few children elsewhere are so beloved by so many. Harsh words are rare, let alone striking of children. But generations of oppression and injustice have taken their toll.

"Natural death" statistics in Fremont County, from 1998 through 2002, involving all 113 Native American and all 696 white deaths where cause of death was known, show that the life expectancy for whites was 75.03 years, while for Native Americans it was 57.13 years. The accidental death rate among Native Americans was twice as high as among whites; the average age of accidental death was 15.56 years younger than among whites. Male and female Native Americans died of suicides and homicides (combined) at a significantly younger age than whites, on average 28.86 versus 42.45 years, a 13.59-year difference.[18]

The 2006 Fremont County coroner's report shows that 100 percent of the seven vehicular homicides in the county involved alcohol or alcohol and drugs; 64.7 percent of vehicular accidental deaths involved drugs or alcohol. These accidental deaths *most often were Indian* in a county where the non-Indian population was well over three times that of the Indians. And that is in a county that has an enormous rate of carnage—it had 7.5 times the national average in drug- and alcohol-related deaths in 2006. These statistics do not give the ethnic group of the perpetrator; four members of a Shoshone family were killed by a reportedly suicidal seventeen-year-old white male as they began their long, middle of the night trip to Salt Lake City for health care in November 2011.[19]

Long distance travel on two-lane county roads is frequent for the majority of reservation residents in order to acquire basic necessities. They must drive even longer distances to attend school and sports-related functions, to attend government-funded educational programs, and for health care, often in other states.

The early age of death for Native Americans has especially tragic implications for the students—it is their brothers, sisters, cousins, and close friends who have been killed. These situations often cause long periods of grieving, defeating many in a given semester with absentee-ism or an inability to concentrate. These heavy losses begin yet another PTSD cycle, involving both the suffering in the first weeks of loss and the smoldering, long-enduring emotional pain and impairment, as the addictions attest.

Grandparent advisors, psychologists, and counselors are essential, given these problems in the Indian schools. These personnel not only provide counseling but are advocates for students. Psychologists put aside the usual tests; assessments are limited to social-emotional his-tories and descriptions of current life circumstances. Peer-mentoring programs are sometimes planned for the students.[20] Peer relationships have several characteristics that give such programs an advantage—trust and understanding felt among well-known, selected companions and often the ability to listen intently to one another. The confidence shown in students by reaching out to them and giving responsibilities congruent with cultural values provides satisfying effects for students on both sides of the equation.

Students and their families often seek counseling at Indian Health Services at Fort Washakie, although allocations for comprehensive Native American health care are shamefully inadequate and the needs are overwhelming. The Department of Health and Human Services reported expected expenditures in the recent decade for Indian Health

Services to be $2,100 per person, compared to approximately $7,600 for Medicare recipients, $5,000 for Medicaid recipients, $5,200 for veterans, and $4,000 for federal prisoners. Antiquated health services buildings at Fort Washakie serve the sick; one stone building is at least seventy years old. The renovated main clinic building is somewhat improved since the days when pharmacists dispensed medications in metal boxes through a near floor level hole in the pharmacy wall "so they wouldn't touch us." Indian people waited for hours in one huge, outdated room until recently. Now personnel require appointments, something not appreciated, since the wait is days longer. There is no hospital or surgical service. In 2005, the Wind River IHS funds limited care to emergency services. Doctors often rotate from other areas. "If it is serious, they fly 'em out," usually to Casper, where the decision is made as to whether to send a patient to Salt Lake City or Denver.[21] Most often family members drive the patient to one of these cities.

These conditions are not unique to the Wind River Indian Reservation. The chair of the U.S. Commission on Civil Rights, Mary Frances Berry, stated in 2003, "It's clear that the programs that they have now are not funded adequately, that they're not staffed adequately. And no matter how hard IHS tries, their needs haven't been given a preferred position within the budget on the part of the national government."[22]

The extreme difficulty in gaining adequate health care is compounded by economic conditions. Local doctors in border towns need to be paid, and Native American payments to private insurance companies are most often out of the question.

The general public often expects reservation incomes to be higher given reservation underground resources. Today the extraction industries negotiate revenue payments to the tribes (as are overseen by federal regulators) and pay taxes to the county and state (over 13 percent). But there are large losses to Native Americans due to well-publicized past federal "mismanagement." A semblance of justice has been slow to come. In 1979 the two Wind River tribes filed suit against the federal government for recovery of trust funds, lost and unaccounted for. Federal courts ruled in the tribes' favor in 2003, but that was appealed in 2005, when the U.S. attorney general asked the Supreme Court to overturn the ruling since it, along with the 1996 *Cobell v. Salazar* case and twenty additional tribal federal court lawsuits, he said, had left the government open to a potential of more than $200 billion in back claims. Claimants tentatively settled the *Cobell* case at a great loss, $3.4 billion, in July 2011 and finalized it in late 2012 after two years in an appeals process.[23]

The tribes have sought a solution to their economic problems through gaming. The Arapaho tribe faced protracted difficulties in negotiations for gaming rights, but the 10th U.S. Circuit Court of Appeals decided in their favor in 2004. According to the court the state did not negotiate in good faith. The "state lost big on (its) casino bet," as the *Casper Star-Tribune* put it. The *Tribune* reported that after eleven years of Northern Arapaho and state negotiations and litigation, the court ruled that "the tribe is entitled to 'the full gamut of casino-style Class III gambling.'" The state was told it would "have no authority" over tribal gaming and, as the *Tribune* put it, "won't get a nickel from it." But the past obstructions have long prevented the tribes from organizing for economic improvements for their communities as a whole.[24]

The historical placement, reductions in reservation size, and competition with settlers for more favored reservation agricultural land and resources all play a fundamental role in economic conditions. The Dubois gerrymandering (see chapter 5) and the McLaughlin agreement reported in chapter 1 serve as examples. And tribal people continue to have severe problems in accessing Wind River Reservation waters.[25] As will be shown in the following paragraphs, poverty has something to do with school performance.

Federal researcher and author Arloc Sherman first used the phrase "no child left behind," in the *Children's Defense Fund Report on the Costs of Child Poverty* in 1994, and it would become the title of 2001 education legislation (NCLB). Sherman showed that the connection between academic performance and poverty was "all but overwhelming"; he found that youth in the economic bottom 20 percent are twice as likely as middle income youths and "11 times more likely than wealthy youths" to drop out of high school. Another study found that racial or ethnic minority status is also related in an independent, powerful, and negative way to academic achievement. Legislators changed the name of the NCLB mandate in 2015 to "Every Student Succeeds."[26] National and state testing may bring down scores for Native American children even more than for most minorities.

Wind River teachers teach local tribal history and governmental structure, but state and national tests did not include this content (see epilogue for 2017 changes). Reservation topics stimulate "intrinsic motivation" and acknowledge that tribal history is significant in the state's story. Teachers have had to set these subjects aside to prepare students for the dominant culture's testing.[27] Their achievement levels are relatively and uncomfortably low except for a few exceptions to be described in the following section.

The state began giving each school a "report card" early in the implementation of NCLB. Internet and local publication reports on results for the Indian schools can be an embarrassment for the tribes, particularly with the lack of general public understanding about the underlying causes for the scores. National tests place the demands of the outer world directly on the student. Several authors point out that there is "a misguided and exaggerated understanding" of what schools and students alone can do to create a more egalitarian society.[28]

Most students in the district qualify for the "English Learners" category. The limitation is not for lack of historic effort to force English language acquisition.[29] In fact the original efforts—that is, boarding school punishments—*combined with present day pressures to perform* are likely to have effects on vulnerable students' academic abilities and on faith in their potential.

Michelle Hoffman, a recent Wyoming Indian Schools superintendent of many years, talked in her interview about how formal test preparation invades the classroom for "weeks and weeks" each year. The high school's social studies teacher noted in 2012 that they had been involved in the testing process from the beginning of the last week of March into May, leaving students "burned out" for further study at the end of the school year. Teachers must "align the curriculum to the tests."[30]

Test results are likely to reflect the quality of teaching as well as population factors over which the teacher and school have no control; that is, economic and cultural factors as well as collective history, generations of language loss, and resistance to control by outsiders. However, the educational hierarchy and some in the larger community may place the blame on the school if the results are not up to par. The state allocates huge educational funds to purchase corporate curriculum and assessment materials to meet testing directives. One Wyoming contract paid Harcourt $13.9 million in 2007. The costs do not end there. Complex administrative procedures require time-consuming cooperation of all staff.[31]

However, administrators and teachers do not seem to consider "personal time" when making decisions about their work load at Wyoming Indian Schools. The staff's small community and cultural pride culminate in dedication. "Our days are longer than any other district in the state," according to Hoffman. The teachers give students who are a year behind in a content area ninety minutes of class time rather than the usual forty-five; the teachers give them an *additional* forty-five minutes, one-on-one, if the student is two years behind. Students who come into the schools three to four academic years behind often have a persistent (although decreasing) lag.[32]

There are complex reasons for the low test scores found for minority students. Some minorities, including Native Americans, see certain dominant group processes as "symbols of identity." They do not view the processes as "barriers they have to overcome" but rather as symbolic of differences "to be maintained."[33] Dominant group processes persist in testing procedures—time pressure, competition showing off individual knowledge, and threats of failure with serious consequences to self and the group.

Many Arapaho and Shoshone children, like those of other Native American groups, are likely to take more time in completing a test simply because they are not individually competitive and usually take seriously questions posed as a matter of thoughtfulness and respect.[34] Most teachers admire these cultural differences and would find them difficult to turn around, even if that were desirable, at the times tests are given.

Native Americans and Alaska Natives in general have been found to have a "wide and persistent" achievement gap with their non-Indian peers. However, in the Wyoming Indian Schools the upper grades' writing proficiency scores have been remarkably high even though the reading scores were relatively low (although consistently higher than in mathematics).[35] Presumably evaluators judge students' writing performance in the test on creativity and accurate use of the English language. Most of these students have listened from their earliest years to Arapaho traditions where the understanding of relationships and analogies are developed.

The science scores for all the Wyoming Indian schools, by contrast are at the bottom of the scale. Ninety percent or more of the students scored at the lowest ("basic" and "below basic") levels for the four years after the subject was first tested (2007–8).[36] Certainly this subject matter involves new language and concepts that require careful explanation. It may be that the relatively new technical words sometimes create heightened anxiety, a factor in low performance.

Limited English has meant that Wyoming Indian students nearly always improve their reading and writing performance by the time they are tested in the eleventh grade. However, by the eighth and eleventh grades, mathematics scores had fallen in the years studied.[37] State evaluators try to determine how and why teaching methods and materials fail the students. High school graduates have been seen to go forward in short order, once liberated from the formal discipline of mathematics in the classroom, to supervise gaming tables at the Wind River Casino, where passing the casino's mathematics test is a requirement for employment.

The introduction to the classroom of topics of relevance in students' lives, such as reservation surface water and air quality near oil wells, could improve math and science scores. These topics contribute to an understanding of regulatory agencies as well. Certainly they would give evidence of the Elders' claim of the interrelatedness of all things. Teaching processes that make the local environment, language, and culture "the centerpiece" are known to give Native students a better chance to succeed.[38]

One group of Wyoming Indian teachers, among them Sandra Iron Cloud and Pamela St. Clair Gambler, developed a local tribal curriculum in the Rural Systemic Initiative and Math Science Partnership in 2006. The initiative outlines standards for the student, educators, school and community to become "culturally responsive." Through the initiative's programs, students learn to become "well grounded in the tribal cultural heritage and traditions." There the development of character is stressed—students' education encourages them to assume lifelong obligations to their home community and to participate in the surrounding cultural environments. These responsibilities include an in-depth understanding of contemporary sociological and political reservation life. Additionally, the initiative stresses "awareness and appreciation of the relationships and processes . . . in the spiritual, natural and human realm," thus many aspects of ancient spirituality and modern science are included.[39] The plans remain on paper, filed away.

For decades Indian educators have noted the negative effects of cultural discontinuity. White Earth Chippewa Patricia Lock, president of the National Indian Education Association in 1978, expressed the resentment that American Indians are "forced to adapt" to the dominant society's educational system *only because they are so numerous, insistent and all-pervasive"—and so sure of their "infallibility."*[40] Arapaho Elder presence is felt less with each passing year in the schools; preparation for the tests takes precedence.

There will be a "culture clash," with all of its adverse effects, as long as one group is dominant and "preparing" another group to take part in *their* world. Strong evidence from several ethnic groups (including Native Americans) and from various periods of history shows that the external control and discrimination often associated with economic exploitation are the main source of the difficulty.[41]

The state has made accommodations for testing English language learners. Testing standards no longer require that sections in mathematics be timed, and monitors may read test questions to the students.

Teachers hope that the state will also adjust the content and assessment methods so that Native American students can see their progress and feel self-worth in the classroom. Testing that shows *individual growth* or lack thereof, is more meaningful and less demeaning than repeated comparisons to students in school districts where the population has been English speaking (with "English" interests) for centuries. Certainly student difficulty with the English language, never adequately taught to parents and grandparents in most of the boarding schools, combined with loss of the original language, go a long way toward explaining low academic performance. Each generation has had to start over, often adjusting from the limited English that they learn at home to schools where English only is used to teach everything from mathematics to science. For many, only a limited language of necessity remained at the turn of this century. Elder Burton Hutchinson (see chapter 1) provides us with a good example. Both of his grandparents (who raised him) attended boarding schools, his grandfather in Genoa, Nebraska, and his grandmother in the government school at Fort Washakie, but neither of them spoke English: "They knew but they didn't speak it." Although Burton fought in the Korean War for ten months in 1951 and then served in France doing construction until October 1953, he sought tutoring from "a bilingual lady," hired by the schools in the mid-1970s.[42]

One among several exceptions to today's limited English phenomenon was Ben Friday Jr. (1933–2003), who spoke fluent English. But the Arapaho language was preferred. His wife Alvena (fluent in both languages) said that in the several days previous to his death, "before he sank into too deep a sleep for talk," he spoke "only in the Arapaho language."[43] Their children, fluent English speakers, are among the most successful on the reservation.

One of the most gratifying outcomes of the establishment of the Wyoming Indian School District is a decrease in the dropout rate. The decrease reflects improvements in teacher-student relationships, classroom content, and the ability of students to feel identified with the schools and their environment. "The reason for starting the school was the high dropout rate," state representative Patrick Goggles pointed out. The graduation rate was 58.62 percent in 2004–5, well above the Wind River Native American graduation rate of less than 30 percent in the 1970s (as discussed in chapter 3), and well above the U.S. Native American graduation rate of less than 50 percent in 2005.[44]

Carol Ward's research findings show that engagement in extracurricular activities corresponds to a reduced dropout rate. The time and efforts put into these traditional activities at Wyoming Indian schools may be paying off.[45] "Virtual school" classes also seem to be helpful to students who are failing. The computer requires correct answers before the student may progress. In this neutral and contemporary environment where no one is watching, approximately 50 percent of these otherwise failing students pass a given class in a given semester.

The external world is evolving in a way that literally touches student development—texting and internet fascination bring all sorts of sophisticated information into the students' environment, and they are moving forward with it. At the same time school administrators have become adept at making the technical efforts necessary for adherence to the state's administrative guidelines. The district passed the accreditation process "with flying colors" in 2011, according to then Federal Program Coordinator Melissa Friday.[46] Neither the state nor the reservation would benefit if the schools were to close.

Social presence and cultural behaviors are powerful characteristics among Wyoming Indian high school teenagers. The students have perfection in grooming and skill in presentation of style. No one today could say that they are not "clean," once the reason given for not allowing them in the local restaurants.[47] The faint scent of exotic flowers sometimes accompanies the girls—some still wear braids, meticulously kept, pleasing the grandmothers. Makeup, if used, is delicate, and clothing, though sometimes short in quantity, is well selected.

Wind River tribal elementary children, like most other children, learn the norms for behavior from familial adults. Repeatedly family members show examples in the traditional stories, usually told in after-hours programs. "The traditions" sometimes tell of children who make decisions in scary circumstances and live with the consequences. One, "Blood-Clot-Boy and White-Owl," tells of a boy who decides to go against the persuasion of his Elders in the face of natural (a fierce snow storm) and supernatural (white-owl) threats. He is able to prove himself and wins the respect of white-owl.[48]

Children who make mistakes in the school environment are likely to be teased in a friendly reminder of their human imperfection and a leveling influence. But the respect for the child's decisions, many of these in the non-Indian community reserved for adults, may help build a sense of dignity and presence often setting Native Americans apart. It is the Native American's almost incredible (to non-Indians) emphasis upon autonomy *and* selflessness that has been called the ultimate of human social development.[49]

There are signs among most students of youthful optimism, personal pride, and a well-incorporated tribal identity. The use of the Native language is limited, and this is no small loss, but at least there are other ways that cultural identity can be felt.[50]

Students, like all teenagers, are part of a peer socialization that sometimes simply has to do with mannerisms of speech, such as the long "eehh—" as a lead-in to teasing and laughter, or the extra time given to the recipient of questions. There is usually a noticeable ease of enjoyment of one another's jokes or silly behavior born of a deep interest in these longtime relatives or friends. They treat parent and grandparent figures in a respectful but confiding way, seen among non-Indians with trusted peers. Their deference to Elders stands out; one outsider commented at a school conference that Elders seemed "almost like royalty."[51] The school environment provides many examples of the students' inclusion of adults and of other culturally tied relationships—the importance of the boyfriend's friendship with the girlfriend's mother, any older relative referred to as a grandparent, and cousins referred to as brothers or sisters.

The peer group tends to monitor itself. Members frown upon and tease those who flaunt frivolous conduct or give too much attention to their own vain interests—vanity is strongly discouraged in the Arapaho traditions. Close-knit groups or cliques are often based upon place

13. Tamara Duran, graduation, 2005. Photograph by author.

of residence and extended family—sometimes, on the negative side, resulting in interfamily group conflicts that have grown out of a long-term history lived in deprivation and overcrowding. Nearly all treat peers with handicaps kindly; there is a cultural norm to take "pity," a word with a deeper meaning among the Arapahos than is usually found among Euro-Americans, one that "generates actions to follow."[52]

The schools do at times provide social events that reflect the customary Euro-American world, although Wyoming Indian students seem very ambivalent about some of these ceremonies. Only a few students place hand on heart during the playing of the national anthem at athletic events, and the direction of attention seems rather vague. This behavior was caught on film in the 2002 documentary *Chiefs*, somewhat humorously. The contrast to the attendant behavior of the opposing team seemingly goes unnoticed by the local people on both sides. And to assure readers that this behavior is not a matter of patriotism, note that at the 2004 prom, although all attendees were fabulously dressed and exciting rock music filled the room dripping with sparkling tinsel, no one danced. I asked a student why not. He told me after some thought that sometimes they dance, "if someone starts it." Students and relatives took hundreds of pictures of couples and cousin groups instead, while at least half of the remainder waited their turn or just watched. As usual, I saw no displays of physical affection. Native Americans who live in close quarters are modest in this regard.[53]

The prom attendee behaviors and that of the observers bear similarities in many ways to the regional Denver Plains Indian powwows, where some participants are "prairie chickens," and some are "warriors," and all like to have their pictures taken. These masters of masquerade were fantastic at the prom in evening gowns and sometimes suits, as was one perfectly decked out as a gangster of the non-Indian world to pose with his delicate date. Everyone loves the community appreciation and the glamour.

14. Jasmin McGill sings a Christmas song with the universal sign language of the Plains Indians, 2006. Photograph by author.

The white-haired photography teacher, some days after the 2004 prom, told me he had decided not to retire but to stay for yet another year. He said one of his students had told him "they would miss me." Such is the power of the student upon the teacher.

The same artistic flair that was apparent at the prom was shown at Halloween in 2003. Unrecognizable ghouls appeared in the early morning, their faces painted in black, white, and sometimes red. Coloring in their hair matched in intricate, tightly pulled designs. And then the ghouls were gone before the noon bell rang, as if it had never happened—a quiet normalcy reigned in the rest of the day. Later the Elders objected to greasepaint on the faces, and this phenomenon has not taken place since.

Group cohesion and organizational skills have played their part in student political protest. Many students along with their reading teacher helped organize Martin Luther King Day marches in Riverton and Casper in 2003 and 2004 to oppose the attempt of a hate group, "World Church of the Creator," to establish itself in Riverton. Students with their families and school staff carried banners saying, "We are all related," reaching out to the whole community. These "church" members had called Native Americans "the mud people," something that quickly circulated around the Indian High School.[54]

The 2003 activities of the Wyoming Indian School students were central to the demise of the "Church of the Creator" in Wyoming, as was reported numerous times in the regional media. A large front page picture in the *Denver Post* in late December 2002 showed WIHS students Cody Lamebear and Rosa Dodge as they contemplated the church's announcement that it would move to Lander. The church's "supreme leader" was awaiting trial for "soliciting the murder of a federal judge" in 2003, and by 2004 the *Casper Star-Tribune* reported that what remained of the group was in Montana "teetering on its last legs."[55]

Fixico argues that it is the Native American holistic approach that underlies the "wider perspective" seen in their artistic and philosophical understandings.[56] Also, it is worth noting that students are more

15. Sherman Chavez at Martin Luther King Day demonstration march, Riverton, Wyoming, 2003. Photograph by author.

successful with less face to face interaction, less use of language, and less of the "English way of doing things" in most K–2 teacher-supervised artistic tasks. The conflict also seems to be put aside in the area of poetry and other writing tasks where contemplation is expected.

Wyoming Indian High School has a right to the claim of outstanding artistic ability among its students. Their drawings have been shown across the state and in museums in Boulder and Fort Collins, Colorado.[57] As they worked, students concentrated on photographs by Sarah Wiles of their Elders and relatives and, sometimes, photographs of members of other tribes by E. S. Curtis. Students often chose photographs of adults with frailties, and children with deformities and worried looks, in projects that took weeks to finish. The results nearly always reflected a deeply meaningful and caring attitude. Their products also include sculpting, remarkable regardless of difficulty, as in a display of sculpted hands.

The high school prepares its students for college, but they may not attend. The high school would like to change that. It offers a class in college orientation and welcomes representatives from the University of Wyoming, Central Wyoming College, the Wind River Tribal College, and several grant programs. The representatives meet with students and assess them for their interests, abilities, and progress and make the assessments available to teachers and staff.

Student continuation in schooling is affected by finances and needs at home. In 2001 it was believed that about 30 percent went on to a college or university. The percentage of students graduating with associate's degrees increased sevenfold from 2001 to 2003 after the Arapaho Endowment of the University of Wyoming began providing financial aid to parents. Most attend near home at Riverton's Central Wyoming College, where ongoing visits with family and tribal community are possible. Student attendees at the University of Wyoming frequently make the long drive home to maintain their emotional and social equilibrium. But students may not choose the advancement that a university education might provide on the reservation or in urban society. Many prefer an alternative choice—to develop "Indian life among Indians."[58]

The foundations for self-determination are found in today's Indian schools. The characteristics are twofold, psychological and cognitive. Psychologically the schools acknowledge and give legitimacy to Indian identity and culture; they confirm respect for Indian identity through the presence of Indian teachers and Indian values. Cognitively, the schools convey knowledge that is specifically important for life on the reservation. Some of that is about tribal, local, and state politics; some of it is about being part of the social and economic context. Leadership skills grow out of both psychological and cognitive dimensions and provide tribal cohesion and self-determination. The overall changes that have taken place since the establishment of the school are a result of its influence and of the Indian people being who they are. The successes described in this book, I believe, were behind the many heartening developments to be seen in the years to follow.

Epilogue

Ethete's people settled in one of the more arid areas of the Wind River Reservation, among islands of sagebrush, its gray stems toughened in winds of all seasons. Then and now, the sky above the nearby Wind River Range of the Rocky Mountains and the northeastern horizon's pale shaded buttes give a rare, ever-changing beauty. The people of the Wind River valley are descendants of families who endured boarding school and federal government deprivations. They survived their physical poverty through communal sharing and with the benefits of a rich spiritual and cultural life. But images of the future were desolate, with threatened cultural loss and generations of teenage children sometimes in white-run schools and sometimes not in school. The tribes' opportunity to coalesce for self-determination was difficult to come by, and chances for it were fading. Things would likely have remained so and taken their course had the Four Old Men not dug up the earth for a cornerstone for the school. Today's image is not about loss, it is about empowerment.

Tribal people established their public school for two reasons; they wanted to give their children an environment that emphasized their history and culture, and they wanted the children to succeed at home and in relationship to the outside world. A high school at the center of their community would in and of itself be a tremendous boost to their economy and a center for community life. In short, the school would be an institution essential to control over their destiny.

There were many subcategories in the national movement for "Indian control of Indian education"; to escape once and for all the boarding school experience, to relieve their children of the experience of prejudice and failure in the local schools, to maintain tribal identity and pride, to see their children make educational and economic advancements, and to be able to foster knowledge specifically useful to the reservation people.[1] To determine one's destiny speaks of independence, as is clear in the words so often used, "self-determination." People have been able to make important strides toward getting beyond obstacles and accomplishing their goal only with some changes in state and national law.

Today's Indian schools in Wyoming, as seen in the last chapter, are environments where local tribal culture is fostered and where most of the children maintain personal presence with self-esteem. They are taught their history, and in this sense they have an advantage over non-Indian children, who all too often have only a murky knowledge of their community's history. When I spoke to the new superintendent of schools at Ethete, Owen St. Clair (the son of Darwin and Sandra St. Clair), he told me of another outcome: increasingly, students are graduating. The Ethete high school saw twenty-eight graduates in 2016 (of an original freshman class of approximately fifty to sixty students). This is more than usually seen at Ethete and percentagewise higher than found in Lander in the 1970s (although this is impossible to calculate specifically because of the unknown number of original students; see chapter 3). The effects of high school graduation are far reaching and difficult to measure, but two major reservation developments external to the school have followed its establishment: improved voting rights and gaming. The tribal people with the help of ACLU attorney Laughlin McDonald filed suit to challenge at-large elections that had diluted their vote for the Fremont County Commission (see McDonald's book *American Indians and the Fight for Equal Voting Rights*). They also gained the economic advantage of reservation gaming (see chapter 11). The confidence, knowledge, and connections that the establishment of a school brought most likely all played a part in making these things happen. Through single-member districts, the Native American community elects representatives for the state legislature (such as Patrick Goggles, an informant in this book), and through the building of the casinos and hotels, and gaming itself, the economy saw hundreds of jobs and other income go directly to the tribes and individuals; the median household or family income at Ethete increased from $24,130 in 2000 to $35,201 in 2009. These changes were fought hard by the local towns; new district boundaries were not needed, they said, and gaming would bring increased illegal activity, neither of which proved to be true.[2] Indians did gain some power and prestige, otherwise overwhelmingly owned by whites.

However, there are some disadvantages that come with having a reservation public high school; reservation resources contribute to the state pool of education funds, and the school receives its portion of the education funds in return. Thus they must deal with state involvement in determining the curriculum as discussed in chapter 11. This is not entirely unwelcome; the school's mission statement directs that students be prepared to be competent in dealings with the external world. But they are not immune to the resulting problems that afflict other public schools. The No Child Left Behind Act began an unwelcome process for many public schools on and off reservations; for example, alignment of the curriculum to the tests, the demeaning of communities when standards are applied across all schools regardless of economic advantage, long weeks of preparation for tests, and loss of local control. The unique complaint of Indian schools until 2017 was that the tests lacked recognition of local tribal history and culture, key components for Indian children (see chapter 11). These components, important enough to give all of us a better sense of our identity, were largely ignored for tribal people. The small tribal numbers (2 percent when including those of mixed descent) were seemingly invisible to educational authorities. Fortunately, this has changed.

Montana, in its program called, "Indian Education for All," has for over a decade required that the state's Indian history be included in the classroom. Maia Rose, board member of the Wyoming Association of Churches, explained to me that in 2017 Wyoming was doing much the same. As she and Melissa Friday explained, the Wyoming Association of Churches (Chesie Lee, director) provided training in 2016 to members of the Wind River Native Advocacy Center (Jason Baldes, executive director) for legislative lobbying. The training resulted in their first project, the lobbying of state legislators to pass the American Indian education program.[3] Wyoming legislators passed the program (HB0076) in 2017. The legislation "requires the State Board of Education—to ensure the cultural heritage, history and contemporary contributions of American Indians are addressed in the standards." The Wind River tribes will have an opportunity to respond to the board's decisions. The state will make the appropriate "materials and resources" available to school districts across the state. The knowledge thus imparted should improve race relations and give Indian students intrinsic motivation to learn. Friday hopes that the ongoing effects of historical Indian loss and trauma—Posttraumatic Stress—will finally be recognized. What was broadly known tended only to cast blame their way.

In a related effort on the reservation, Wind River Native Advocacy (WRNA), their mission "to empower Native Americans in Wyoming," has several ongoing projects. Melissa Friday, the Wind River Reservation's White Buffalo Youth prevention coordinator (Sunny Goggles, director), told me in 2017 that WRNA had hired Community Builders Incorporated to "figure out what we need" to have an economic base. She said that according to their findings the three things the reservation needs are "wellness, youth leadership, and civic engagement." One of their most important findings was that approximately 80 percent of the reservation population was less than twenty-five years of age (Jason Baldes, director of WRNA, similarly noted that the population is 85 percent less than thirty years of age). This finding reflects the dire circumstances of health on the reservation and emphasizes the importance of the involvement of youth in determining the future. Melissa related that now they are conducting leadership forums and that already several are ready to develop marked trails in their mountains, lead hunting expeditions, and become involved in health-related programs such as the Northern Arapaho Diabetes Program. The Elders are opening the inner circle of ceremonial practices to include youth, always prohibited before. If we are 80 percent youth, "then we have no time to wait."[4]

The local Indian peoples' history and its relationship to Posttraumatic Stress were explained at a Wyoming Indian High School conference in 2006. Now, there is a Northern Arapaho Tribal Historic Preservation Office. This office made arrangements for the burial repatriation of the three Arapaho children who died at the Carlisle Indian Industrial School: Little Chief, Horse, and Little Plume. It is believed that Little Plume, whose gravestone is pictured in the introduction to this book, was "Hayes" (his English name), the grandson of the first Friday (see introduction). The Carlisle cemetery was moved in 1927 to make way for buildings and a parking lot. Apparently at the time, Little Plume's body was either buried with another (or others) or numbered improperly; his remains were missing from the grave. The Indian School's gravediggers had put the bones of two older boys in his place. Tribal representatives placed a handful of Carlisle dirt in Little Plume's coffin to have symbolism of his physical presence.[5]

The spirits of Little Plume, Horse, and Little Chief were present on a still and clear day when brightly decorated horses circled, one missing its rider in each of three funerals, conducted in the dry grass and sage of the reservation's graveyards. Arapaho men slowly lowered the small caskets wrapped in white ruffled quilts, into Wind River ground, on August 18, 2017.

There are other reminders of culture clash and loss. According to Superintendent St. Clair, the Indian school's graduates are still not well represented at the University of Wyoming.[6] Many instead attend Central Wyoming College in Riverton; too many financial and social problems remain for Indian students at the university. As shown in the documentary *Chiefs* (see chapter 10), the stars often leave home with scholarships and then, to their family's heartbreak, return, avoiding them, lost and ashamed, no longer with a vision of where to go next. While on the basketball court they are agile and brilliant in team play, the academic world challenges language limitations and cultural belonging.

Being a university student is not a team sport—individualism comes first. Ironically, suspicions of the prejudice that on the court helped them win can in the larger world play a part in defeat.

Native American students are required to gain the basic knowledge long held by the Euro-American society. It takes time to establish these concepts and language from early childhood forward. And when they are not available or well integrated, each generation must start over. This is particularly noticeable where language is concerned and it is, of course, interwoven with the new concepts. When a language is eradicated (as it was for most in the boarding schools) without the new language being carefully and adequately established, recovery is going to take the contributions of language specialists, educators, and again, time.

There remains another discontinuity and schism discussed in the earlier chapters, although temporarily overcome at times and by certain tribal members; the Northern Arapahos and Eastern Shoshones have long struggled to overcome the conflict created when federal troops "escorted" the Arapahos onto the Shoshone reservation (in spite of the Arapahos' desire at the time to be placed in Sweetwater River country) and the forced permanent sharing of land and resources. The Joint Tribal Council ceased meeting and became defunct for a lengthy period in recent years. However, in 2017 tribal officials agreed to governmental system overhauls that promise dramatic improvements. Already there is an Intertribal Council that replaces the Joint Tribal Council. Significantly, too, an Intertribal Court will soon begin ruling in misdemeanor cases. In these cases this court will replace the Courts of Indian Offenses that functioned under the Code of Federal Regulations, known as CFR courts. These major changes may eventually affect tribal prejudices and attitudes across reservation life; both tribes will be reminded of the strength of joint work.[7]

There are other old schisms; the schism between the towns and the tribes, where issues have sometimes changed and sometimes not. The behaviors are well known yet still shocking; one interviewee, Richard Ortiz, a fifty-year-old BIA employee, told of being called "a 'f—' Indian lover" as he left a restaurant with his wife and friends. The name caller was a county commissioner. "I had never talked to the guy before in my life!" exclaimed Ortiz in his 2006 interview. And in the broader picture, it was not just the towns' opposition to casinos but the aspersions that were made; there would be illegal activity because of gambling itself and because these casinos were run by Indians. And there is factionalism within each tribe, such as that between Lower and Upper Arapahos, that extends further down to within each family. Relationships of grand-children of stepchildren or half siblings may be more contentious and jealous than were those their grandparents; "that's how the Arapaho are," said one in-law in the tribe. But when offense is taken Elders urge the offended to "let it go." From ancient times they have worked hard to unify and keep the peace.[8]

The Shoshones established a charter high school at Fort Washakie about ten years ago and went forward to develop a public high school in 2012. Like the school at Ethete, it is starting small, and many Sho-shones still attend high school in Lander and a few at Ethete. Similarly, the school protects Shoshone identity and history although, as always, with critical competitiveness as well.[9]

An educational endeavor that is without competition on the reserva-tion is the Wind River Tribal College (next door to the Wyoming Middle School in Ethete). In recent years it partnered with the University of Wisconsin at Oshkosh. Together they graduated twenty-four students— mostly from the tribal communities. Their degrees are in the fields of early and elementary education. The funding from the Arapaho Tribal Council and two federal grants has now ended, and so the Tribal Col-lege has closed. Every attempt must be made to find money if classes are to resume.[10] A Tribal College success is helpful for the students and communities to achieve their potential and essential for those whose care and attention is needed at home.

Reservation parents have long looked with apprehension at the mile-age and social gap between the reservation and advanced schooling. However, Alfred Redman's statement that he would "like to see the kids I coach go to college and come back and work here on the reservation," is coming true for many. Owen St. Clair was a player in 1986; Redman's daughter, Josephine Redman, has been a mathematics teacher at WIHS since 1998; WIHS alumna Aleta Moss is in charge of coaching for high school girls and the health curriculum, and the list is growing. Other WIHS college and university graduates work in tribal government offices, the Indian Health Service, Social Services, or the BIA. And as mentioned earlier, for hundreds of high school graduates, the construction and the management of the tribes' casinos have meant accessible training and work in skilled positions such as electrician, carpenter, computer programmer, surveillance officer, and administrator. The Arapahos' Wind River Casino, one of the three reservation casinos, was the largest employer on the Wind River Indian Reservation in 2009. With completion of its new hotel, it became the largest employer in Fremont County in 2012, employing nearly seven hundred people.[11]

There is another positive change as well, one having to do with the Episcopal Church. As will be remembered, the tribal relationship with the Episcopal Church took a downturn when the Church sold reservation land to the Ethete school board (see chapter 10). It is possible that the schools played a part in alerting Church officials to tribal community feelings; the history, both good and bad, of the Church's involvement with the school was outlined at more than one school conference where Episcopal officials were in attendance. They have now more than made up for the financial transactions in question. Episcopalians are active members in the Wyoming Association of Churches in support of reservation leadership; the Episcopal Foundation of Wyoming is giving $50,000 in three installments to fund Wind River Native Advocacy Center activities. Native Advocacy is using the money to determine needs as described earlier and for the education and training of the tribal leadership and health care specialists. It seems that the Church is forgiven entirely; Rawlin Friday, son of Alvena and Ben Friday Jr., recently took his place as the first full-time Episcopal priest at the Ethete mission since Reverend Duncombe's death; Roxanne Friday, daughter-in-law of Alvena Friday, is the newly appointed priest at Robert's Episcopal Mission at Fort Washakie.[12]

And 645 tribes saw a positive economic change that had its beginning with the success of the Coalition of Indian Controlled School

Boards. The story is one of twists and turns that ends well. As will be remembered, Michael Gross of Santa Fe, New Mexico, was the coalition's attorney from the time it was established in 1971 (see chapter 4), and it was the coalition that lobbied Congress for self-determination legislation that was passed in 1975 (see chapter 9). The legislation provided contracts for services to the tribes that were to be administered by the federal government. The legislation was good, but the government did not live up to its responsibilities. And so the Ramah Chapter of the Navajo Nation initiated a lawsuit for more than 645 tribes that was settled in 2016—for $940 million. Attorney Gross stuck with the tribes for the decades it took to see it through. This was certainly more than a professional and personal vindication for him—after the heartbreaking defeat in Wyoming. "Mr. Gross never gave up on the school board and the chapter," said one member of the Navajo tribe in the *Navajo Times*.[13]

There have been many sad losses since the writing of this book began. Only some of the Elders who were interviewed are still alive. A few of the students died in tragic circumstances. And the school superintendent who required the study, Lonn Hoffman, died in 2004 covering his children from a rock slide in the mountains. I so regret that they are not here to see the outcome of their contributions and the work as a whole. Happily Verna Thunder, Alvena Friday, Alberta Friday, Alfred Redman, Nelson and Crawford White, Barbara Sage, Hubert Friday, and William C'Hair, all of the oldest generation interviewed, are still with us. Several of the teachers are still teaching at the high school as well.

As many of the outcomes described indicate, I am a proponent of WIHS. There is hardly a way to make a comparison between where the reservation communities are now and where they might have been without the school. But most directly, I have observed the school in its role as an educational and conference center and as a center for community life: for cultural ceremonies, local and regional basketball games, awards ceremonies, funerals, and as a place where many Elder-student or other connections can be made. Residents strongly associate the school and its educational potential with home and tribal community. I have no doubt that it has had great influence in all of these outcomes; its very existence is a confidence builder. In a local town school, decisions would have been made by residents of that town, and teachers would have been hired who had little knowledge of Indian culture; enculturation would be unilateral. The town, not the reservation, would have gained the economic advantage of the students' federal funds, of the salaries paid to the teachers and all other employees. Tribal people would have remained embittered by the injustice. The tribes, I believe, would have made gains without the school, particularly in the development of gaming as was accomplished nationally, but students educated in their own community school are prepared in greater numbers to enhance their own family life and every aspect of the community. They are better able to thrive, to find and self-determine a brighter future.

The state, school personnel, and all Wyoming communities continue to need to work to overcome the damage done by Euro-American prejudice and their use of the tools of extreme economic advantage. Since 1868 no family on the reservation has been without those who have been weakened, fallen ill, or been cut down. However, as the Elders ensured, the schools now impart knowledge of their history and of their identity with which to determine future directions. It can also be said that no family on this reservation is without persons of hindsight, foresight, and interconnectedness in this place. They were the leaders who made possible this school and all of its potential.

NOTES

ABBREVIATIONS

CDW   Curriculum Development Workshop

CS-T   *Casper Star-Tribune*

FCRC   Fremont County Reorganization Committee

WRSAEA   Wind River Shoshone and Arapaho Education Association

WSJ   *Wyoming State Journal*

INTRODUCTION

1. Fowler, *Arapahoe Politics*, 52–53.
2. Fowler, *Arapahoe Politics*, 73–74.
3. Szasz, *Education and the American Indian*, 192–97.
4. Prucha, *The Great Father*, 1030–31, 1047; Fowler, *Arapahoe Politics*, 209.
5. Fowler, *Arapahoe Politics*, 178, 182, 212, 215, 39–42, 74–75; Leroy R. Hafen, *The Life of Thomas Fitzpatrick*, 326–28, 330; Friday, *The Story of Friday*, 1–10; Kruse, *Wind River Reservation*, 14. Kruse's booklet may be found at the Wyoming Indian High School Library, District No. 14.

1. PRECURSORS

Records of interviews, letters, emails, and telephone and personal communications are in the author's collection.

1. Fowler, *Arapahoe Politics*, 57; Fosher, Report of Agent, 350–51; Fowler, *Arapahoe Politics*, 71–72.
2. Fowler, *Arapahoe Politics*, 32–35, 46–47; Prucha, *The Great Father*, 481–82; Hoig, *The Sand Creek Massacre*, 129, 143; Brown, *Bury My Heart*, 302–7; Mooney, *The Ghost-Dance Religion*, 869.
3. Prucha, *Documents of Indian Policy*, 26–27, 238, 246–47, 250; Jones, Sixty-Sixth Annual Report of the Commissioner, 13; Prucha, *The Great Father*, 7–9, 693, 704.

4. U.S. Congress, "For Support of Schools," 51st Cong., 1014; Prucha, *Documents of Indian Policy*, 27; Prucha, *The Great Father*, 689, 704; Stamm, *People of the Wind River*, 242–43.

5. Prucha, *Documents of Indian Policy*, 246–50; Prucha, *The Great Father*, 707–11.

6. Prucha, *The Great Father*, 707; Hoferer, "Some Facts and Incidents," 3; Kurth, quoted in Stansell, "The Jesuits in Wyoming," 31–32.

7. Prucha, *Documents of Indian Policy*, 235, 253; Reyhner and Eder, *American Indian Education*, 4; Getches and Wilkinson, *Federal Indian Law*, 121.

8. Markley and Crofts, *Walk Softly*, 5, 59, 148–52, 160.

9. Markley and Crofts, *Walk Softly*, 8–9.

10. Hoferer, "Some Facts and Incidents," 2; Father Jutz was gravely wounded in the massacre at Wounded Knee, as reported by Mooney in *The Ghost-Dance Religion*, 872.

11. Daly, "For God and Country," 3; Hoferer, "Some Facts and Incidents," 3.

12. Daly, "For God and Country," 5.

13. Markley and Crofts, *Walk Softly*, 59.

14. Markley and Crofts, *Walk Softly*, 5, 59–63, 65, 103.

15. Bernadine G. Friday (1932–2009) and Annette Bell (b. 1933), Elder panel discussion #1 at Wyoming Indian High School, May 24, 2005, 10–11; Lone Bear, letter to Rev. William H. Ketchum, January 13, 1912, 1, Saint Stephen's Mission Jesuit Papers, Department of Special Collections and University Archives, Raynor Memorial Libraries, Marquette University, Milwaukee, Wisconsin (hereafter St. Stephen's Papers); Burton Hutchinson, interview 1, September 20, 2004, 2; Rupert Weeks interview, "Portrait of Boy at Government School," #14 in Kahin, "From Trout Creek to Gravy High," Warm Valley Historical Project; Melissa Friday (b. 1964), discussion, August 19, 2017; Hoferer, "Some Facts and Incidents," 1; Markley and Crofts, *Walk Softly*, 69.

16. Fosher, Report of Agent, 352; Wilson, Report of Agent, 316; Putney, "Fighting the Scourge," 141–45, 151; Markley and Crofts, *Walk Softly*, 61–63.

17. Markley and Crofts, *Walk Softly*, 70; Wilson, Report of Agent.

18. Cedartree, *Wind River Memories*, 4–5; Anderson, *Four Hills of Life*, 14; cf. Curriculum Development Workshop (hereafter CDW), *Wind River Reservation Yesterday* (1972), 39.

19. Cohen, *Handbook of Federal Indian Law*, Section 5: "The End of Treaty-Making" and Section 6: "Indian Agreements," 66–67; Prucha, *The Great Father*, 668, 671; Getches and Wilkinson, *Federal Indian Law*, 110–12, 114.

20. O'Brien, *American Indian Tribal Governments*, 78; Stamm, *People of the Wind River*, 243–45; Fowler, *Arapahoe Politics*, 93–96, 156, 230–31, 238; Equality

State Policy Center, "The Wind River Reservation Boundary Dispute," 4–5; U.S. Environmental Protection Agency, Region 8, "Attachment 1," 9; "Riverton, Wyoming," https://en.wikipedia.org/wiki/Riverton,_Wyoming (accessed October 28, 2015); Arno Rosenfeld, "Wyoming Tribes Don't Have Sovereignty over Riverton, Court Rules," *Casper Star-Tribune* (hereafter CS-T), February 22, 2017, 19, https://trib.com/news/state-and-regional/wyoming-tribes-don-t-have-sovereignty-over-riverton-land-north/article_328a9206-0a23-5ae5-a2bf-192426b6cea9.html (accessed January 23, 2018).

21. "The Nicholas Biddle Notes," in Jackson, *Letters of the Lewis and Clark Expedition*, 519.

22. Coutant, *History of Wyoming*, 2:390–94; CDW, *Wind River Reservation Yesterday* (1999), 13–15, 17–18; U.S. Environmental Protection Agency, "Attachment 1," 3–4.

23. Shimkin, "Eastern Shoshone," 309–10; Stamm, *People of the Wind River*, 81, 250–51; Fowler, *Arapahoe Politics*, 102–4, 69, 103.

24. Prucha, *The Great Father*, 208–11.

25. Prucha, *The Great Father*, 760–61; Fowler, *Arapahoe Politics*, 136, 142–43, 147, 168–69.

26. Fowler, *Arapahoe Politics*, 106–7, 175.

27. Fowler, *Arapahoe Politics*, 136–37, 177–82.

28. Prucha, *The Great Father*, 668, 793–94; Stamm, *People of the Wind River*, 244–45; McDonald, *American Indians and the Fight for Equal Voting Rights*, 206–7.

29. CDW, *Wind River Reservation Yesterday*, 32, 41; Fowler, *Arapahoe Politics*, 106; Wyoming state representative Patrick Goggles (b. 1952), pers. comm., April 18, 2009, 2.

30. Verna Thunder, pers. comm., November 6, 2006, 4.

31. Kelly, "Charles Henry Burke," 259–60; Philp, "John Collier 1933–45," 275; Meriam and Staff, *The Problem of Indian Administration*, 8–15; Reyhner and Eder, *American Indian Education*, 209.

32. Philp, "John Collier 1933–45," 276; Prucha, *The Great Father*, 772–79.

33. U.S. Congress, "An Act Authorizing . . . (Johnson-O'Malley Act)," 596; Kelly, "Charles Henry Burke," 268.

34. Fishman and McCarthy, *John Dewey*, 7; Reyhner and Eder, *American Indian Education*, 210–11, 216–21; Rosenfelt, "Toward a More Coherent Policy," 211–12.

35. CDW, *Wind River Reservation Yesterday* (1999), 35–36, 39; Markley and Crofts, *Walk Softly*, 69.

36. State of Wyoming Archivist, email, November 26, 2003, 1; Oakleaf, "Origins of Fremont County Library," 1.

37. Bruce Chavez (1952–2016), WIHS history and tribal government teacher, 1992–93 to 2016, interview 2, May 30, 2007, 1.

38. Kruse, *Wind River Reservation*, 9.

39. Lloyd Dewey, interview 1, April 5, 2005, 6.

40. Dewey interview, 6–7.

41. Dewey interview, 7–8; Fowler, *Arapahoe Politics*, 198–99.

42. Anonymous (likely Stansell), "Black Coal and Missionaries," 27; Prucha, *The Great Father*, 646–47, 801–3.

43. Stansell, "The Jesuits in Wyoming," 27–28; Friday and Bell, Elder panel #1, May 24, 2005, 11; Zuercher, letter to "Father Superior" (no name given), February 18, 1938, 1, St. Stephen's Papers; Prendergast, letter to Father Provincial, May 31, 1942, 2, St. Stephen's Papers.

44. Prendergast, letter to Father Provincial, May 31, 1942; Kellam, letter to Rev. Patrick A. McGovern, May 14, 1942, 1, St. Stephen's Papers.

45. Friday and Bell, Elder panel #1, May 24, 2005, 2; Nelson White (b. 1939), interview 1, February 17, 2006, 2–3, and 6; Ralph "Pat" Kniffin (b. 1918), Elder panel discussion, May 23, 2005, 6–7.

46. Crawford White (b. 1941), interview 2, October 29, 2005, 1, 3.

47. Prucha, *The Great Father*, 698, 814–15; Meriam, *The Problem of Indian Administration*, 12–13; U.S. Congress, "For Support of Schools"; Nelson White, interview 1, February 17, 2006, 2–4; Anderson, *Four Hills of Life*, 2.

48. Nelson White, interview 1, February 17, 2006, 3; Crawford White, interview 2, October 29, 2005, 2; Elder panel discussion #2, May 24, 2005, 8; Burton Hutchinson, interview 1, September 20, 2004, 2.

49. Starr Weed (1918–2015), interview 2, October 22, 2001, 1; Hutchinson, interview 4, March 21, 2005, 5–6.

50. Caroline Goggles, pers. comm., August 27, 2001; Caroline Goggles (b. 1930), interview 4, April 15, 2005, 12. See Anderson, *Four Hills of Life*, 60, and Coleman, *American Indian Children at School*, 97.

51. Goggles, interview 4, 12; Verna Thunder, Elder panel discussion at Wyoming Indian High School, May 23, 2005, 4–5.

52. Bernadine Friday, Elder panel discussion at Wyoming Indian High School, May 24, 2005, 2–4.

53. "Jesuits Say 13 Accused Abusers," *Denver Post*, December 8, 2018, 4A; Anderson, *Four Hills of Life*, 286–88.

54. Rosenfelt, "Indian Schools," 497–502; Rosenfelt, "Coherent Policy," 198–201.

55. Gerald Sage (b. 1932), interview 1, January 15, 2002, 1–2; interview 2, August 13, 2004, 1; Fowler, *Arapahoe Politics*, 194–95.

56. Sage, interview 2.

57. Sage, interview 1, 1.

58. Forrest D. Stone (1927–2003), telephone interview, July 11, 2002, 2.

59. Sage, interview 1, June 4, 2001, 2; Sandra (1936–2005) and Darwin St. Clair (b. 1933), interview 1, October 10, 2001, 1.

60. Darrell Howarth (b. 1926), Lander high school student in the 1940s, pers. comm., February 13, 2005; telephone comm., January 19, 2005, 1; Goggles, interview 3, December 2, 2004, 1.

61. Vera Trosper, pers. comm., September 25, 2006; December 2, 2009.

62. Caroline Goggles, pers. comm., December 2, 2009. See Uchida, *Desert Exile*.

63. Sage, interview 3, August 19, 2004, 3; Patch, Deposition, October 2, 1973, 15, in *Alfred Ward, et al., . . . v. Robert Schrader, et al.*; A. Redman (b. 1936), pers. comm., April 7, 2006; Elder panel #2, May 24, 2005, 21; H. Friday plaques kept at Friday residence; V. Thunder and Caroline Goggles, discussion with author at Wyoming Indian High School, April 10, 2006.

64. Hubert Friday, pers. comm., June 27, 2007, 1.

65. Fowler, *Arapahoe Politics*, 209; Prucha, *The Great Father*, 1047; Ward in *Alfred Ward, et al., . . . v. Robert Schrader, et al.*, 153–54; Thomas J. Duran, chairman, Arapahoe General Council, letter, April 12, 1946; P. Goggles, pers. comm., May 18, 2009; State of Wyoming, *Constitution of the State of Wyoming*, 35.

66. Fowler, *Arapahoe Politics*, 199–201; Prucha, *The Great Father*, 1047, 1079–81; Fowler, *Arapahoe Politics*, 210.

67. Fowler, *Arapahoe Politics*, 183, 184; Verna Thunder and Bernadine Friday, pers. comm., November 13, 2003; Fowler, *Arapahoe Politics*, 210, 212.

2. SELF-DETERMINATION

1. Hertzberg, *American Indian Identity*, 31, 180, 208–9; Philp, "John Collier 1933–45," 277–80.

2. "African-American Civil Rights Movement (1954–1968)," https://en.wikipedia .org/wiki/African-American_Civil_Rights_Movement(1954–1968); *Plessy v. Ferguson*; *Brown v. Board*, 3.

3. Fowler, *Arapahoe Politics*, 202; Caroline Goggles, telephone comm., September 10, 2006.

4. Prucha, *The Great Father*, 1090, 1115–16, 1203–4; Zerga, "A Study," 23. Zerga was a teacher in Wyoming Indian schools from 1960 and superintendent, 1973–83.

5. "Title I: Improving Academic Achievement." See Graham, *The Civil Rights Era*, 142; Loevy, "A Chronology," 359–60.

6. Martin Luther King Jr., "I Have a Dream," www.usconstitution.net/dream.html (accessed July 4, 2009).

7. William C'Hair (b. 1943), interview 5, May 9, 2005, 2; "burning eloquence" from Coutant, *History of Wyoming*, 2:547–48.

8. O'Brien, *American Indian Tribal Governments*, 87; Calloway, *First Peoples*, 434–35.

9. Prucha, *The Great Father*, 1098–99.

10. U.S. Congress, Senate, *Indian Education*, 1–2; Brewton Berry Research Foundation, *Education of American Indians*, 1–121; Szasz, *Education and the American Indian*, 150.

11. U.S. Congress, Senate, *Indian Education*, Part 1, 21.

12. U.S. Congress, Senate, *Indian Education*, 21.

13. U.S. Congress, Senate, *Indian Education*, 105, 116; Gross, "Indian Self-Determination," 1204.

14. William C'Hair, telephone comm., June 27, 2008; U.S. Congress, "An Act Authorizing . . . (Johnson-O'Malley Act)," 596; Rosenfelt, "New Regulations," 23–24.

15. Reyhner, *American Indian/Alaska Native*, 14; Platero, "Multicultural Teacher Education Center," 45; Fuchs and Havighurst, *To Live*, 252, 254, 257–58; Lomawaima and McCarty, *To Remain an Indian*, 117; McCarty, *A Place to Be Navajo*, 76.

16. Szasz, *Education and the American Indian*, 162–64; Schierbeck, "Indian Education: Community Control," in "Education = Cultural Politics," 9. See Fuchs and Havighurst, *To Live*, 256–57.

17. BoBo Dean, email, April 1, 2008, 1; Gaillard, "'We'll Do It Our Own Way Awhile,'" 22, 26. Research for the Gaillard article was funded by the Edward Elliot Foundation (see p. 22 in article); see Judy Weeks, "South Florida's Miccosukee Seminoles," http://www.think-inc.com/Stuff/Seminoles.html (accessed August 8, 2011); Flannery, "The Indian Self-Determination Act," graph 5.3, 114. See Ward, *Native Americans*, for current issues in the Busby school. Dean represented the Association of American Indian Affairs in providing legal assistance to the Miccosukee Tribe in negotiating the 1971 contract (in 2008, with Hobbs, Straus, Dean and Walker, LLP, a law firm specializing in representing tribes, in Washington DC).

18. Rosenfelt, "Indian Schools and Community," 497–99; U.S. Congress, "Public Law 92-318": "Indian Assistance Act," sec. 302 (a) and (b), 334–35.

19. Reyhner and Eder, *American Indian Education*, 273; Flannery, "The Indian Self-Determination Act"; Wind River Shoshone and Arapaho Education Association (hereafter WRSAEA), "Fact Sheet," April 1971, 2–4; Szasz, *Education and the American Indian*, 162–63.

20. Nixon, "Special Message," 1–5.

21. Nixon, "Special Message," 3.

22. Castile, "Native North Americans," 273; Senese, *Self-Determination*, 113; Roxanne Ortiz, foreword to Forbes, *Native Americans and Nixon*, 11; Nixon, "Special Message," 1.

23. Nixon, "Special Message," 4.

24. Nixon, "Special Message," 3–4.

25. Forbes, *Native Americans and Nixon*, 39; Szasz, *Education and the American Indian*, 149.

26. Forbes, *Native Americans and Nixon*, 31; Castile, "Native North Americans," 273, 286.

3. WHY THE PEOPLE WANTED A SCHOOL

1. Wilkins, *American Indian Politics*, 217–18; Melissa Friday (b. 1964), telephone interview, October 19, 2015; Ben Friday Jr. (1933–2003), interview 1, November 1, 2001, 1.

2. Ben Friday, interview 1; Caroline Goggles, interview 1, November 30, 2001, 1.

3. Alberta Friday, interview 1, July 11, 2002, 1.

4. Ben Friday, interview 1. See Fowler, *Arapahoe Politics*, 268–69.

5. Anderson, *Four Hills of Life*, 15–16; Buckanaga (member of the Minnesota Indian Education Committee), "Interracial Politics," 53.

6. Ben Friday Jr., interview 3, December 23, 2002, 1; Buckanaga, "Interracial Politics," 53.

7. Friday, interview 3, 1–2.

8. Fowler, *Arapahoe Politics*, 231–33; Councilman Henry Lee Tyler in Fowler, *Arapahoe Politics*, 194; Friday, interview 1, 1; U.S. Congress, "Public Law 97-451."

9. Fowler, *Arapahoe Politics*, 232, 90, 208–9; Minnie Woodring, "4,987 Indian Recipients—Announce Per-Capita Pay for Shoshone, Arapaho," *Wyoming State Journal* (hereafter *WSJ*), December 28, 1970, 2; Friday, interview 1, 1.

10. Rosenfelt, "Toward a More Coherent Policy," 195, 211–12; Gross, in "Indian Control v. Segregation," 1, appendix B to Gress, "Statement of the Coalition of Indian Controlled School Boards, Inc." See Szasz, *Education and the American Indian*, 184–85.

11. Caroline Goggles, interview 1, November 30, 2001, 2; Draft Proposal of the Wind River Wyoming Indian Leadership Council to John Elliot, Edward Elliott Foundation, n.d., 1, courtesy of Michael P. Gross; Fuchs and Havighurst, *To Live*, 257.

12. William C'Hair, interview 4, November 29, 2004, 2.

13. Chris Goggles, interview, August 27, 2001, 2.

14. Hoferer, "Some Facts and Incidents," 3. See Caroline Goggles, interview 6, April 15, 2005, 3.

15. See *WSJ* articles "... and one who missed!" September 21, 1970, 1; "Gov. Love Big Fan" and "Squaw Dance" (picture caption), "At Victory Banquet Saturday Night," September 20, 1971, 1, 4-SS; Jan Wilkinson, "Legend 'Fascinating,'" August 31, 1972, 1, and "One-Shot Activities," September 4, 1972, 8; "The Lander One-Shot Antelope Hunt," September 19, 1974, 4; Alicia Giuffrida and Susan Gray Gose, "One Shot Hunt Criticized," October 15, 2003, A1, A3.

16. See *WSJ* articles "The Lander One-Shot Antelope Hunt" and Wilkinson, "One-Shot Activities"; "Astronauts Win One-Shot," September 18, 1972, 1; William Sniffin, "The Hunt," September 21, 1972, 17, and "It's One-Shot Time!" September 19, 1974, 1; "Hathaway, Saxbe Both Score Kills," September 26, 1974, 17–19. Organizers dropped the "squaw dance" decades later when Sarah St. Clair-Robinson, of the Shoshone tribe (daughter of Darwin and Sandra St. Clair), complained about the demeaning nature of the use of the word "squaw." See Giuffrida and Gose, "One-Shot Hunt Criticized."

17. Zerga, "A Study," 28–29. See Deyhle, "Navajo Youth and Anglo Racism," 406.

18. Lana Johnson, "Indian Leaders Push Ahead," *CS-T*, May 11, 1971, 8.

19. Pamela St. Clair Gambler, master's degree in educational leadership from Montana State University, interview 1, January 12, 2006, 1; panel discussion, June 10, 2005, workshop at Holiday Inn, Riverton, Wyoming. "Ours to Recover," vol. 3, videotape, in author's collection.

20. "Great Tradition, Little Tradition, and Formal Education," in Wax et al., *Anthropological Perspectives on Education*, 6; McDermott, "Achieving School Failure," 83; Luftig, "Effects of Schooling," 252.

21. Alberta Friday, interview 1, July 11, 2002, 2.

22. William C'Hair, interview 5, May 9, 2005, 2.

23. Sandra C'Bearing (b. 1954), interview 1, January 23, 2006, 1; Sandra C'Bearing, pers. comm., April 3, 2006; Alberta Friday (b. 1931), telephone discussion, September 18, 2015.

24. C'Bearing, interview 1. See Wells et al., "How Society Failed," 89–91.

25. C'Bearing, interview 1, 1–2; Gàndara, Moran, and Garcia, "Legacy of *Brown*," 33; Wells et al., "How Society Failed," 83–85.

26. C'Bearing, interview 1, 1, 3; pers. comm., February 10, 2006; pers. comm., January 31, 2006.

27. C'Hair, interview 5, May 9, 2005, 2; Gross, letter to Dennis Sun Rhodes, September 9, 1970, courtesy of Gross; William Sniffin, "Re-organization: What Does It Mean to People of Lander Area?" *WSJ*, August 22, 1971, 2; William Greider, "Indian Runaround," *Washington Post*, November 7, 1971, B3.

28. A. Sage, interview, in Bordeaux, *Our Children, Our Schools, Our Tribes*, 22; Alfred Redman, pers. comm., May 22, 2006; William C'Hair, interview, May 9, 2005, 2.

29. "High School Name Change," *WSJ*, June 16, 1969, 1; William Sniffin, "'Getting the Facts Straight,'" *WSJ*, May 13, 1971, 2.

30. Sniffin, "'Getting the Facts Straight'"; I. St. Clair and R. Spoonhunter, in Johnson, "Indian Leaders Push Ahead," *CS-T*, May 11, 1971, 8; Sage, interview, in Bordeaux, *Our Children, Our Schools, Our Tribes*; "Congratulations Class of

1970," *WSJ*, May 28, 1970, 9–11; *WSJ*, May 31, 1971, 7–9; reservation residents A. Trosper (b. 1949), V. Trosper (1948–2011), and D. Chavez did the counts on February 20, 2004; Data/Technology Unit, Wyoming State Department of Education, email, February 19, 2004.

31. Bass and Burger, *American Indians and Educational Laboratories*, 6; Bill Neikirk, 1967 Census Bureau in "Educational Gap Shown in Census," *Riverton Wyoming Ranger*, January 14, 1971, 9; Jackson, chair of the Senate Interior Committee, quoted in "Want Indian Schools Out of BIA Authority," *Riverton Wyoming Ranger*, March 29, 1971, 4; Bordeaux, *Our Children, Our Schools, Our Tribes*, 6; Brewton Berry Research Foundation, *Education of American Indians*, 28. See Deyhle and Swisher, "Research in . . . Native Education," 132.

32. Sniffin, "'Getting the Facts Straight,'" 2.

33. Michael Gross, attorney, email, May 30, 2002, 5; Dennis Sun Rhodes (b. 1947), email, February 1, 2006; Barbara Sage, interview 1, June 4, 2001, 2; Alfred Redman, pers. comm., May 22, 2006.

34. Edward Duncombe, letter, January 9, 1974, 3–5, courtesy of Michael Gross; Gross email, May 30, 2002, 2.

35. Duncombe letter, 3–5; Fowler, *Arapahoe Politics*, 35–37, 210.

36. Duncombes' letter, February 15, 1971, 1–2; P. Duncombe (1925–2010), letter, n.d., received January 30, 2003, 1; Sandra St. Clair (1936–2005), pers. comm., October 13, 2005; Duncombe, "Ethete: Episcopal Churchwork," iv; P. Duncombe, telephone interview, November 11, 2003, 3–6.

37. St. Clair, pers. comm.

38. P. Duncombe, telephone interview, 5–6.

39. Duncombes' letter, 1.

40. Duncombes' letter, 1.

41. Lander Valley High School, FCVHS District, Lander, Wyoming, Minutes, April 1971, 1, courtesy of Edward Duncombe.

42. Wind River Shoshone and Arapaho Education Assn., Inc., "Proposal for the Establishment of a Reservation High School" (rough draft), n.d., 3 (file #5).

4. FALSE PROMISES

1. Sandra St. Clair (1936–2005), pers. comm., October 13, 2005; Siebert, "A History," 105.

2. A. Sage, letter to the Shoshone and Arapaho Joint Business Council, March 21, 1970; Draft Proposal of the Wind River Wyoming Indian Leadership Council to John Elliot, Edward Elliot Foundation, n.d.; Articles of Incorporation filed with the State of Wyoming, March 18, 1971; Gross, email, May 30, 2002, 3; "Guest Editorial, Reservation High School . . . ," including "Fact Sheet" news release

published by the WRSAEA, *WSJ*, June 7, 1971, 2; United States Department of the Interior cover page, Cost Reimbursable Contract for Operation of the Wyoming Indian High School, contract no. K51C14200682, July 1, 1972.

3. B. Sage, telephone comm., September 24, 2011; Sage, letter, received October 5, 2011.

4. William C'Hair, interview 1, July 3, 2003, 1; M. Groesbeck (b. 1947), St. Stephen's principal, telephone interview, January 12, 2016, 2; CDW, *Wind River Reservation Yesterday* (1972), 42.

5. Fowler, *Arapahoe Politics*, 261, 264–65.

6. Ben Friday Jr., interview 1, November 1, 2001, 1; Draft Proposal, n.d., 1; John Elliott, "A note in haste" to Michael Gross, n.d., courtesy of Gross; Louis R. Bruce, letter, March 31, 1971, 1–2, courtesy of Gross; Means, *Where White Men Fear*, 191–92.

7. Alberta Friday, interview, July 11, 2002, 1; Barbara Sage, pers. comm., March 4, 2006, 1.

8. WRSAEA, "Fact Sheet," April 9, 1971, paragraph #6, 1; Bruce, letter, March 31, 1971, 1; Gaillard, "'We'll Do It Our Own Way Awhile,'" 21, 27.

9. "Reservation Gets High School," *WSJ*, April 8, 1971, 1.

10. "Reservation Gets High School."

11. WRSAEA, "Fact Sheet," April 9, 1971, 2–3; "Want Indian Schools Out of BIA Authority," *Riverton Ranger*, March 29, 1971, 4; anonymous advocate, pers. comm., February 25, 2006; W. Terry Ward, "Threshold of an Era," *WSJ*, January 12, 1970, 2.

12. Fowler, *Arapahoe Politics*, 64–66; Barbara Sage, interview 1, June 4, 2001, 3.

13. "School up for Approval," *WSJ*, July 26, 1971, 1.

14. Gaillard, "'We'll Do It Our Own Way Awhile,'" 26–27.

15. Forbes, *Native Americans and Nixon*, 38–44.

16. Forbes, *Native Americans and Nixon*, 39, 44, 54; Gaillard, "'We'll Do It Our Own Way Awhile,'" 26; Gaillard, "Indians Demand Bureau Reform," 10.

17. Gaillard, "'We'll Do It Our Own Way Awhile,'" 26; Forbes, *Native Americans and Nixon*, 49–50.

18. Forbes, *Native Americans and Nixon*, 53–54, 70–73.

19. Gaillard, "Indians Demand Bureau Reform," 7–8; Means, *Where White Men Fear*, 192. Means confused the date, saying it was mid-November, but Gaillard's early October report clears the confusion.

20. Merrell, secretary pro tem, and D. Duncombe, vicar, letter, April 12, 1971, 1, courtesy of E. Duncombe; Ben Friday Jr., interview 1, November 1, 2001, 1; Lease agreement by and between the Episcopal Diocese of Wyoming (Lessor) and the Wind River Shoshone and Arapahoe Education Association, Inc. (Lessee), September 26, 1971, 1 (file #21); Cedartree, *Wind River Memories*, 7.

21. Emery, Episcopal chancellor, letters, Diocese of Wyoming, July 6, 1971, 1, and July 15, 1971, 1, courtesy of E. Duncombe.

22. Wilkins, *American Indian Politics*, 217; Gaillard, "Indian Community Control Coalition," 1; Gross, "Reckoning for Legal Services," 90.

23. Gross, "Reckoning for Legal Services"; William Greider, "Indian Runaround," *Washington Post*, November 7, 1971, B3; Gaillard, "'We'll Do It Our Own Way Awhile,'" 27; Gross, email, January 15, 2017, 1; William C'Hair, interview 4, November 29, 2004, 2.

24. "Reorganization Hearing . . . ," *WSJ*, October 14, 1971, 12.

25. Michael Gross, email, May 30, 2002, 3.

26. Gross, Conference: "The Struggle for Self-Determination," February 3, 2006, disc. #1; Szasz, *Education and the American Indian*, 162; Gross, email, May 30, 2002, 1.

27. Jerry Reynolds, Washington DC correspondent for *Indian Country Today*, email, November 2, 2017; Gross, email, January 2, 2006, 2.

28. Barbara Sage, telephone comm., August 23, 2002; Sage, pers. comm., February 28, 2004; Means, *Where White Men Fear*, 167; Sandra St. Clair, interview, October 10, 2001, 2.

29. "Wind River A.I.M.," *Tribe Talk*, Wyoming Indian High School, October 31, 1972, 2.

30. Fowler, *Arapahoe Politics*, 52; Harvey Major (Chippewa and member of AIM's "Trial of Broken Treaties Caravan"), quoted in "Indian Believes Force Necessary," *WSJ*, December 7, 1972, 6, from Kaul in the *Des Moines Register*.

31. Forbes, *Native Americans and Nixon*, 39, 75, 76–80, 104; Prucha, *The Great Father*, 1118; *Wassaja*, January 1, 1973, cited in Forbes, *Native Americans and Nixon*, 79; Means, *Where White Men Fear*, 233.

32. White, *Breach of Faith*, 132–33; Alexander, *The New Jim Crow*, 40–41; Means, *Where White Men Fear*, 235.

33. Yellowtail, "Montana Chief Condemns," *WSJ*, December 7, 1972, 6.

34. "P.I.E. Members Angry over Campaign Letter," *WSJ*, November 30, 1972, 6.

35. Forbes, *Native Americans and Nixon*, 54, 119.

36. Forbes, *Native Americans and Nixon*, 119–20; Means, *Where White Men Fear*, 236–37, 253; Prucha, *The Great Father*, 1119–20; Peltier, preface to *Prison Writings*, viii–xv.

37. Means, *Where White Men Fear*, 227–29; Ortiz, in foreword to Forbes, *Native Americans and Nixon*, 2–4.

5. THE FIGHT OVER INDIAN RESOURCES

1. Dawson, "School District Reorganization," 82–84; Wilkerson, "The Road to Freedom," *Smithsonian*, September 2016, 40–42 (47 percent of blacks fled into the North and West beginning in 1916 and lasting into the 1970s); United

States Census Bureau, "History, Urban and Rural," https://www.census.gov->History>Programs>Geography (accessed July 24, 2017); National Center for Educational Statistics, "The Landscape of Public Education," 1–8. See Lieberman, *The Future of Public Education*, 34–37.

2. Dawson, "School District Reorganization," 82–84; State of Wyoming, "Wyoming Education Code," in Session Laws of Wyoming, 1969 (Ch. 111), Original Senate File No. 10, sec. 106, 176–77; "Education Code," sec. 109 (e), 178; "Education Code," sec. 107 (a) (i) and (d), 177.

3. "Education Code," sec. 107 (c) and (d), 177; "Education Code," sec. 109 (b), 178.

4. FCRC Minutes, April 21, 1969, 1, Wyoming State Archives; Starrett, "S. J. Starrett Writes Letter," *WSJ*, September, 27, 1971, 1; Jan Jibben, "At Reorganization Meeting . . . . , More Petitions Presented Opposing Reservation H. S.," *WSJ*, May 13, 1971, 1.

5. "County School Organization Committee Starts Planning," *WSJ*, May 8, 1969, 9; "Education Code," sec. 111, 178, and sec. 112 (g), 179; Painter and Johnson, "Wyoming Education Code," 534; "One District Proposed," *WSJ*, February 12, 1970, 1–8.

6. State of Wyoming, *Wyoming Highway Map and More* (2001); CDW, *Wind River Reservation Yesterday* (1999), 18.

7. Larson, *History of Wyoming*, 9–10; State of Wyoming, *Wyoming Highway Map*.

8. Wyoming State Archives, email, November 26, 2003, 1; Amundson, *Yellowcake Towns*, xviii–xix, 38.

9. Office of Natural Resources Revenue, email, August 25, 2011; Melissa Friday, telephone interview, October 19 2015; Alvena Friday (b. 1931), telephone interview, November 1, 2015; Larson, *Wyoming: A Bicentennial History*, 169; Wyoming State Archives, email.

10. "Wind River Country," http://www.windrivercountry.com/other/hudsonfrontpage .html (accessed May 24, 2006); "Hudson," Wyoming's Wind River Country, http://www.windriver.org/ingo/communities/hudson.php (accessed May 19, 2012); Caroline Goggles, regarding her father, Ben Friday Sr. (b. 1903), interview 4, April 15, 2005, 6; M. Friday, email, January 15, 2013. See Burton Hutchinson (1929–2011), pers. comm., December 6, 2005.

11. Wyoming State Archives, email, November 26, 2003; "One District Proposed," *WSJ*, February 12, 1970, 1; FCRC Minutes, December 15, 1969, 1.

12. Wyoming State Archives; Stamm, *People of Wind River*, 244–45; Wind River Oil and Gas Commissioner, (hand drawn) map, February 15, 2003.

13. Wyoming State Archives; B. Sage, pers. comm., September 8, 2005.

14. Stamm, *People of Wind River*, 35; Starr Weed (1918–2015), telephone comm., November 25, 2008.

15. Office of Natural Resources Revenue, telephone comm., January 6, 2018; Anderson, *Four Hills of Life*, 13.

16. State of Wyoming, *Constitution of the State of Wyoming*, Article 7, sec. 1; "Education Code," sec. 109 (e), 178.

17. P. Goggles, telephone interview, September 29, 2003; Fixico, *Invasion of Indian Country*, 143–44; Office of Natural Resources Revenue, emails, March 24 and 28, 2011, and November 13, 2015. The tribes received a royalty rate from the sales value/gross oil and gas proceeds of between 12.5 and 16.667 percent prior to 1982. The industry now pays a "severance tax" (which is the sales value [minus royalties paid] × the 8.5 percent severance tax rate) to the tribes for removal of the oil and gas. Approximately 20 percent of these extraction contracts are held by individual mineral owners, mostly Indian; 80 percent are held in common by the tribes.

18. Wyoming Oil and Gas Conservation Commission, www.wogcc.state.wy.us (accessed March 7, 2006); Wind River Commissioner map, February 15, 2003; "S. J. Starrett Writes Letter," *WSJ*, September 27, 1971, 4; Oil and Gas Conservation Commission, Wyoming Fields Data 1978.

19. "School Reorganization Committee: Proposes," *WSJ*, November 19, 1970, 8; "One District Proposed," *WSJ*, February 12, 1970, 1; "Valuation $2 Million Jump," *WSJ*, July 31, 1969, 1; Fowler, *Arapahoe Politics*, 48; Dan Hudson, former AFL, CIO union officer at the mines and for many years (to 2009), finance officer for Jefferson County District 14 Schools, interview 2, March 11, 2006, 6.

20. FCRC Minutes, April 21, 1969, 1, Wyoming State Archives; "County School Organization Committee," *WSJ*, May 8, 1969, 9; RoJean Thayer, "Jeffrey City High School," *WSJ*, May 10, 1973, 1; Jan Wilkinson, "LVHS in Bind," *WSJ*, June 14, 1973, 1; Minutes, October 13, 1969, 1; "Committee Starts Planning," *WSJ*, May 8, 1969, 1; "One District Proposed," 1; Barbara Sage, telephone comm., February 4, 2010.

21. "Education Code," sec. 109 (c), 178; Wyoming State Archives, email; Wind River Oil and Gas Commissioner map, February 15, 2003; Cooper, Native American Voting Rights Case Report for the Court, September 15, 2006, 3. District 6's "any part Indian" population ranged from 2.4 percent in the town of Pavillion to 49.7 percent in Crowheart in 2000.

22. FCRC Minutes, February 16, 1955, 1–3. These minutes at Wyoming State Archives were discontinued until 1964.

23. Wind River Oil and Gas Commissioner map; Minutes, October 13, 1969, 1; "Reorganization Board Seeks Help from Boundary Board," *WSJ*, May 14, 1970, 1.

24. FCRC Minutes, April 21, 1969; Minutes, October 13, 1969; "A Riverton View," *Riverton Ranger*, in *WSJ*, May 3, 1973, 4; William Sniffin, "Re-organization," *WSJ*, August 22, 1971, 2.

25. FCRC Minutes, October 13, 1969.

26. William C'Hair, interview 1, November 30, 2001, 1; Sandra and Darwin St. Clair, interview 1, October 10, 2001, 1; C'Hair, interview 3, September 9, 2003, 4.

27. Alberta Friday, telephone comm., August 19, 2007; FCRC Minutes, November 10, 1969, 1.

28. Minutes, November 10, 1969.

29. Minutes, December 15, 1969, 1; Minutes, January 12, 1970, 1.

30. "School Reorganization Committee: Proposes Five Districts for Fremont County," WSJ, November 19, 1970, 8; Minutes, January 12, 1970; Minutes, February 9, 1970, 1–2; Minutes, March 9, 1970, 1.

31. "County Reorganization Board Considers Four Proposals," WSJ, October 15, 1970, 1; CDW, *Wind River Reservation Yesterday* (1972), 43.

32. FCRC Minutes, February 9, 1970, 2; "One District Proposed," WSJ, February 12, 1970, 1; CDW, *Wind River Reservation Yesterday* (1972), 39; Minutes, March 9, 1970, 1.

33. Minutes, April 13, 1970; Minutes, May 11, 1970.

34. Minutes; "Reorganization Board Seeks Help from Boundary Board," WSJ, May 14, 1970, 1.

35. Traveler, pers. comm., February 24, 2006.

36. Traveler, pers. comm.; Capehart, "A Boy, a President," *Washington Post*, in *Denver Post*, June 3, 2012, 5D.

37. FCRC Minutes, July 13, 1970, 1.

38. "District 14 Election," WSJ, September 21, 1970, 2; Office of Natural Resources Revenue, email, November 12, 2015, 1; "District 14 to Ballot," WSJ, September 28, 1970, 1.

39. "Mill Creek Votes 'Yes,'" WSJ, October 1, 1970, 1; "Arapahoe Says Yes," WSJ, October 5, 1970, 1; Louis Twitchell, Shoshone Business Council Minutes, October 20, 1971, 6.

40. "County Reorganization Board Considers Four Proposals," WSJ, October 15, 1970; "County School Organization Committee Starts Planning," WSJ, May 8, 1969, 1–8.

41. FCRC Minutes, October 26, 1970, 1.

42. Jan Jibben, "Fremont County's Reorganization Necessary under 1969 School Law," WSJ, November 23, 1970, 1.

43. Jibben, "Fremont County's Reorganization"; Wyoming Department of Education, Data/Technology Unit, emails, March 9 and 10, 2006; "School Reorganization Committee: Proposes Five Districts for Fremont County," WSJ, November 19, 1970, 8; Oil and Gas Commission map; "Committee Starts Planning," WSJ, May 8, 1969, 1.

44. "Indian School District Discussed," WSJ, March 1, 1971, 1; "School Reorganization Committee: Proposes Five Districts for Fremont County," WSJ, November

19, 1970, 8; Hodgson, superintendent, Dubois School District 2, letter, October 21, 1971, 1–2.

45. "On High School; Problems . . . 150 at Fort Washakie Meetings," *WSJ*, May 31, 1971, 1–8; "At Monday Meeting . . . 5-District Plan Stays Despite Opposition," *WSJ*, September 16, 1971, 1; William Sniffin, "'Getting the Facts Straight,'" *WSJ*, May 13, 1971, 2.

46. "S. J. Starrett Writes Letter," *WSJ*, September 27, 1971, 1, 4; Sage letter, received May 30, 2012. See Saville-Troike, "Language Instruction and Multicultural Education," 58, for the statistics on the "retarded" perception among teachers of black students.

47. "Squaw Dance" (picture caption), "At Victory Banquet Saturday Night," *WSJ*, September 20, 1971, 1, 4-SS; "Gov. Love Big Fan of One-Shot Hunt," *WSJ*, September 20, 1971, 1; "County School Reorganization . . . What the Five-District System Looks Like," *WSJ*, September 20, 1971, 1.

48. Tom Shakespeare, quoted in Jan Jibben, "200 at Riverton Hearing," *WSJ*, October 7, 1971, 1.

49. "Big Turnout: Over 400 at Hearing Wednesday; Most Opposed 5-District Plan," *WSJ*, October 11, 1971, 1–2; "Reorganization Hearing," *WSJ*, October 14, 1971, 12; "7–5 Vote Tuesday, 5-District Plan," *WSJ*, October 21, 1971, 1.

50. Diamond, *Guns, Germs and Steel*, 90; William Sniffin, "Tired Committee," *WSJ*, October 21, 1971, 4.

51. Jan Wilkinson, "Rejected! State Throws out 5-District Plan," *WSJ*, November 15, 1971, 1.

52. "Reorganization Committee Bemoans Rejection of Plan," *WSJ*, December 2, 1971, 1; Wilkinson, "Rejected!"

53. Wilkinson, "Rejected!"

54. Wilkinson, "Rejected!"

6. ORGANIZATIONS OPPOSE THE SCHOOL

1. Minnie Woodring, "Group Opposes Reservation H. S.," *WSJ*, April 15, 1971, 1; "On Reservation . . . Opposition to High School Grows," *WSJ*, May 6, 1971, 1, 6.

2. Woodring, "Group Opposes Reservation H. S."; WRSAEA, "Fact Sheet," April 9, 1971.

3. WRSAEA, "Fact Sheet," 3; WINDS 2 Executive Summary, in CDW, *Wind River Reservation Yesterday* (1999), 68. See 2000 U.S. Census in "Report of William S. Cooper," *Large v. Fremont County, Wyoming*, Pl. Ex. 234, September 15, 2006, 3.

4. Merle Haas, telephone comm., March 23, 2006; pers. comm., June 5, 2007. See Jeffrey D. Anderson, introduction, in Dorsey and Kroeber, *Traditions of the Arapaho* (1997), xxiv.

5. See *Lawlor v. Board of Education* and Open Jurist, http://openjurist.org (accessed May 20, 2014).

6. Dennis Sun Rhodes was then also curator of the Arapahoe Cultural Museum at St. Michael's Mission (see "Sun Rhodes Named Curator of Arapahoe Museum," *WSJ*, April 22, 1971, 9); letter to the editor, "Indian School?" *WSJ*, April 26, 1971, 2; Spoonhunter and Iva St. Clair, quoted in Johnson, "Indian Leaders Push Ahead," *CS-T*, May 11, 1971, 8; "On Indian School," *WSJ*, October 16, 1972, 2.

7. Alberta Friday, interview 4, October 27, 2003, 1; Property Owners on the Reservation (POOR), "Report of Meeting," September 14, 1971, 1–2.

8. Warren, Opinion of the Court, in *Brown v. Board of Education of Topeka*, 3; Getches and Wilkinson, *Federal Indian Law*, 114.

9. Szasz, *Education and the American Indian*, 9.

10. Zerga, "A Study," 33–34; Barbara Sage, interview 2, August 24, 2001, 8, 10; Sage, telephone comm., January 24, 2004; Sage, interview 1, November 30, 2001, 1; Caroline Goggles, telephone comm., July 31, 2002.

11. *Alfred Ward, et al., . . . v. Robert Schrader, et al.*, 161, 167–69, 170–71; "Decision Soon on Reorganization," *WSJ*, February 14, 1974; "30 Days to Appeal, State's 4-District Plan Upheld by Judge Liamos," *WSJ*, February 18, 1974, 1.

12. Pratt, "Arts of the Contact Zone," 34.

13. Fowler, *Arapahoe Politics*, 3, 6, 144, 249, 286; Starr Weed (1918–2015), interview 2, October 22, 2001, 1.

14. Sage, telephone comm., June 6, 2004.

15. Sturm, *Blood Politics*, 78–81, 87; Fowler, *Arapahoe Politics*, 164–65, 222.

16. Wendy Rose, interview in Coltelli, *Winged Words*, 123; Hertzberg, *American Indian Identity*, 39; Sturm, *Blood Politics*, 151, 203–4; Churchill, "A Question of Identity," 63. See Bieder, "Attitudes Toward Indian Mixed-Bloods," 17–27.

17. Fowler, *Arapahoe Politics*, 144.

18. See Means, *Where White Men Fear*, 11.

19. Sage, telephone comm., January 24, 2004.

20. Sage, telephone comm.; Fowler, *Arapahoe Politics*, 144–45.

21. Fowler, *Arapahoe Politics*.

22. Front pages, *WSJ*, June 26 and September 25, 1972.

23. Alberta Friday, pers. comm., August 28, 2001; interview 1, July 11, 2002, 2–3; interview 3, October 14, 2002; telephone comm., August 19, 2007. See Zerga, "A Study," 5.

24. *Alfred Ward, et al., . . . v. Robert Schrader, et al.*, 156–58, 160–61, 168–69; "State Committee Meets on Reorganization Friday," *WSJ*, March 29, 1973, 1.

25. Barbara Sage, telephone comm., November 17, 2001; "Indian Education Coordinator Sets January Office Opening," *WSJ*, December 4, 1969, 1; "Court Dilemma 'What Is an Indian?'" *WSJ*, November 26, 1973, 1.

26. "Johnson-O'Malley Conference Held at Fort Washakie," *WSJ*, December 7, 1970; "Reservation H.S. Topic of Meeting May 27–28," *WSJ*, May 20, 1971, 1; "Indian Conference Wednesday, Thursday at Fort Washakie," *WSJ*, May 27, 1971, 1; "On High School; Education Problems . . . 150—Fort Washakie Meetings," *WSJ*, May 31, 1971, 1–8.

27. Shimkin, "Eastern Shoshone," 309; Fowler, *Arapahoe Politics*, 67; Wright, "Washakie," 137–38; Mrs. Alfred Ward and Mr. and Mrs. Alfred McAdam, "Indians Ask: 'Let Public Decide Issue,'" *WSJ*, June 15, 1972, 6; Fowler, *Arapahoe Politics*, 248–51.

28. Kruse, *Wind River Reservation*, 25; Fowler, *Arapahoe Politics*, 196–97; Minnie Woodring, "4,987 Indian Recipients—Announce Per-Capita Pay for Shoshone, Arapaho," *WSJ*, December 28, 1970, 1; Fowler, *Arapahoe Politics*, 232; Jan Jibben, "At Reorganization Meeting . . . More Petitions Presented Opposing H.S.," *WSJ*, May 13, 1971, 1.

29. *Alfred Ward, et al., . . . v. Robert Schrader et al.* (February 11, 1974), 156.

30. Shoshone Business Council Minutes, October 20, 1971, 1–2, 6–7 (courtesy of Starr Weed); B. Sage, telephone comm., March 27, 2003. See *Alfred Ward et al., . . . v. Robert Schrader et al.*, 158.

31. Starr Weed, interview, October 22 and 23, 2001, 1; pers. comm., December 3, 2002, 1.

32. Shoshone Business Council Minutes, October 20, 1971, 3, 9.

33. Shoshone Business Council Minutes, 1, 5.

34. Shoshone Business Council Minutes, 6.

35. Shoshone Business Council Minutes, 7 (Ward), 2, 8 (Weed), 9.

36. Starr Weed, interview, 2.

37. Jan Wilkinson, "Rejected! State Throws out 5-District Plan," *WSJ*, November 15, 1971; Sandra and Darwin St. Clair, interview; Darwin St. Clair, interview, July 13, 2007, 1.

7. INDIAN SCHOOL OPENS

1. Burton Hutchinson, interview, March 21, 2005, 5 (several interviewees remembered the German in-laws who lived with their coach and his wife; Hutchinson remembered people commenting that the German in-laws "couldn't hardly talk—English"); Darwin St. Clair, pers. comm., July 13, 2007; Dennis Sun Rhodes, telephone comm., January 19, 2006; Darwin and Sandra St. Clair, interview 1, October 10, 2001, 2.

2. Michael Gross, email, May 30, 2002, 1; interview 1, July 11, 2002, 1.

3. Alberta Friday; Conference at Wyoming Indian High School: "The Struggle for Self-Determination," panel discussion, "Political Activity," February 4, 2006, disk 6. Storytelling is an ancient art, still apparent when interviewees tell of humorous but nearly catastrophic experiences.

4. St. Clairs, interview 1, 1–2.

5. St. Clairs, interview 1, 2.

6. St. Clairs, interview 1; email, May 30, 2002, 3; obituary brochure, "A Celebration of the Life of Sandra May (Glover) St. Clair," November 24, 2005.

7. Starr Weed, interview 2, October 22, 2001, 2; Weed, pers. comm., March 9, 2004; Sage, telephone comm., May 31, 2006; St. Clairs, interview 1; Ben Friday Jr., interview 1, November 1, 2001, 2.

8. William Greider, "Indian Runaround: How the Bureaucracy Vetoes a Nixon Vow on Schools," *Washington Post*, November 7, 1971. The *Washington Post*'s editor Ben Bradlee guided publication of the Watergate scandal, and coverage won the Pulitzer Prize. The paper also covered the Pentagon Papers, which were about the government's secretive Vietnam War decisions.

9. Greider, "Indian Runaround"; Gaillard, "'We'll Do It Our Own Way Awhile,'" January 3, 1972, 27.

10. Greider, "Indian Runaround."

11. Greider, "Indian Runaround"; Nixon, "Special Message," 3; Michael Gross, email, May 30, 2002, 1.

12. Ben Friday Jr., interview 1, November 1, 2001, 2; Senators McGee and Hansen, letter (unsigned copy, but later events show that the letter was signed and sent), November 2, 1971, 1, courtesy of Michael Gross.

13. Michael Gross, email, May 30, 2002, 3.

14. Gross, email.

15. Hawkins, Memorandum, November 10, 1971, courtesy of Michael Gross; Allen, engineering contract adviser, letter, November 11, 1971, 1, courtesy of Gross.

16. "Resources Center Opens," *WSJ*, January 17, 1972, 2; McGee and Hansen, letter, November 2, 1971.

17. Forbes, *Native Americans and Nixon*, 39; Rosenfelt, "Toward a More Coherent Policy," 191, footnote 14; Jack Anderson, "Shameful Treatment of Indians," *Anniston (AL) Star*, July 19, 1976, 4A; Mankiewicz, *U.S. v. Richard M. Nixon*, 119; Ted Duncombe, "Abuse," *Anniston (AL) Star*, July 22, 1976, 4A.

18. Forbes, *Native Americans and Nixon*, 65; Castile, "Native North Americans and the National Question," 273–76, 284; White, *Breach of Faith*; Ortiz, in foreword to Forbes, *Native Americans and Nixon*, 11.

19. Senese, *Self-Determination*, 113.

20. Forbes, *Native Americans and Nixon*, 39.

21. Michael Gross, email, January 1, 2006, 1; Prucha, *The Great Father*, 1202; Fowler, *Arapahoe Politics*, 50, 56; Crum, *The Road*, 162. The Wind River alliance with the government to maintain survival came just less than a hundred years after a similar alliance with a similar purpose: the Shoshone warriors served with the U.S. government in attacking the Northern Arapahos at Nowood Creek in Bates Battle (1874), and the Arapahos scouted out the Sioux for General George Crook (1876).

22. "Reservation School Starts in January," *WSJ*, November 18, 1971, 1; McGee and Hansen, letter, November 2, 1971, 1; "Resources Center Opens," *WSJ*, January 17, 1972, 2; "Contract Signed for Resources Center," *WSJ*, November 25, 1971, 1; "Contract Signed for Center," *WSJ*, November 29, 1971, 1; Gross, "Indian Self-Determination," 1218; Ben Friday Jr., interview 1, November 1, 2001, 2; Bruce Chavez, interview 1, June 7, 2001, 2.

23. Alfred Redman, pers. comm., September 9, 2002; email, May 30, 2002, 3; William C'Hair, interview 5, May 9, 2005, 7.

24. Redman, pers. comm.; "After Five-District Rejection," *WSJ*, November 29, 1971, 1; Darwin St. Clair, pers. comm., July 13, 2007; telephone comm., November 7, 2008.

25. Barbara Sage, telephone comm., June 5, 2006; Patrick Goggles, telephone comm., October 18, 2004.

26. Alberta Friday, interview 1, July 11, 2002, 2; Marilyn Groesbeck, interview 1, December 20, 2001, 1–2. Groesbeck was principal at the BIA St. Stephen's Indian School in 2011, her position for ten years; Senese, *Self-Determination*, 128.

27. Groesbeck, interview 1, 2; B. Sage, telephone comm., August 23, 2002; Annette Bell (b. 1933), interview 1, June 30, 2003, 1.

28. William C'Hair, interview 5, May 9, 2005, 8–9; "W.I.H.S. Nears Accreditation," *Tribe Talk*, October 31, 1972, 1.

29. B. Sage, telephone comm., June 11, 2009. A reservation automobile accident killed Irene Mountain Sheep (1938–2002) on her way to a high school basketball game (February 21) shortly after the interviews for this study began.

30. B. Sage, interview, June 4, 2001, 2; Jan Wilkinson, "Noble Hotel Shuts Down," *WSJ*, January 17, 1972, 1.

31. G. Groesbeck, in Hipp, "'Something They Haven't Told,'" *Wyoming Indian Schools Newsletter*, December–January, 2002, 3; pers. comm., June 29, 2007. See Pratt, "Arts of the Contact Zone," 35, and Lyons, "A Captivity Narrative," 102.

32. Ben Friday Jr., interview 2, January 10, 2002, 1.

33. Alberta Friday, in Conference at Wyoming Indian High School: "The Struggle for Self-Determination," panel discussion, "Political Activity," February 4, 2006, disk 6; Rosenfelt, "Toward a More Coherent Policy," 211–12.

34. M. Groesbeck, interview, December 20, 2001, 1; Duncombe, "Ethete: Episcopal Churchwork," 65; Alvena Friday, telephone comm., December 20, 2011. Honoraria gifts are given in "giveaways" to individuals, often to the singers and drummers, and sometimes to younger children as a group. The gifts are often of significant value, ranging from wool blankets, star quilts, and quality jewelry to children's toys and candy. Interspersed with the announcements of gifts, slow dancers honor guests with their families.

35. "Ethete! New Classroom," *WSJ*, November 9, 1972, 10; Sandra C'Bearing, interview, January 23, 2006, 2. See Anderson, *Four Hills of Life*, 201.

36. M. Groesbeck, interview 2, December 21, 2001, 1; Ben Friday Jr., interview 2, January 10, 2002; Alberta Friday, in Conference at Wyoming Indian High School: "The Struggle for Self-Determination," panel discussion, "Political Activity," February 4, 2006, disk 6.

37. P. Goggles, telephone interview, June 26, 2003, 1; "Indian School District Discussed," *WSJ*, March 1, 1971, 1; Smith, "Why Different Education?" 43. See Apple, *Cultural Politics and Education*, 14–15.

38. "Wyoming Education Code," sec. 109 (b), 177.

39. "Committee Bemoans Rejection of Plan," *WSJ*, December 2, 1971, 1; "After Five-District Rejection," *WSJ*, November 29, 1971, 1; "Education Code," sec. 109 (e), 178.

40. "Reorganization Committee Discusses Three Plans," *WSJ*, December 16, 1971, 8.

41. "New Plans from Old," *WSJ*, January 13, 1972, 1; "One District; Opposite Sides," *WSJ*, January 27, 1972, 1, 8.

42. "Board Opposes One District," *WSJ*, February 10, 1972, 1.

43. "Trustees, Bonds Discussed," *WSJ*, February 17, 1972, 1.

8. INDIAN PEOPLE SPEAK

1. Jan Wilkinson, "Now It's 4 Districts!" *WSJ*, May 1, 1972, 1; Wilkinson, "Future of New Plan," *WSJ*, May 8, 1972, 1 (map).

2. "The Five-District System," *WSJ*, September 20, 1971, 1 (map); Jan Wilkinson, "Four-District Plan Withstands," *WSJ*, May 11, 1972, 1; Wilkinson, "Committee 'Threatened' with AIM Action," *WSJ*, June 8, 1972, 1; Fowler, *Arapahoe Politics*, 140.

3. Chester Armajo, in Wilkinson, "Committee 'Threatened' with AIM Action," 1.

4. Quoted in Wilkinson, "Committee 'Threatened' with AIM Action," 1, 8.

5. Quoted in Wilkinson, "Committee 'Threatened' with AIM Action."

6. Quoted in Wilkinson, "Committee 'Threatened' with AIM Action."

7. Joan Wheel, "Fremont Schools Decison [*sic*] July 24," *CS-T*, June 12, 1972, 2; Alberta Friday, interview 2, September 6, 2002, 1; ". . . and one who missed!" *WSJ*, September 21, 1970, 1; "Squaw Dance" (picture caption), "At Victory Banquet Saturday Night," *WSJ*, September 20, 1971, 1, 4-SS.

8. Friday, interview 2; Wheel, "Fremont Schools Decison."

9. Wheel, "Fremont Schools Decison."

10. Fowler, *Arapahoe Politics*, 47.

11. Jan Wilkinson, "Cheyenne Hearing," *WSJ*, June 12, 1972, 1.

12. Wheel, "Fremont Schools Decison."

13. Michael Gross, email, May 30, 2002, 3; interview 1, July 11, 2002, 1; Wilkinson, "Cheyenne Hearing," 8.

14. Alberta Friday, interview 2, September 6, 2002, 1.

15. "Indian Charges Board Retaliates," *CS-T*, June 16, 1972, 3.

16. "Indians Ask: 'Public Decide,'" *WSJ*, June 15, 1972, 6; Shoshone Business Council Minutes, 7.

17. "Indians Ask: 'Public Decide.'" See Fowler, *Arapahoe Politics*, 197.

18. "Urges Shoshones to Attend," letter, *WSJ*, June 22, 1972, 6; Jan Wilkinson, "Tribes Differ," *WSJ*, June 26, 1972, 1; "Indians Back High School," *CS-T*, June 24, 1972, 1; Wilkinson, "No! State Committee Rejects," *WSJ*, July 24, 1972, 1; Stephen Hendricks, "Memorial a Whitewash," *CS-T*, June 3, 2003, A8.

19. Jan Wilkinson, "Status of Johnson-O'Malley Funds," *WSJ*, June 29, 1972, 1.

20. Wilkinson, "No! State Committee Rejects," 1, 8; "Will State Committee Accept?" *WSJ*, July 20, 1972, 1.

21. Wilkinson, "No! State Committee Rejects."

22. Rosenfelt, "Toward a More Coherent Policy," 192–93; U.S. Congress, "Public Law 92-318," sec. 303 (a) and (b), sec. 304 (1) and (2), sec. 305 (b), 335–37; U.S. Congress, *Statutes at Large* (January 4, 1975), sec. 5 (a), 2213.

23. U.S. Congress, *Statutes at Large* (June 23, 1972), sec. 307 (b), (2), (C), 338, and sec. 411 (a), 334; Rosenfelt, "Toward a More Coherent Policy"; U.S. Congress, "An Act Authorizing . . . (Johnson-O'Malley Act)."

24. "Activities for Indian Program," *WSJ*, April 1, 1974, 8; "'Nothing More Appropriate,'" *WSJ*, September 2, 1974, 4.

25. William Sniffin, "Tribes Threaten," *WSJ*, July 17, 1972, 1; Sniffin, "Commissioners to Consider Indian," *WSJ*, July 2, 1972, 1.

26. "Indians Seek Cooperation," *WSJ*, July 17, 1972, 2; "Kail Responds to Indians," *WSJ*, July 20, 1972, 1. McDonald, *American Indians and the Fight for Equal Voting Rights*, 198, 232.

27. John P. Manges Jr., "On Indian Situation," letter, *WSJ*, July 24, 1972, 2; "Commissioners Appoint White Man," *WSJ*, July 27, 1972, 1; letter, "Disagrees with Commissioners," July 31, 1972, 2; William Sniffin, "Commissioners Erred in Appointment," *WSJ*, July 27, 1972, 4.

28. Fremont County Planning Committee, "Plan of Organization," September 11, 1972, 12–13 (hereafter Fremont Committee, "Plan").

29. Fremont Committee, "Plan," 12; Wilkinson, "No! State Committee Rejects," *WSJ*, July 24, 1972, 8; U.S. Congress, *Statutes at Large* (June 23, 1972); Rosenfelt, "Toward a More Coherent Policy."

30. Fremont Committee, "Plan."

31. Fremont Committee, "Plan," 12; Stamm, *People of Wind River*; Fowler, *Arapahoe Politics*, 93–96.

32. Fremont Committee, "Plan,"13–14.

33. Jan Wilkinson, "Committee Proposes One District—Again," *WSJ*, September 14, 1972, 1, 8.

34. "New Project Director," *Tribe Talk*, 1; Michael Gross, email, January 20, 2003, 1; Alfred Redman, telephone interview, August 6, 2009, 1; "Indian—Vows Court Fight," *CS-T*, September 23, 1972, 7; "'I'm Not Representing Tribes' Says Redman," *WSJ*, September 28, 1972, 1; "Committee Agrees to Try Again," *WSJ*, December 4, 1972, 1. One District 6 resident argued that Indian children were not alone in having "special needs"; she saw District 6's school programs as being for "the special needs of white children," as was reported in the latter *WSJ* article.

35. "'I'm Not Representing Tribes' Says Redman," *WSJ*; "Schools Hit," *CS-T*, September 24, 1972, 3.

36. "'Abysmal' Level Cited for Indians' Education," *Denver Post*, September 24, 1972, 2.

37. "'Abysmal' Level."

38. "Shoshones Protest," *WSJ*, September 25, 1972, 1; "'I'm Not Representing Tribes' Says Redman," *WSJ*.

39. Wilkinson, "A Better Plan?" *WSJ*, September 28, 1972, 4; "Public Hearing Held," *WSJ*, October 5, 1972, 1; "Reorganization Struggle Five Hardworked Plans— Four Confusing Failures," *WSJ*, February 7, 1974, 10; Gross, "Indian Control for Quality," 243, 256. Another of Gross's arguments concerned the compromises "to religious beliefs . . . and community life" of the Indian children.

40. Jan Wilkinson, "Motion Is Filed to Dismiss Four-District Re-organization Suit," *WSJ*, October 19, 1972, 1; as quoted in Cynthia Boyhan, "Go to State Board," *WSJ*, November 6, 1972, 1.

41. "Another Hearing Set," *WSJ*, October 16, 1972, 1; "No Decision Made, State Committee Hesitates on One-District Proposal," *WSJ*, November 13, 1972, 1.

42. "School Plan Is Rejected," *WSJ*, November 23, 1972, 1.

43. Fremont County Planning Committee, "Six District Plan," December 18, 1972; "Committee Agrees to Try," *WSJ*, December 4, 1972, 1; "LVHS Endorses Six District Plan; Combines Graduation," *WSJ*, December 14, 1972, 5; "Hearing Held Monday: Six-District Plan to State Committee," *WSJ*, December 21, 1972, 1.

44. "Hearing Held Monday," *WSJ*.

45. *Riverton (WY) Ranger*, January 5, 1973, 8.

46. "At Casper Hearing," *WSJ*, February 8, 1973, 1.

47. Minnie Woodring, "Snow and Cold!" *WSJ*, March 1, 1973, 1; Jan Wilkinson, "School Boards 'Wait,'" *WSJ*, March 12, 1973, 1; William Sniffin, "We Have Much to Lose," *WSJ*, March 22, 1973, 6.

48. Jan Wilkinson, "Lawsuits Being Prepared," *WSJ*, March 5, 1973, 1; Wilkinson, "School Boards 'Wait'"; Wilkinson, "Lander Gets Some Relief," *WSJ*, April 2, 1973, 1; "A Riverton View," *Riverton Ranger*, May 3, 1973, 4; "State Meets on Reorganization," *WSJ*, March 29, 1973.

49. Victor Zerga, interview, November 29, 2002, 1; Zerga, telephone comm., April 21, 2006.

50. Wilkinson, "Lawsuits Being Prepared," 1, 8; Wilkinson, "Lander Gets Some Relief," 1–5.

51. Jan Wilkinson, "Administrators 'Plan,'" *WSJ*, February 15, 1973, 1; Wilkinson, "Lander Gets Some Relief"; Wilkinson, "School Boards 'Wait,'" 1.

52. "Cody Judge," *WSJ*, May 3, 1973, 1; "Another Motion on Reorganization," *WSJ*, May 3, 1973, 7; Minnie Woodring, "Snow!" *WSJ*, April 23, 1973, 1; "A Riverton View," *Riverton Ranger*, in *WSJ*; Principal Starrett, letter to the *WSJ* editor, "Lander Administrator Replies to Riverton Reorganization View," *WSJ*, May 7, 1973, 2; Jan Wilkinson, "'Tables Turned' on WEA," *WSJ*, June 18, 1973, 5.

53. "Meier Criticizes," *WSJ*, July 12, 1973, 4; Jan Wilkinson, "Taxes Will Be Levied," *WSJ*, July 19, 1973, 1; Wilkinson, "Boards Face Problems on Lander School Budgets," *WSJ*, July 30, 1973, 1.

54. RoJean Thayer, "Jeffrey City," *WSJ*, May 10, 1973, 1; Jan Wilkinson, "LVHS in Bind on Jeffrey City Plea," *WSJ*, June 14, 1973, 1; Wilkinson, "Boards Face Problems on Lander School Budgets," *WSJ*, July 30, 1973, 4.

55. Jan Wilkinson, "Author of Acclaimed Program Larry Murray Resigns from Home-School Post," *WSJ*, August 30, 1973, 15; Wilkinson, "Status of Johnson-O'Malley Funds," *WSJ*, June 29, 1972, 1.

56. "Tribes Say No!" *WSJ*, June 4, 1973, 1; "Spiro Agnew," *WSJ*, October 18, 1973, 1.

57. "With Governor—Advisory Council Discusses Current Problems," *WSJ*, September 3, 1973, 1; "Traffic Light for Ethete," *WSJ*, November 8, 1973, 1.

9. FIGHTS IN THE COURTS

1. *Alfred Ward, et al., . . . v. Robert Schrader, et al.*; also *Geraud, et al., Petitioner, vs. Schrader, et al., Respondents*, Brief in Support of Motion to Dismiss. No. 16342, filed November 5, 1973; "Cody Judge to Hear Protest," *WSJ*, May 3, 1973, 1. See *Wright v. Council of City of Emporia*.

2. Michael Gross, "Outline of Legal Theories in *Ward v. Schrader*" (draft), n.d., copy in possession of author. See *Keyes v. Denver School District No. 1.*

3. Getches and Wilkinson, "The Rights of Individual Indians," 559–60; Gross, "Indian Control for Quality Indian Education," 239.

4. *Alfred Ward, et al., . . . v. Robert G. Schrader, et al.*, Civil Cases No. 16307 and 16342; "New Judge to Hear Reorganization Suit," *WSJ*, October 1, 1973, 1; Rosenfeld, *"Shut Those Thick Lips!": A Study of Slum School Failure*, 110.

5. Patch, Deposition, October 2, 1973, 3, in *Alfred Ward, et al., . . . v. Robert G. Schrader, et al.*

6. Patch Deposition, 7–9.

7. Patch Deposition, 15–16.

8. Duncombe, letter to Gross, January 9, 1974; Patch Deposition, 18.

9. Patch Deposition, 30.

10. Patch Deposition, 31–32.

11. William Sniffin, "'Getting the Facts Straight,'" *WSJ*, May 13, 1971, 2; Patch Deposition, 35.

12. Phibbs, Gross and Forhan, Attorneys for Intervenors, Brief and Supplementary Brief (Gross only), Case No. 16342, November 2, 1973, 1–5, and November 16, 1973, 1–2; *Wyo. Stats.*, sec. 9–276.32 (1957), in Phibbs, Gross and Forhan, November 2, 1973, 1; "'What Is an Indian?'" *WSJ*, November 26, 1973, 1.

13. The sweat lodge ceremony is described in Michael Gross, email, January 20, 2003, 1. "Decision Soon on Reorganization," *WSJ*, February 14, 1974, 1; Reyhner and Eder, *American Indian Education*, 264–68; Gross, email, October 28, 2003, 1; U.S. Congress, Senate, *Indian Education; Alfred Ward, et al., . . . vs. Robert G. Schrader, et al.* (February 1974), 157–61, 167–69.

14. "30 Days to Appeal," *WSJ*, February 18, 1974, 1.

15. "Reorganization Appeals Filed," *WSJ*, July 15, 1974, 1. In *Alfred Ward, et al., . . . vs. Robert G. Schrader, et al.*, see *Geraud, et al., Appellants v. Schrader, et al., Appellees*, and the *WRIEA, Inc., et al.*, and *Ward, et al. v. (same) Appellees*, and *F.C.V.H.S. District and Lander School District No. 1 v. (same) Appellees*. In the Supreme Court of the State of Wyoming (February 7, 1975), No. 4389, 4390, and 4391. Chief Justice Guthrie. Justices McEwan, McClintock, Raper, and Thomas heard the case (title page 2). Justice Raper wrote the majority opinion.

16. *Geraud v. Schrader*, 875, 879, 880.

17. *Geraud v. Schrader.*

18. *Geraud v. Schrader*, 881.

19. *Geraud v. Schrader*, 881, 882; Getches and Wilkinson, *Federal Indian Law*, 591. In 1975 HEW "took the position that state agencies . . . may establish schools exclusively for Indians without offending Title VI of the Civil Right Act of 1964."

20. Larson, "Toward a Psychology of Positive Youth Development," 174; Deyhle and Swisher, "Research in American Indian and Alaska Native Education," 169; *Geraud v. Schrader*, 881.

21. *Geraud v. Schrader*, 883.

22. *Geraud v. Schrader*, 879–80, 884.

23. Michael Gross, email, May 30, 2002, 3; Jan Wilkinson, "Legalities Overwhelming If Indians Want 'Out,'" WSJ, June 12, 1975, 6; "U.S. Supreme Court Postpones School Reorganization Decision," WSJ, July 24, 1975, 1; "Supreme Court to Make Reorganization Decision," WSJ, July 17, 1975, 1; "Reorganization Committee Frustrated by Pending Constitutionality Ruling," WSJ, September 11, 1975, 7; Art Werner, "All-Indian District Improbable," WSJ, October 20, 1975, 1, 6.

24. U.S. Congress, House, *Statement of Information*, 5; "Complaint for Declaratory and Injunctive Relief," John Charles Redman, a minor, by and through his father and next friend, Alfred Paul Redman and Millcreek School District No. 14 of Fremont County, Wyoming, Fort Totten School District, No. 30, Ft. Totten, N. Dakota, Mandaree School District, No. 36, Mandaree, N. Dakota, the WRIEA, Inc., Ethete, Wyoming, Hannahville Education Committee, Wilson, Michigan and the Coalition of Indian Controlled School Boards, Plaintiffs v. Ottina, Acting Commissioner of Education, U.S. Department of HEW, Defendant. Civil Action No. 62873 (March 30, 1973), 9, courtesy of attorney Kirke Kickingbird.

25. Letter to Senator Bible, chairman, Interior Appropriations Subcommittee, Committee on Appropriations, April 10 1973, 1, courtesy of Kickingbird; "Opposition to Plaintiffs' Motion for Preliminary Injunction" of Civil Action No. 628-73, Hallington Wood Jr., assistant attorney general and other attorneys for the defendant, Department of Justice, April 17, 1973, 9, courtesy of Kickingbird; "The Impeachment Inquiry," *Congressional Quarterly, Almanac*, 93rd Cong., 2nd sess. (1974), vol. 30, 869, 888; U.S. Congress, House, *Statement of Information*, 94–95.

26. Coalition of Indian Controlled School Boards press release, May 7, 1973, courtesy of Kickingbird; Jerry Reynolds, email, August 12, 2009, 1, with reference to Kickingbird, Ghostbear, and Gross interviews in Reynolds, "The Rebecca Adamson Archive"; Reynolds, emails, August 12, 2009, and November 2, 2017; "Complaint for Declaratory and Injunctive Relief."

27. Kickingbird, telephone comm., August 13, 2009; Reynolds, email, 1–2; *Order: The Minnesota Chippewa Tribe, et al., Plaintiffs v. Carlucci, etc., et al., Defendants*, Civil Action No. 175-73 (and) *Redman, John Charles et al. v. John R. Ottina*, Civil Action No. 628-73 (May 8, 1973), 1–3, courtesy of Kickingbird; Affidavit (re. Civil Actions No. 175-73 and 628-73), Mattheis, Acting Commissioner of Education, U.S. Office of Education, Department of HEW, in the temporary absence of

Ottina (April 19, 1973), 1–3; Jones, Special Assistant to the President, Affidavit, for Civil Action No. 628-73 (May 7, 1973), 1–2. Copies of both courtesy of Kickingbird. See U.S. Congress, House, *Statement of Information*, 24; White, *Breach of Faith*, 29–35.

28. U.S. Congress, "Public Law 93-638," 2203; Gross, emails, May 30, 2002, 1, and January 2, 2006, 2; Gross, "Indian Self-Determination," 1197; U.S. Congress, *Statutes at Large*, sec. 3 (a), 2203–4, sec. 4, and sec. 5; U.S. Congress, (a), 2213; U.S. Congress, sec. 7 (b), (1) and (2), 2205; Senese, *Self-Determination*, 121–28; Wilkins, *American Indian Politics*, 234. See O'Brien, *American Indian Tribal Governments*, 89.

29. Frank No Runner, St. Stephen's superintendent, telephone interview, August 24, 2016; M. Groesbeck, St. Stephen's principal, telephone interview, January 12, 2016, 2.

10. CONTROL OF THEIR DESTINY

1. "County Committee on Reorganization," *WSJ*, February 13, 1975, 1; "Committee Re-forms," *WSJ*, April 24, 1975, 1, 8; B. Sage, telephone comm., February 4, 2010; "Reorganization Committee Discusses," *WSJ*, May 15, 1975, 1; Jan Wilkinson, "Legalities Overwhelming," *WSJ*, June 12, 1975, 1.

2. "Arapahoe Council Seeks Ouster," *WSJ*, June 26, 1975, 1; anonymous source, pers. comm., March 18, 2002.

3. *Common Sense* was the title of Thomas Paine's 1776 pamphlet that gave reasons to seek independence from Great Britain. It is also preferred by the Arapahos over pedantic reasoning. Art Werner, "All-Indian School District," *WSJ*, October 20, 1975, 1, 6; *Geraud, et al. v. Appellees Schrader, et al. and the WRIEA, Inc., et al.*, 880.

4. *Chiefs' Souvenir Edition*, *WSJ*, February 1986, 8.

5. Amundson, *Yellowcake Towns*, 156, 158–59; Rabe (referencing Boyhan of Dubois), "Reorganization Committee Okays $800,000," *WSJ*, January 15, 1976, 1; "State Committee Thwarts County Reorganization Plans," *WSJ*, February 12, 1976, 1; Severt Rist, Fort Washakie superintendent, and Principal John Williams, letter to the FCRC, August 9, 1976, 1, courtesy of Starr Weed.

6. Dick George, "Committee Given Some Help," *WSJ*, April 26, 1976, 1; Rist and Williams, letter to FCRC, 1, 2.

7. "Rev. Duncombe Killed," *WSJ*, April 26, 1976, 1; "Guilty," *WSJ*, June 14, 1976, 1; "Brothers Accused in Death," *CS-T*, March 15, 1978, 1; "Defense: Agents Failed," *CS-T*, May 18, 1978, 27; Barron, "Murder Charges Dropped," *CS-T*, May 26, 1978, 1 (articles regarding Reverend Duncombe's death, courtesy of E. Duncombe); John Yellow Plume, pers. comm., September 18, 2003.

8. Yunker, "Tillman—New Indictment," *Boomerang*, March 15, 1978, 2; "Rose Tillman Explains Testimony," *CS-T*, May 20, 1978, 1; Barron, "Jury Finds Youth Guilty," *CS-T*, May 25, 1978, 1; Barron, "Murder Charges Dropped," May 26, 1978, 1.

9. Barron, "Murder Charges Dropped"; "Billy Tillman Critically Injured," *WSJ*, August 21, 1978, 1; "Billy Tillman, 18, Died," *WSJ*, August 24, 1978, 1.

10. Michael Gross, email, May 30, 2002, 4; Duncombe, "Ethete: Episcopal Church-work," v.

11. Dennis Sun Rhodes, quoted from the eulogy in Duncombe, "Ethete: Episcopal Churchwork," v–vi; Alvena Friday, pers. comm., February 19, 2009.

12. "School Reorganization Committee Works," *WSJ*, July 15, 1976, 1.

13. Rist and Williams, letter to FCRC, 1; "Plan Ruled Out," *WSJ*, August 12, 1976, 1; "County School Receive $142,358," *WSJ*, July 26, 1976, 1; U.S. Congress, *Statutes at Large* (June 23, 1972).

14. Alfred Redman, pers. comm., May 20, 2005; "School Reorganization Committee Works," *WSJ*, July 15, 1976, 1; "Plan Ruled Out," *WSJ*, August 12, 1976, 1.

15. "Plan Ruled Out."

16. Cynthia Boyhan, "Committee Pushes Eight Districts," *WSJ*, September 16, 1976, 5.

17. Cynthia Boyhan, "Committee Seeks Nine Districts," *WSJ*, September 30, 1976, 8; Scott Dewey, quoted in Boyhan, "Nine-District School Plan Passes Hearing Thursday," *WSJ*, November 1, 1976, 1.

18. "County Reorganization Plan Rejected," *WSJ*, December 20, 1976, 1; William Sniffin, "Meier, Jennings Consider Five-District School Bill," *WSJ*, January 20 1977, 1; "Five District Plan," *WSJ*, February 3, 1977, 1; "Students Start Classes," *WSJ*, January 3, 1977, 4; "Board Discusses Re-organization," *WSJ*, January 31, 1977, 5.

19. George Zerga, telephone interview 2, April 21, 2006, 1–3; Cynthia Boyhan, "County Reorganization Board Puzzles," *WSJ*, March 10, 1977, 1; "New Reorganization Bill," *WSJ*, March 14, 1977, 1; State of Wyoming, "School District Organization Law," *Wyoming Statutes 1977* (21-5-132, b and c), 54.

20. State of Wyoming, "School District Organization Law," *Wyoming Statutes 1977* (21-5-132, c), 54; (21-5-136, a), 56; (21-5-135, b), 55; Smith, "School Boards Discuss Confusing Reorganization," *WSJ*, March 10, 1977, 1; Boyhan, "County Reorganization Board Puzzles."

21. "Committee Re-forms," *WSJ*, April 24, 1975, 8; Alfred Redman, email, May 22, 2012; Fowler, *Arapahoe Politics*, 286; Sage, *Tribal Government at Wind River*, 2; Alvena Friday, telephone comm., April 30, 2012.

22. "Congressional Report," *WSJ*, March 24, 1977, 8.

23. State of Wyoming, "School District Organization Law," *Wyoming Statutes 1977* (21-5-132, b), 54; eleven letters dated between March 9 and 29, 1977, Wyoming

State Archives; Fremont County Boundary Board, "Plan of Organization of the Public Schools of Fremont County, Wyoming," January 10, 1978, 17, Wyoming State Archives.

24. George Zerga, interview 1, November 29, 2002, and telephone interview 2, April 21, 2006, 1; "New Organization Bill," *WSJ*, March 14, 1977, 1; Fremont Reorganization Committee Minutes, November 18, 1977, Eager, Secretary-Treasurer, 1–3, Wyoming State Archives.

25. Alvena Friday, pers. comm., January 20, 2003; Fremont Reorganization Committee Minutes.

26. State of Wyoming, "School District Organization Law," *Wyoming Statutes 1977* (21-5-135, a and b), 55; Minutes, May 13, 1977; Zerga, letter to Fremont County Boundary Board, April 5, 1977, Wyoming State Archives; Minutes, November 18, 1977, 2–3; "A Salute to the Good People of Jeffrey City," *WSJ*, October 6, 1977, 2; Cynthia Boyhan, "It's Nine-District Plan," *WSJ*, November 21, 1977, 1.

27. Richard G. Hodgson, letter, March 9, 1977; Richard G. Hodgson, superintendent, and William Ideker, vice-chairman of Dubois District, letter to Lorraine Ocenas, Boundary Board, December 6, 1977, Wyoming State Archives.

28. Fremont County Boundary Board Minutes, December 7, 1977, Ocenas, Boundary Board Secretary, Wyoming State Archives; Zerga, telephone interview 2; Boundary Board Minutes, December 20, 1977; Fowler, *Arapahoe Politics*, 91; Fremont County Boundary Board, "Plan of Organization of the Public Schools," January 10, 1978, 8–9, Wyoming State Archives.

29. Boundary Board, "Plan of Organization," 2–4, 6, 15.

30. Resolution of State Organization Committee on School District Organization adopted February 28, 1978, Wyoming State Archives; *Schraeder and Wyoming State Board of Education, acting as the State Committee on School District Organization v. District Boundary Board of Fremont County and Fremont County Planning Committee*, March 3, 1978, District Court of Fremont County, Wyoming, Ninth Judicial District, Civil No. 18833, ruling signed April 7, 1978, 2, Wyoming State Archives.

31. Dwight D. Bonham, state examiner, letter, December 6, 1978, Wyoming State Archives; Amundson, *Yellowcake Towns*, 153, 158–59, 165; Wyoming Department of Education, "School Program Information," September 25, 2002, 6; M. Hoffman, email, February 25, 2018.

32. State representative P. Goggles, telephone interview, December 4, 2009; M. Friday, interview, October 4, 2016; No Runner, St. Stephen's superintendent, telephone interview, August 24, 2016; anonymous canvasser, pers. comm., February 19, 2009; O. St. Clair, superintendent of Fremont County District 14 Schools, telephone interview, June 30, 2016, 1. In 2009 the State Legislature

again considered trying to decrease the number of small districts, some wanting to set a "1,000 student count benchmark" and some wanting only countywide districts. Representative Goggles commented that the latter "would not work here" in his telephone interview, June 26, 2003.

33. State of Wyoming, *Constitution of the State of Wyoming*, 36; anonymous participant, discussion, March 26, 2011.

34. Office of Indian Affairs, Fort Washakie, Wyoming, Allotment No. 1270, Land-Sales 48131-1912, from Seth Willow, July 3, 1913; Office of Indian Affairs, Allotment No. 1271, Land-Sales 97980-1918, from J. Dresser, June 21, 1919. These sales are only partially documented; Episcopal Bishop Thornberry, D.D., letter, July 15, 1971, 1.

35. Anonymous school board member, pers. comm., February 19, 2009, 1; Hudson, pers. comm., February 17, 2009; Episcopal Diocese of Wyoming, signatory, Jones, Warranty Deed, February 19, 1986, Fremont County book 262 of microfilm page 306 (March 21, 1986), 1082222.

36. Anonymous school board member, pers. comm.; Episcopal Bishop Thornberry, letter; Tara M. Berg, Fremont County assessor, email, May 16, 2012.

37. Ben Friday Jr., interview, November 1, 2001, 2; P. Goggles, interview 3, August 30, 2006, 2; Dan Hudson, email, February 25, 2004, 1; Hudson, pers. comm., February 17, 2009; M. Hoffman, email, February 2, 2018; P. Goggles, telephone interview, June 26, 2003; Goggles, telephone comm., October 18, 2004.

38. Courtesy of Hudson; Hudson, interview 1 (written response), February 23, 2004, 1; Hudson, interview 2, March 11, 2006, 2. See *Campbell County School Dist. v. State*; Hudson, notation, February 25, 2004, 1; Hudson, notation, February 13, 2004, 1.

39. Joan Barron, "House Defeats District Consolidation," CS-T, February 13, 2003, 1, 12; Hudson, interview 1; "Starrett Writes Letter," WSJ, September, 27, 1971, 1. See Lieberman, *Future of Public Education*, 51.

40. May, *Indigenous Community-Based Education*, 1; Indian Schools Mission Statement; Duran, chairman, Arapahoe General Council, letter, April 12, 1946. See Fowler, *Arapahoe Politics*, 209.

41. Dick, Estell, and McCarty, "Restructuring the Teaching of Language," 32; Holm and Holm, "Rock Point," 184; McCarty, "Bilingual Education Policy and the Empowerment of American Indian Communities," 5–6; Deyhle and Swisher, "Research in American Indian and Alaska Native Education," 172–73; Kamanā, "Reflections and Feelings Deriving from a Pulakaumaka within My Heart," 200–211; Wellington, New Zealand, Department of Education, 1984 *Annual Report*, in Barrington, "New Zealand Experience," 321.

42. Greymorning, "Language Survival," 213–14, 217, 223; Alvena Friday, discussion, February 15, 2017. See Skinner, "Teaching through Traditions," 115.

43. *Chiefs* won the First Annual Tribeca Film Festival's "Best Feature Documentary" award in New York, May 12, 2002.

44. "Something to Yell About," *Chiefs' Souvenir Edition*, WSJ, February 1986, 7; "History Set Nov. 23, 1985: Chiefs Shatter Old Record of 46 Consecutive Wins with 112–68 Victory over Dubois; Set New Record at 50," *Chiefs' Souvenir Edition*, WSJ, February 1986, 8–9, courtesy of M. A. Redman; Dennis Durband, "March to Record Brought Attention to WIHS," CS-T, November 25, 1985, B4.

45. Alfred Redman, interview 1, March 28, 2006; "Myron 'The Magician' Chavez," *Chiefs' Souvenir Edition*, WSJ, February 1986, 3, courtesy of M. A. Redman; Bill Landen, "It's Still Hard to Get By Wyoming Indian," CS-T, November 22, 1984, D1; Wiles, "Indian Basketball: Two Films," 106.

46. "State Champions," *Riverton Ranger*, March 8, 2001, 1; "Chiefs Down Lander," *Riverton Ranger*, January 4, 2003, Extra, 1; "WIHS Girls Win Rematch with Tigers to Capture Girls Shootout Championship," *Lander Journal*, January 4, 2006, B1; Randy Tucker, "Lady Chiefs Roll to Title," *Lander Journal*, March 9, 2003, C1; Jack Daly, "Basketball Championships: Showstopper: Wyoming Indians' SoundingSides Capable of 3-Point Performance," CS-T, March 3, 2004, D3; "SoundingSides Featured in *Sports Illustrated*," *Lander Journal*, February 25, 2004, B1. SoundingSides died in a highway accident on May 31, 2012. The driver had overcorrected in an attempt to avoid a deer, according to the *Riverton Ranger* (courtesy of M. Friday).

47. Steve Peck, "Shootout," *Lander Journal* and *Riverton Ranger*, January 2, 2004, Opinion page; "Racism in Wyoming Athletics: Unfortunate Reality," CS-T, January 28, 2004, A1–A9.

48. Alfred Redman, interview 1, March 28, 2006; Wyoming Coaches' Association, Nineteenth Annual Hall of Fame and Awards, courtesy of M. A. Redman; award trophy and pictures at Redman home, February 23, 2009.

11. AS SEEN FROM THE SUN DANCE GROUNDS

1. O. St. Clair, telephone interview, July 16, 2016; P. Goggles, telephone interview, June 26, 2003, 2.

2. Phil Tingley, president, National Indian Social Workers Association, interviewed in Gale, "Post-Traumatic Stress," 13; Getches and Wilkinson, *Federal Indian Law*, "Section B. Rights and Benefits," 560; Hampton, "Toward a Redefinition," 267.

3. G. Sage, Elder panel discussion, May 24, 2005, 5–6; Larson, *History of Wyoming*, 39–41; O. St. Clair, telephone interview, June 30 and July 1, 2016, 2.

4. Cohen, "The Shaping of Men's Minds," 22; G. Coan, director of education for Rough Rock Demonstration School, November 24, 1987, testimony in the

Oversight Hearing on Culturally Relevant Early Education Programs, 5–9, Senator Inouye, chairman, 100th Cong., 2nd sess., S. Hrg.100-570, Washington DC: GPO, 1988, 8–9.

5. Klug and Whitfield, *Widening the Circle*, 165, 205–6; Fishman, "Minority Mother Tongues in Education," 55; Pewewardy and Hammer, "Culturally Responsive Teaching," 2.

6. Landes, "Teachers and Their Family Cultures," 401.

7. Mann, "Of This Red Earth," 51; Reyhner, "American Indians Out of School," 1–4; Deyhle and Swisher, "Research in American Indian and Alaska Native Education," 116, 153; Reyhner, *American Indian/Alaska Native*, 24; Brewton Berry Research Foundation, *Education of American Indians*, 39; Luftig, "Effects of Schooling," 257; McDermott, "Achieving School Failure," 105; Erikson, *Gandhi's Truth*, 74; Pewewardy and Hammer, "Culturally Responsive Teaching," 24–25.

8. Barnhardt, "Being Native," 137–38; Wolcott, "The Teacher as an Enemy," 411; Hampton, "Toward a Redefinition."

9. Sanders, "Cultural Conflicts," 82–83; Hampton, "Toward a Redefinition," 289; Calsoyas, "Considerations," 307; Fixico, *The American Indian Mind*, 5–6.

10. Klug and Whitfield, *Widening the Circle*, 3, 137; Sanders, "Cultural Conflicts," 86; McDermott, "Achieving School Failure," 105; Christensen, quoted in Gallagher, "Teaching (Native) America," 36.

11. Skinner, "Teaching through Traditions," 111.

12. Christensen, quoted in Gallagher, "Teaching (Native) America"; Deyhle and Swisher, "Research in American Indian and Alaska Native Education," 129–31; McGoldrick and Giordano, "Overview," 1. See Ward, *Native Americans*, 43.

13. Fixico, *The American Indian Mind*, 5; Anderson in introduction to Dorsey and Kroeber, *Traditions of the Arapaho*, xxiii–xxiv; Ruby K. Payne, aha! Process, Inc. Seminar: "A Framework for Understanding Poverty," 2, 12b, February 16, 2004; "Franz Boas," http://en.wikipedia.org/wiki/Franz Boas (accessed September 19, 2012).

14. Reyhner, "American Indians Out of School," 7.

15. Faulkner, *Intruder*, 237; McGoldrick and Giordano, "Overview," 1.

16. Rosenheck, "Impact of Posttraumatic Stress," 326; Rosenheck, "Secondary Traumatization in Children," 539; Childers, *Soldier from the War*, 7–8, 271, 288; Harkness, "Transgenerational Transmission," 635; Davidson and Mellor, "The Adjustment of Australian Vietnam Veterans," 345, 347–48.

17. Scurfield, "Posttraumatic Stress Disorder," 285–86; Whiting et al., "Intergenerational Transmission of Violence," 640; Phil Tingley, president, National Indian Social Workers Association, interviewed in Gale, "Post-Traumatic Stress," 8–10; Klug and Whitfield, *Widening the Circle*, 76–77.

18. Ed McAuslan, Fremont County, Wyoming, coroner, death data, June 16 and 29, 2010, summed by author; Cheryl Beseler, PhD, Colorado State University epidemiologist, email, August 10 and 12, 2010, 1–2 (.05 level of significance), based on data originating from the Fremont County coroner. For race ratios, see 2000 U.S. Census in "Report of William S. Cooper," *Large v. Fremont County, Wyoming*, Pl. Ex. 234, September 15, 2006, 3.

19. McAuslan, chart: "Involvement of Drugs and Alcohol," 2006, received January 5, 2007, 1; U.S. Department of Health and Human Services, CDC, "National Vital Statistics—Deaths: 2006," vol. 57, no. 14, 93, 95; Neary and Moen, "Coroner: Head-on Crash Killed 5," *Washington Post*, November 18, 2011, courtesy of Melissa Friday.

20. Cummins, "Empowering Minority Students," 9–10; Reyhner, "American Indians Out of School," 10. See Leacock, "The Concept of Culture," 424.

21. Department of Health and Human Services, "2005 HIS Expenditures Per Capita Compared to Other Federal Health Expenditure Benchmarks" (a Health and Human Services chart), January 2006; Melissa Friday, pers. comm., September 8, 2012; "Tribes Target Health Problems: Reservation Can Only Handle Emergency Care," CS-T, May 19, 2005, 1, A16; Alvena Friday, telephone comm., August 7, 2012.

22. Patricia L. Garcia, "Commission Discusses Indian Health Care," CS-T, October 18, 2003, B6.

23. Shoshone and Arapaho Minerals Compliance Office, "Oil and Gas Taxes within the Wind River Reservation" (flyer), August 27, 2003; Brodie Farquhar, "Feds Appeal Suit," CS-T, April 8, 2005, B1; "Native Americans Could Win $10B," *USA Today*, February 14, 2002, 1A–4A; "U.S. Finalizes $3.4 Billion," CNN, November 27, 2012, http://edition.cnn.com/2012/11/26/politics/American-indian-settlement /index.html?hpt=us c2 (accessed November 27, 2012).

24. Brodie Farquhar, "Court Gives Green Light to Gambling," CS-T, November 25, 2004, 1, A7; Farquhar, "Tribe Gets Green Light for Gambling," CS-T, July 12, 2005, 1. See Wilkins, *American Indian Politics*, 167–72.

25. Jeff Gearino, "Tribes Seek Return," CS-T, January 17, 2004, 1.

26. U.S. Congress, *No Child Left Behind Act of 2001*; Sherman, *Wasting America's Future*, 62, 63 (statistics from National Center for Education Statistics); Wong, Meyer, and Shen, "Educational Resources and Achievement," 35; O. St. Clair, telephone interview, June 30, 2016, 2; Alyson Klein, "ESEA Reauthorization," *Education Week*, November 30, 2015, blogs.edweek.org/edweek/campaign-k -12/2015/11/esca-reauthorization-the-every.html (accessed July 21, 2019).

27. Manuelito, "The Role of Education," 84; Larson, "Toward a Psychology of Positive Youth Development," 170; Fishman and McCarthy, *John Dewey*, 21.

28. "Leaders Defend Schools," *Lander Journal*, November 3, 2002, 1; "WRIR Schools Named," *Wind River News*, August 7, 2003, 1; Apple, *Cultural Politics and Education*, 32–33; Wells et al., "How Society Failed," 58.

29. Commissioner Atkins, September 21, 1887, Extract from Annual Report, in Prucha, *Documents of Indian Policy*, 174–75.

30. Michelle Hoffman, pers. comm., August 14, 2006; Pamela St. Clair Gambler, interview, May 21, 2012, 1; "Teaching to a Test," CS-T, December 15, 2002, E1; "Wyoming Schools," CS-T, February 23, 2004, 1; Office of English Language Acquisition, U.S. Department of Education, "Celebrate Our Rising Stars!" conference, Washington DC, November 13–15, 2002. See Greg Winter for the *New York Times*, "Rigorous Testing Impedes Student Progress: Scores Decline on Other Key Exams," in *Denver Post*, December 29, 2002, 4A.

31. Johnson, "A New Road?" 33; Apple with Zenk, "American Realities," 68; Michael Dobbs, "NEA, States Challenge 'No Child' Program," *Washington Post*, http://www.washingtonpost.com/wp-dyn/articles/A4741–2005Apr20.html (accessed July 30, 2006); Scott Wiblemo, curriculum director, pers. comm., June 4, 2007; Aimee Tabor, "Wyoming Overhauls PAWS Test," CS-T, April 28, 2007, 5; U.S. Department of Education, *State of Wyoming Consolidated State Application Accountability Workbook*, 2005–6, 22–23.

32. Michelle Hoffman, email, May 31, 2012.

33. Ogbu, "Immigrant and Involuntary Minorities," 8–9, 14–15. See Foley, Levinson, and Hurtig, "Anthropology Goes Inside," 47. See Luftig, "Effects of Schooling," 251; Lyons, "A Captivity Narrative," 97.

34. Klug and Whitfield, *Widening the Circle*, 139; Hani, "Teaching Native American Students," 46. See Deyhle and Swisher, "Research in . . . Native Education," 144–46.

35. Sarah D. Sparks, "NAEP Scores Still Stalled for Native American Students," *Education Week*, July 3, 2012, 1, https://www.edweek.org/ew/articles/2012/07/03/36indian.h31.html (accessed July 21, 2018); PAWS Public Mean Scale Score—District Level (and) State Level (years beginning 2006–7), http://www.k12.wy.us (accessed August 17, 2011); Wiblemo, "WyCAS—PAWS," 1999–2006 graphs by grade and academic year (in-service seminar); PAWS Results, http://fusion.edu.wyoming.gov/Login/web/Pages/PAWSPublicResults. Assessment. PAWS Results (accessed July 12, 2012), see "Final results" section.

36. PAWS Results.

37. PAWS Results.

38. Klug and Whitfield, *Widening the Circle*, 192–94, 203–4; Fishman and McCarthy, *John Dewey*, 30–32; Elizabeth Shogren, "Loophole Lets Toxic Oil Water Flow over Indian Land," NPR, http://www.npr.org/2012/11/15/164688735 (accessed

November 16, 2012); Tippeconnic, quoted in Gallagher, "Teaching (Native) America," 37; Reyhner, "American Indians Out of School," 5.

39. Rural Systemic Initiative and Math and Science Partnership, April 28 and 29, 2006, 1–19, courtesy of Wyoming Indian High School teachers Pamela Gambler and Sandra Iron Cloud. See Calsoyas, "Considerations," 306.

40. Lock, "An Ideal School System," 118, 120.

41. Christensen with Demmert, "The Education of Indians," 139; Kramer, "Education and American Indians," 287–307; Skinner, "Teaching through Traditions," 112; Lee, "Koreans in Japan and the United States," 151–52. See Deyhle and Swisher, "Research in . . . Native Education," 138–50.

42. 2012 Proficiency Assessments for Wyoming Students (PAWS) Standard Accommodation FAQ, http://wyoming.gov/Programs/accomodations.aspx (accessed July 27, 2012); J. Redman, mathematics teacher, interview, May 18, 2012; Bruce Chavez, interview, May 18, 2012; Hoffman, email, May 31, 2012, 1–2; Burton Hutchinson, interviews, September 20, 2004, and October 24, 2005; "Arapaho Veteran Survived," CS-T, December 22, 2006, B1–2.

43. Alvena Friday with Verna Thunder, discussion, January 20, 2003.

44. Patrick Goggles, telephone interview 1, June 26, 2003, 1; Education Statistics, http://www.k12.wy.us (accessed August 17, 2006); Susan C. Faircloth and John W. Tippeconnic, "The Dropout/Graduation Crisis," January 1, 2010, 1, Civil Rights Project, Graduate School of Education and Information Services, UCLA, https://civilrightsproject.ucla.edu/research/k-12-education/school-dropouts/the-dropout-graduation-crisis-among-american-indian-and-alaska-native-students-failure-to-respond-places-the-future-of-native-peoples-at-risk/ (accessed March 24, 2013).

45. Ward, *Native Americans in the School System*, 193.

46. Melissa Friday, email, August 15, 2011.

47. Nell Scott, in Fowler, *Arapahoe Politics*, 202.

48. Dorsey and Kroeber, *Traditions of the Arapaho*, 304–9.

49. Smith, "Why Different Education?" 43.

50. Brenzinger, Heine, and Sommer, "Language Death in Africa," 35.

51. Ken Kidder, photographer, pers. comm., February 3, 2006. See Cohen, "The Shaping of Men's Minds," 27.

52. Anderson, *Four Hills of Life*, 47.

53. Life Size Entertainment and Releasing. See Klug and Whitfield, *Widening the Circle*, 133.

54. "State Rallies," CS-T, January 21, 2003, A1, A10; "White Makes Plight," *Rocky Mountain News*, December 26, 2002, 4A,12A–13A; "Supremacists Not Welcome," *Denver Post*, December 20, 2002, A1, A11.

55. "Landerites—for Diversity," *Lander Journal*, January 1, 2003, A1, A10; "Fighting Hate with Love," *Lander Journal*, January 22, 2003, A1, A10; "Supremacist Arrested," *CS-T*, January 9, 2003, A1, A10; "World Church of the Creator," *CS-T*, March 28, 2004, C1, C2; "Racist Church Pulls up Stakes," *CS-T*, March 29, 2004, A3, A4.

56. Fixico, *The American Indian Mind*, 15.

57. "Continuing the Tradition," *CS-T*, March 6, 2003, C1.

58. Marilyn Groesbeck, interview 2, from unpublished research, December 21, 2001, 2; Deyhle and Swisher, "Research in American Indian and Alaska Native Education," 131; "Progress in Education?" Supplement, *American Demographics* 24 (November 2002): 1–2, EBSCO Host Data Bases, http://web18.epnet.com (accessed May 1, 2004); Melissa Friday, Sky People Higher Education, set of bar graphs, March 18, 2004, 1–6; Iron Cloud, pers. comm., May 5, 2005; Cazden and John, "Learning," 269.

EPILOGUE

1. Barbara Sage, interview 1, June 4, 2001, 1.

2. O. St. Clair, telephone interview, June 30, 2016, 1; City-Data, http://www.city-data.com (accessed August 29, 2011); Jared Miller, "Betting for Better," *CS-T*, September 23, 2007, 1.

3. Neyooxet Greymorning, email, June 18, 2018; Melissa Friday, interview, October 6, 2016, 2; Maia Rose, interview, August 29, 2017.

4. M. Friday, interview; Alejandra Silva, "Development on the Reservation," *Riverton Ranger*, July 27, 2017, 3 (quoting Jason Baldes, at "Wind River Gathering on Economic Development" conference).

5. Heather Richards, "The Remains of Three Northern Arapaho Children Will Be Returned Home to Wyoming," *CS-T*, August 4, 2017, 2; "Student Remains Returned," *Riverton Ranger*, August 17, 2017, 1, 7; Melissa Friday, interview, August, 19, 2017; Betty Friday, discussion, August 19, 2017.

6. Owen St. Clair, telephone interview, June 30, 2016, 1.

7. Fowler, *Arapahoe Politics*, 227, 286; U.S. Department of the Interior, Indian Affairs, https://www.bia.gov/regional-offices/southern-plains/court-indian-offenses; Melissa Friday, interview, November 18, 2017.

8. Richard Ortiz, interview, April 4, 2006; Fowler, *Arapahoe Politics*, 260, 286.

9. Pamela Kaulaity, discussion, September 19, 2017.

10. Finkel-Hoffman, "From Wisconsin to Wyoming," 28–30.

11. "New Wind River Casino to open May 1," *Wyoming Business Report*, http://www.wyomingbusinessreport.com/article.asp?id=92214 (accessed October 11, 2009); "Casino Hotel Has Ceremony," *Riverton Ranger*, March 8, 2012, 1.

12. M. Friday, interview, October 6, 2016; Alvena Friday, telephone interview, February 18, 2009, and October 28, 2017.

13. Alysa Landry, "Ramah Chapter Wins $940M Settlement," *Navajo Times*, September 24, 2015, 1, and "The Ramah Settlement," A11; Associated Press, "U.S. to Pay $940 Million to Settle Claims Over Tribal Contracts," *Wall Street Journal*, September 17, 2015, 1–3.

BIBLIOGRAPHY

ARCHIVAL AND UNPUBLISHED SOURCES

Anonymous. "Black Coal and Missionaries," 1–32. Saint Stephen's Mission Jesuit Papers, microfilm (series 7-1, reel 2), n.d. (1983?), Department of Special Collections and University Archives, Raynor Memorial Libraries, Marquette University, Milwaukee, Wisconsin.

Gress, Betty L., acting executive director, Coalition of Indian Controlled School Boards, Inc. "Statement of the Coalition of Indian Controlled School Boards, Inc." Report, communicated to the House Subcommittee on Elementary, Secondary and Vocational Education in conjunction with the Advisory Study Group on Indian Education of the Committee on Education and Labor (May 18, 1977), 1–17.

Hoferer, Michael J., SJ. "Some Facts and Incidents Taken from the Annuals of the Sisters of St. Francis Relating to St. Stephen's Mission" (1924), 1–6. Saint Stephen's Mission Jesuit Papers, microfilm (series 7-1), Department of Special Collections and University Archives, Raynor Memorial Libraries, Marquette University, Milwaukee, Wisconsin.

Kahin, Sharon, project director. "From Trout Creek to Gravy High: The Boarding School Experience at Wind River." Warm Valley Historical Project, sponsored by the Shoshone Episcopal Mission's Warm Valley Historical Project, 1992–93.

Kellam, Harry M., warden, St. Michael's Episcopal Church Mission. Letter to Office of the Rector, Rev. Patrick A. McGovern, May 14, 1942, 1. Saint Stephen's Mission Jesuit Papers, microfilm (series 1-1), Department of Special Collections and University Archives, Raynor Memorial Libraries, Marquette University, Milwaukee, Wisconsin.

Lone Bear, chief of Arapahoe Tribe of Indians. Letter to Rev. William H. Ketchum, Washington DC, January 13, 1912, 1. Saint Stephen's Mission Jesuit Papers, microfilm (series 1-1), Department of Special Collections and University Archives, Raynor Memorial Libraries, Marquette University, Milwaukee, Wisconsin.

Patch, Eugene G., assistant principal at Lander Valley High School. Deposition by attorneys W. A. Smith, R. I. Leedy, and Michael P. Gross, October 2, 1973. In *Alfred Ward, et al. . . . v. Robert G. Schrader, et al.* Civil No. 16307 and Civil No. 16342.

Prendergast, George P. Letter to Father Provincial, P.C., May 31, 1942. Saint Stephen's Mission Jesuit Papers, microfilm (series 1-1), Department of Special Collections and University Archives, Raynor Memorial Libraries, Marquette University, Milwaukee, Wisconsin.

Reynolds, Jerry. "The Rebecca Adamson Archive." Under a grant from the W. K. Kellogg Foundation and the Bay and Paul Foundation. Sophia Smith Collections, Smith College, Northampton, Massachusetts.

Stansell, Harry L. "The Jesuits in Wyoming: The First Hundred Years" (n.d.), 5–40. Saint Stephen's Mission Jesuit Papers, microfilm (series 7-1), Department of Special Collections and University Archives, Raynor Memorial Libraries, Marquette University, Milwaukee, Wisconsin.

Zuercher, Albert C. Letter to "Father Superior" (no name given), February 18, 1938, 1. Saint Stephen's Mission Jesuit Papers, microfilm (series 1-1), Department of Special Collections and University Archives, Raynor Memorial Libraries, Marquette University, Milwaukee, Wisconsin.

PUBLISHED SOURCES

Alexander, Michelle. *The New Jim Crow: Mass Incarceration in the Age of Colorblindness.* New York: New Press, 2010.

Alfred Ward, et al., Appellants, Lawrence J. Geraud, et al., Appellants, Fremont County Vocational High School District and Lander School District No. 1, Appellants, v. Robert G. Schrader, et al., Appellees, Wind River Indian Education Association, Appellee, Geraud v. Schrader, 1975 WY 9, 531 P. 2d 872.

Amundson, Michael A. *Yellowcake Towns: Uranium Mining Communities in the American West.* Louisville: University Press of Colorado, 2002.

Anderson, Jeffrey D. *The Four Hills of Life.* Lincoln: University of Nebraska Press, 2001.

Apple, Michael W. *Cultural Politics and Education.* New York: Teachers College Press, Columbia University, 1996.

Apple, Michael, with Christopher Zink. "American Realities: Poverty, Economy, and Education." In *Cultural Politics and Education,* edited by Michael W. Apple, 68–90. New York: Teachers College Press, Columbia University, 1996.

Barnhardt, Raymond J. "Being Native and Becoming a Teacher in the Alaska Rural Teacher Training Corps." In *The Collected Papers of the Northern Cross-Cultural Education Symposium,* edited by F. Berry, 129–80. Fairbanks: University of Alaska, 1974.

Barrington, John M. "The New Zealand Experience: Maoris." In *Minority Status and Schooling: A Comparative Study of Immigrant and Involuntary Minorities,*

248 BIBLIOGRAPHY

edited by Margaret A. Gibson and John U. Ogbu, 309–26. New York: Garland Publishing, 1991.

Bass, Willard P., and Henry G. Burger. *American Indians and Educational Laboratories*. Publication No. 1-1167, Contract No. OEC-4-7-062827-3078. Albuquerque: U.S. Department of Health, Education and Welfare, Southwestern Cooperative Educational Laboratory, 1967.

Bieder, Robert E. "Scientific Attitudes Toward Indian Mixed-Bloods in Early Nineteenth Century America." *International Migration Review* 14, no. 2 (Summer 1980): 17–30.

Bordeaux, Roger. "Assessment for American Indian and Alaska Native Learners." ERIC Clearinghouse on Rural Education and Small Schools, September 1995.

———. *Our Children, Our Schools, Our Tribes: Thirty Years of Local Control of Indian Education 1966–1996*. Sisseton SD: Association of Community Tribal Schools, 1996.

Boyer, Paul. "It Takes a Native: Educators Reform Schools in an Era of Standards." *Tribal College Journal of American Indian Higher Education* 17, no. 4 (Summer 2006): 14–19.

Brenzinger, Matthias, Bernd Heine, and Gabriele Sommer. "Language Death in Africa." In *Endangered Languages*, edited by Robert H. Robins and Eugenius M. Uhlenbeck, 19–44. Oxford: Berg, 1991.

Brewton Berry Research Foundation. *The Education of American Indians: A Survey of the Literature*. Prepared at the request of the Special Subcommittee on Indian Education of the (Senate) Committee on Labor and Public Welfare, Project No. 7-0813. Washington DC: U.S. Department of Health, Education, and Welfare, Office of Education, Bureau of Research, 1968.

Brown, Dee. *Bury My Heart at Wounded Knee*. New York: Holt, Rinehart and Winston, 1970.

Brown v. Board of Education of Topeka, 347 U.S. 483 (May 17, 1954).

Buckanaga, Jerome. "Interracial Politics: The Pressure to Integrate an Experimental School." In *The Schooling of Native America*, edited by Thomas Thompson, 52–71. Washington DC: American Association of Colleges for Teacher Education in collaboration with the Teacher Corps United States Office of Education, 1978.

Calloway, Colin G. *First Peoples: A Documentary Survey of American Indian History*. 2nd ed. Boston: Bedford–St. Martin's, 2004.

Calsoyas, Kyril. "Considerations in the Educational Process Relative to Native Americans." *Cambridge Journal of Education* 35, no. 3 (November 2005): 301–10.

Campbell County School Dist. v. State, 1995 WY 184, 907 P.2d 1238.

Castile, George P. "Native North Americans and the National Question." In *The Political Economy of North American Indians*, edited by John H. Moore, 270–94. Norman: University of Oklahoma Press, 1993.

Cazden, Courtney B., and Vera P. John. "Learning in American Indian Children." In *Anthropological Perspectives on Education*, edited by Murray L. Wax, Stanley Diamond, and Fred O. Gearing, 252–72. New York: Basic Books, 1971.

Cedartree, Helen. *Wind River Memories*. Wyoming Indian High School Library, District No. 14. Ethete WY: Title IV Curriculum Development Project, 1984.

Chiefs. Directed by Daniel Junge. Parsippany NJ: Life Size Entertainment and Releasing, 2002.

Childers, Thomas. *Soldier from the War Returning: The Greatest Generation's Troubled Homecoming from World War II*. Boston: Houghton Mifflin Harcourt, 2009.

Christensen, Rosemary Ackley, with William G. Demmert. "The Education of Indians and the Mandate of History." In *The Schooling of Native America*, edited by Thomas Thompson, 139–52. Washington DC: American Association of Colleges for Teacher Education in collaboration with the Teacher Corps United States Office of Education, 1978.

Churchill, Ward. "A Question of Identity." In *A Will to Survive: Indigenous Essays on the Politics of Culture, Language, and Identity*, edited by Stephen Greymorning, 59–94. Boston: McGraw-Hill, 2004.

Cohen, Felix S. *Handbook of Federal Indian Law*. Washington DC: GPO, 1942.

Cohen, Yehudi A. "The Shaping of Men's Minds: Adaptations to Imperatives of Culture." In *Anthropological Perspectives on Education*, edited by Murray L. Wax, Stanley Diamond, and Fred O. Gearing, 19–50. New York: Basic Books, 1971.

Coleman, Michael C. *American Indian Children at School, 1850–1930*. Jackson: University Press of Mississippi, 1993.

Coltelli, Laura. *Winged Words: American Indian Writers Speak*. Lincoln: University of Nebraska Press, 1990.

Cornell, Stephen, Joseph Kalt, Matthew Krepps, and Jonathan Taylor. *American Indian Gaming Policy and Its Socio-Economic Effects: A Report to the National Gambling Impact Study Commission*. Cambridge MA: Economics Resource Group, 1998.

Coutant, C. G. *History of Wyoming*. 3 vols. 1899; reprint, Laramie WY: Spafford and Mathison, 1966.

Crum, Steven J. *The Road on Which We Came: Po'i Pentun Tammen Kimmappeh*. Salt Lake City: University of Utah Press, 1994.

Cummins, Jim. "Empowering Minority Students: A Framework for Intervention." *Harvard Educational Review* 71, no. 4 (Winter 2001): 1–17.

Curriculum Development Workshop (CDW). *The Wind River Reservation Yesterday, Today and Tomorrow*. Dir. Larry Murray, revision editors Gloria Goggles, Gary Miller, and Donnie Chavez. First published as *The Wind River Reservation Yesterday and Today*, Wyoming State Department of Education and Wind River Agency, 1972; rev. ed. Wyoming Council for the Humanities, 1999.

Daly, Lowrie J., "For God and Country: The Story of St. Stephen's Mission." *Jesuit Bulletin* 39, no. 6 (1960): 3–6, 18.

Davidson, Ann C., and David J. Mellor. "The Adjustment of Australian Vietnam Veterans: Is There Evidence for the Transgenerational Transmission of the Effects of War-Related Trauma?" *Australian and New Zealand Journal of Psychiatry* 35 (2001): 345–51.

Dawson, Howard A. "A Current Look at School District Reorganization in the United States." *Teachers College Journal* 29, no. 6 (May 1958): 82–86.

Deloria, Vine, Jr. *Indian Education in America.* Boulder CO: American Indian Science and Engineering Society, 1994 (first published in *Winds of Change* magazine).

Deyhle, Donna. "Navajo Youth and Anglo Racism: Cultural Integrity and Resistance." *Harvard Educational Review* 65, no. 3 (Fall 1995): 403–44.

Deyhle, Donna, and Karen Swisher. "Research in American Indian and Alaska Native Education: From Assimilation to Self-Determination." In *Review of Research in Education*, edited by Michael W. Apple, 113–94. Washington DC: American Educational Research Association, 1997.

Diamond, Jared. *Guns, Germs and Steel: The Fates of Human Societies.* New York: W. W. Norton and Company, 1999.

Dick, Galena Sells, Dan W. Estell, and Teresa L. McCarty. "Saad Naakih Bee'enootíílji Na'alkaa: Restructuring the Teaching of Language and Literacy in a Navajo Community School." *Journal of American Indian Education* (1994): 31–47.

Dorsey, George A. *The Arapaho Sun Dance: The Ceremony of the Offerings Lodge.* Field Columbian Museum Publication 75. Chicago: Field Museum, 1903.

Dorsey, George A., and Alfred L. Kroeber. *Traditions of the Arapaho.* Trans. Southern Arapaho Cleaver Warden. Field Museum, 1903; reprint, Lincoln: University of Nebraska Press, 1997.

Duncombe, Edward S. "Ethete: Episcopal Churchwork among the Northern Arapahoes 1883–1925." MA thesis, University of Wyoming, December 1981.

Equality State Policy Center. "The Wind River Reservation Boundary Dispute— Some Facts." http://equalitystate.org/assets/media/ESPC_FAQ_WRR _BoundaryDispute.pdf.

Erikson, Erik H. *Gandhi's Truth: On the Origins of Militant Nonviolence.* New York: W. W. Norton and Company, 1969.

Faulkner, William. *Intruder in the Dust.* New York: Vintage International, 1948.

Finkel-Hoffman, Susan. "From Wisconsin to Wyoming and Back Again: The Journey to a Bachelor's Degree and Teacher Licensure." *Tribal College: Journal of American Indian Higher Education* 27, no. 3 (Spring 2016): 28–30.

Fishman, Joshua A. "Minority Mother Tongues in Education." *Prospects* 14, no. 1 (1984): 51–61.

Fishman, Stephen, and Lucille McCarthy. *John Dewey and the Challenge of Classroom Practice.* New York: Teachers College Press, 1998.

Fixico, Donald L. *The American Indian Mind in a Linear World: American Indian Studies and Traditional Knowledge.* New York: Routledge, Taylor and Francis Group, 2003.

———. *The Invasion of Indian Country in the Twentieth Century: American Capitalism and Tribal Natural Resources.* Niwot: University of Colorado Press, 1998.

Flannery, Thomas Patrick. "The Indian Self-Determination Act: An Analysis of Federal Policy." PhD diss., Northwestern University, August 1980.

Foley, Douglas A., Bradley A. Levinson, and Janise Hurtig. "Anthropology Goes Inside: The New Educational Ethnography of Ethnicity and Gender." In *Review of Research in Education,* edited by Walter G. Secada, 37–98. Washington DC: American Educational Research Association, 2001.

Forbes, Jack D. *Native Americans and Nixon: Presidential Politics and Minority Self-Determination, 1969–1972.* Los Angeles: University of California, American Indian Studies Center, 1981.

Fosher, John. Report of Agent. Shoshone Agency, Wyoming, July 31, 1893. In *Report of the Secretary of the Interior,* 53rd Cong., 2nd sess., H. Executive Docs. (Washington DC, 1893–94).

Fowler, Loretta Kay. *Arapahoe Politics, 1851–1878: Symbols in Crises of Authority.* Lincoln: University of Nebraska Press, 1982.

Friday, Ben, Sr. *The Story of Friday (Sitting in the Meek).* Edited by William J. C'Hair. Wyoming Indian School Library, District No. 14. Ethete WY: Office of Indian Education, Title IV, Indian Education Act, grant no. G007604575, n.d.

Fuchs, Estelle, and Robert Havighurst. *To Live on This Earth.* Albuquerque: University of New Mexico Press, 1972.

Gaillard, Frye. "Indian Community Control Coalition." *Race Relations Reporter* 2, no. 19 (October 18, 1971): 1.

———. "Indians Demand Bureau Reform." *Race Relations Reporter* 2, no. 18 (October 4, 1971): 7–12.

———. "'We'll Do It Our Own Way Awhile.'" *Race Relations Reporter* 3, no. 1 (January 3, 1972): 21–27.

Gale, Nancy. "Post-Traumatic Stress: What Some Indian Youth and Vietnam Veterans Have in Common." U.S. Department of Education, Office of Educational Research and Improvement, Educational Resources Information Center, 1990, 1–19.

Gallagher, Brian Thomas. "Teaching (Native) America." *Nation,* June 5, 2000, 36.

Gàndara, Patricia, Rachel Moran, and Eugene Garcia. "Legacy of *Brown: Lau* and Language Policy in the United, States." In *Review of Research in Education,* edited by Robert E. Floden, 27–46. Washington DC: American Educational Research Association, 2004.

Gay, Geneva. "Curriculum Theory and Multicultural Education." In *Handbook of Research on Multicultural Education*, edited by James A. Banks and Cherry A. McGee Banks, 30–49. San Francisco: Jossey-Bass, 2004.

Getches, David H., and Charles F. Wilkinson. *Federal Indian Law: Cases and Materials, Second Edition.* American Casebook Series. St. Paul MN: West Publishing Company, 1986.

———. "The Rights of Individual Indians." In Getches and Wilkinson, *Federal Indian Law*, 548–98.

Graham, Hugh Davis. *The Civil Rights Era: Origins and Development of National Policy.* New York: Oxford University Press, 1990.

Greymorning, Stephen (Hiitoo3oobetit Neniice'ooke). "Hinono'eitiino'oowu' and the Work of Language Survival." In *A Will to Survive: Indigenous Essays on the Politics of Culture, Language, and Identity*, edited by Stephen Greymorning, 212–24. Boston: McGraw-Hill, 2004.

Gross, Michael P. "Indian Control for Quality Indian Education." *North Dakota Law Review* 49, no. 2 (1973): 237–65.

———. "Indian Self-Determination and Tribal Sovereignty: An Analysis of Recent Federal Indian Policy." *Texas Law Review* 56, no. 7 (1978): 1195–224.

———. "Reckoning for Legal Services: A Case Study of Legal Assistance in Indian Education." *Notre Dame Lawyer* 49, no. 78 (October 1973): 78–104.

Hafen, Leroy R. *Brokenhand, The Life of Thomas Fitzpatrick: Mountain Man, Guide and Indian Agent.* Lincoln: University of Nebraska Press, 1973.

Hampton, Eber. "Toward a Redefinition of American Indian/Alaska Native Education." *Canadian Journal of Native Education* 20, no. 2 (1993): 261–309.

Hani, Morgan. "Teaching Native American Students: What Every Teacher Should Know." *Education Digest* 75, no. 6 (February 2010): 44–47.

Harkness, Laurie Leydic. "Transgenerational Transmission of War-Related Trauma." In *International Handbook of Traumatic Stress Syndromes*, edited by John P. Wilson and Beverley Raphael, 635–43. New York: Plenum Press, 1993.

Hertzberg, Hazel W. *The Search for an American Indian Identity: Modern Pan-Indian Movements.* New York: Syracuse University Press, 1971.

Hoig, Stan. *The Sand Creek Massacre.* Norman: University of Oklahoma Press, 1961.

Holm, Agnes, and Wayne Holm. "Rock Point, A Navajo Way to Go to School: A Valediction." *Annals of the American Academy of Political Science* 508 (March 1990): 170–84.

Ilutsik, Esther A. "The Founding of Ciulistet: One Teacher's Journey." *Journal of American Indian Education*, Spring 1994, 6–13.

Jackson, Donald, ed. *Letters of the Lewis and Clark Expedition with Related Documents, 1783–1854*. Urbana: University of Illinois Press, 1962.

Johnson, Richard. "A New Road to Serfdom? A Critical History of the 1988 Act." In *Education Limited, Schooling, Training and the New Right in England since 1979*, edited by Education Group II, Department of Cultural Studies, University of Birmingham, 31–86. London: Unwin Hyman, 1991.

Joint Business Council of the Eastern Shoshone and Northern Arapaho Tribes. *Looking to the Future of the Wind River Indian Reservation: Executive Summary of the Wind River Indian Needs Determination Survey (Winds-2)*. Fort Washakie: Joint Business Council of the Eastern Shoshone and Northern Arapaho Tribes, 1999.

Jones, William A. Sixty-Sixth Annual Report of the Commissioner of Indian Affairs, Washington DC, September 10, 1897, 13.

Josephy, Alvin M., Jr. *Red Power: The American Indians' Fight for Freedom*. New York: American Heritage Press, 1971.

Kamanā, Kauanoe, "Reflections and Feelings Deriving from a Pulakaumaka within My Heart." In *A Will to Survive: Indigenous Essays on the Politics of Culture, Language, and Identity*, edited by Stephen Greymorning, 200–211. Boston: McGraw-Hill, 2004.

Kelly, Lawrence C. "Charles Henry Burke 1921–29." In *The Commissioners of Indian Affairs, 1824–1977*, edited by Robert M. Kvasnicka and Herman J. Viola, 251–61. Lincoln: University of Nebraska Press, 1979.

———. "Charles James Rhoads 1929–33." In *The Commissioners of Indian Affairs, 1824–1977*, edited by Robert M. Kvasnicka and Herman J. Viola, 263–71. Lincoln: University of Nebraska Press, 1979.

Keyes v. Denver School District No. 1, 413 U.S. 184 (June 21, 1973), 412 U.S. 200. http://supreme.justia.com/us/413/189/case.html (accessed October 13, 2008).

Klug, Beverly J., and Patricia T. Whitfield. *Widening the Circle: Culturally Relevant Pedagogy for American Indian Children*. New York: RoutledgeFalmer, 2003.

Kramer, Betty Jo. "Education and American Indians: The Experience of the Ute Indian Tribe." In *Minority Status and Schooling: A Comparative Study of Immigrant and Involuntary Minorities*, edited by Margaret A. Gibson and John U. Ogbu, 287–307. New York: Garland Publishing, 1991.

Kroeker, Wally. *An Introduction to the Russian Mennonites: A Story of Flights and Resettlements*. Intercourse PA: Good Books, 2005.

Kruse, Babs, ed. *The Wind River Reservation, 1865–1910: Historical Photographs and Anecdotes*. Wyoming Indian High School Library, District No. 14. Ethete WY: Title IV Curriculum Development Project, 1984.

Landes, Ruth. "Teachers and Their Family Cultures." In *Schooling in the Cultural Context*, part 6, edited by Joan I. Roberts and Sherrie K. Akinsanya, 401–18. New York: David McKay Company, 1976.

Larson, Reed W. "Toward a Psychology of Positive Youth Development." *American Psychologist* 55, no. 1 (January 2000): 170–83.

Larson, T. A. *History of Wyoming*. Lincoln: University of Nebraska Press, 1965.

———. *Wyoming: A Bicentennial History*. New York: W. W. Norton and Company, 1977.

Lawlor v. Board of Education of City of Chicago, 458 F.2d 660 (7th Cir. April 10, 1972).

Leacock, Elanor Burke. "The Concept of Culture and Its Significance for School Counselors." In *Schooling in the Cultural Context*, part 6, edited by Joan I. Roberts and Sherrie K. Akinsanya, 418–26. New York: David McKay Company, 1976.

Lee, Yongsook. "Koreans in Japan and the United States." In *Minority Status and Schooling: A Comparative Study of Immigrant and Involuntary Minorities*, edited by Margaret A. Gibson and John U. Ogbu, 131–67. New York: Garland Publishing, 1991.

Lieberman, Myron. *The Future of Public Education*. 1960; reprint, Chicago: University of Chicago Press, 1963.

Lipka, Jerry. "Culturally Negotiated Schooling: Toward a Yup'ik Mathematics." *Journal of American Indian Education*, Spring 1994, 14–30.

Lock, Patricia. "An Ideal School System for American Indians: A Theoretical Construct." In *The Schooling of Native America*, 119–36. Washington DC: American Association of Colleges for Teacher Education in Collaboration with the Teacher Corps, 1978.

Loevy, Robert D. "A Chronology of the Civil Rights Act of 1964." In *The Civil Rights Act of 1964: The Passage of the Law That Ended Racial Segregation*, edited by Robert D. Loevy, 353–61. New York: State University of New York Press, 1997.

Lomawaima, K. Tsiannina, and Teresa L. McCarty. *To Remain an Indian: Lessons in Democracy from a Century of Native American Education*. New York: Teachers College Columbia University, 2006.

Luftig, Richard L. "Effects of Schooling on the Self-Concept of Native American Students." *School Counselor* 30, no. 4 (March 1983): 251–60.

Lyons, Scott. "A Captivity Narrative: Indians, Mixedbloods, and 'White' Academe." In *Outbursts in Academe: Multiculturalism and Other Sources of Conflict*, edited by Kathleen Dixon, 87–108. Portsmouth NH: Boynton/Cook Publishers, 1998.

Mankiewicz, Frank. *U.S. v. Richard M. Nixon: The Final Crisis*. New York: Quadrangle—New York Times Book Company, 1975.

Mann, Henrietta. "Of This Red Earth." In *A Will to Survive: Indigenous Essays on the Politics of Culture, Language, and Identity*, edited by Stephen Greymorning, 47–58. Boston: McGraw-Hill, 2004.

Manuelito, Kathryn. "The Role of Education in American Indian Self-Determination: Lessons from the Ramah Navajo Community School." *Anthropology and Education Quarterly* 36, no. 1 (2005): 73–87.

Markley, Elinor R., and Beatrice Crofts. *Walk Softly, This Is God's Country*. Lander WY: Mortimer Publishing, 1997.

May, Stephen. Introduction to *Indigenous Community-Based Education*, edited by Stephen May. Clevedon: Multilingual Matters, 1999.

McCarty, Teresa L. "Bilingual Education Policy and the Empowerment of American Indian Communities." *Journal of Educational Issues of Language Minority Students* 14 (Winter 1994): 23–40. http://www.ncela.gwu.edu/pubs/jeilms/vol14/mccarty.htm (accessed July 13, 2005).

——— . *A Place to Be Navajo: Rough Rock and the Struggle for Self-Determination in Indigenous Schooling*. Mahwah NJ: Lawrence Erlbaum Associates, 2002.

McDermott, R. P. "Achieving School Failure: An Anthropological Approach to Illiteracy and Social Stratification." In *Education and Cultural Process: Toward an Anthropology of Education*, edited by George Dearborn Spindler, 82–118. New York: Holt, Rinehart and Winston, 1974.

McDonald, Laughlin. *American Indians and the Fight for Equal Voting Rights*. Norman: University of Oklahoma Press, 2010.

McGoldrick, Monica, and Joe Giordano. "Overview: Ethnicity and Family Therapy." In *Ethnicity and Family Therapy*, edited by Monica McGoldrick and Joe Giordano. New York: Guilford Press, 1996.

Means, Russell. *Where White Men Fear to Tread*. New York: St. Martin's Griffin, 1995.

Meriam, Lewis, and Staff at the Institute for Government Research Studies in Administration. *The Problem of Indian Administration*. Baltimore: Johns Hopkins Press, 1928.

Milliken v. Bradley, 418 U.S. 717 (July 25, 1974). http://laws.findlaw.com/us/418/717.html (accessed November 15, 2012).

Mooney, James. *The Ghost-Dance Religion and the Sioux Outbreak of 1890*. Lincoln: University of Nebraska Press, 1991.

The Multi-Ethnic Think Tank. *Call to Action: Mandating an Equitable and Culturally Competent Education for All Students in Washington State*. Washington State: Community Outreach of the Office of Superintendent of Public Instruction, October 2002.

National Center for Educational Statistics. "The Landscape of Public Education: A Statistical Portrait Through the Years." *Epicenter*, April 2011. http://www.educationalpolicy.org/publications/EPI%20Center/EPICenter_K-12.pdf (accessed July 24, 2017).

Nixon, Richard. "Special Message to the Congress on Indian Affairs," July 8, 1970. American Presidency Project, http://www.presidency.ucsb.edu/ws/?pid=2573.

Oakleaf, Barbara. "Origins of Fremont County Library Date to 1906." *Wind River Mountaineer* 19, no. 1 (April 2007).

O'Brien, Sharon. *American Indian Tribal Governments*. Norman: University of Oklahoma Press, 1989.

Ogbu, John U. "Immigrant and Involuntary Minorities in Comparative Perspective." In *Minority Status and Schooling: A Comparative Study of Immigrant and Involuntary Minorities*, edited by Margaret A. Gibson and John U. Ogbu, 3–33. New York: Garland Publishing, 1991.

Ourada, Patricia. "Dillon Seymour Meyer." In *The Commissioners of Indian Affairs, 1824–1977*, edited by Robert M. Kvasnicka and Herman J. Viola, 251–61. Lincoln: University of Nebraska Press, 1979.

Painter, Donald L., and Robert H. Johnson. "The Wyoming Education Code of 1969." *Land and Water Law Review* 5, no. 2 (1970): 531–76.

Peltier, Leonard. *Prison Writings: My Life Is My Sun Dance*. Edited by Harvey Arden. New York: St. Martin's Griffin, 1999.

Pewewardy, Cornel, and Patricia Cahape Hammer. "Culturally Responsive Teaching for American Indian Students." ERIC Clearinghouse on Rural Education and Small Schools, 2003.

Philp, Kenneth R. "John Collier 1933–45." In *the Commissioners of Indian Affairs, 1824–1977*, edited by Robert M. Kvasnicka and Herman J. Viola, 273–82. Lincoln: University of Nebraska Press, 1979.

Platero, Dillon. "Multicultural Teacher Education Center at Rough Rock." In *The Schooling of Native America*, edited by Thomas Thompson, 44–51. Washington DC: American Association of Colleges for Teacher Education in collaboration with the Teacher Corps United States Office of Education, 1978.

Plessy v. Ferguson, 163 U.S. 537, 165. Ct. 1138, 41 L. Ed. 256, 1896 U.S. 339.

Pratt, Mary Louise. "Arts of the Contact Zone." *Profession*, 1991, 33–40.

Prucha, Francis Paul. *The Churches and the Indian Schools, 1888–1912*. Lincoln: University of Nebraska Press, 1979.

——, ed. *Documents of United States Indian Policy*. Lincoln: University of Nebraska Press, 1975.

——. *The Great Father: The United States Government and the American Indians*. Lincoln: University of Nebraska Press, 1984.

Putney, Diane T. "Fighting the Scourge: American Indian Morbidity and Federal Policy, 1897–1928." PhD diss., Marquette University, Milwaukee, Wisconsin, April 1980.

Redman, John Charles et al. v. John R. Ottina. Civil Action No. 628-73. United States District Court for the District of Columbia.

Reyhner, Jon Allen. *American Indian/Alaska Native Education.* Bloomington IN: Phi Delta Kappa Educational Foundation, 1994.

——. "American Indians Out of School: A Review of School-Based Causes and Solutions." *Journal of American Indian Education* 31, no. 2 (1992): 1–14.

Reyhner, Jon Allen, and Jeanne Eder. *American Indian Education: A History.* Norman: University of Oklahoma Press, 2004.

Rosenfeld, Gerry. *"Shut Those Thick Lips!": A Study of Slum School Failure.* New York: Holt, Rinehart and Winston, 1971.

Rosenfelt, Daniel M. "Indian Schools and Community Control." *Stanford Law Review* 25, no. 4 (April 1973): 489–533.

——. "New Regulations for Federal Indian Funds." *Inequality in Education*, no. 10 (December 1971): 22–26.

——. "Toward a More Coherent Policy for Funding Indian Education." In *Law and Contemporary Problems: Indian Education*, edited by Lawrence Rosen, 190–223. Durham NC: School of Law, Duke University, 1976.

Rosenheck, Robert. "Impact of Posttraumatic Stress Disorder of World War II on the Next Generation." *Journal of Nervous and Mental Disease* 174, no. 6 (1986): 319–27.

——. "Secondary Traumatization in Children of Vietnam Veterans." *Hospital and Community Psychiatry* 36, no. 5 (May 1985): 538–39.

Sage, Barbara. *Tribal Government at Wind River: The Modern Era.* Wyoming Indian High School Library, District No. 14. Ethete WY: Title IV Curriculum Development Project, 1982–85.

Sanders, Danielle. "Cultural Conflicts: An Important Factor in the Academic Failures of American Indian Students." *Journal of Multicultural Counseling and Development*, April 1987, 81–90.

Saville-Troike, Muriel. "Language Instruction and Multicultural Education." In *Multicultural Education: Commitments, Issues, and Applications*, edited by Carl A. Grant, 52–59. Washington DC: Association for Supervision and Curriculum Development, 1977.

Schierbeck, Helen. "Education = Cultural Politics." *Inequality in Education*, no. 7 (February 10, 1971): 3–14.

Scurfield, Raymond Monsour. "Posttraumatic Stress Disorder in Vietnam Veterans." In *International Handbook of Traumatic Stress Syndromes*, edited by John P. Wilson and Beverley Raphael, 285–95. New York: Plenum Press, 1993.

Senese, Guy B. *Self-Determination and the Social Education of Native Americans.* New York: Praeger Publishers, 1991.

Shakespeare, Tom. *The Sky People.* New York: Vantage Press, 1971.

Sherman, Arloc. *Wasting America's Future: The Children's Defense Fund Report on the Costs of Child Poverty*. Boston: Beacon Press, 1994.

Shimkin, Demitri B. "Eastern Shoshone." In *Handbook of North American Indians*, vol. 11, *Great Basin*, edited by Warren L. D'Azevedo, 308–35. Washington DC: Smithsonian Institution Press, 1986.

Siebert, Roger David. "A History of the Shoshone Indians of Wyoming." MA thesis, University of Wyoming, 1961.

Skinner, Linda. "Teaching through Traditions: Incorporating Languages and Culture into Curricula." In *Next Steps: Research and Practice to Advance Indian Education*, edited by Karen Gayton Swisher and John W. Tippeconnic III, 107–34. Charleston WV: ERIC Clearinghouse on Rural Education and Small Schools, 1999.

Smith, William L. "Why Different Education for Different Groups?" In *Multicultural Education: Commitments, Issues, and Applications*, edited by Carl A. Grant, 40–44. Washington DC: Association for Supervision and Curriculum Development, 1977.

Spindler, George D. "Why Have Minority Groups in North America been Disadvantaged by Their Schools?" In *Education and Cultural Process: Toward an Anthropology of Education*, edited by George D. Spindler, 69–81. New York: Holt, Rinehart and Winston, 1974.

Stamm, Henry E., IV. *People of the Wind River: The Eastern Shoshones 1825–1900*. Norman: University of Oklahoma Press, 1999.

State of Wyoming. *Constitution of the State of Wyoming Including All Amendments Adopted to January 1, 1957*. Compiled and reprinted by Everett T. Copenhaver, Secretary of State.

——. "School District Organization Law." *Wyoming Statutes 1977*.

——. "Wyoming Education Code of 1969." In Session Laws of Wyoming, 1969 (Ch. 111), Ch. 6, "School District Organization," Original Senate File No. 10, 176–84.

——. *Wyoming Education Code of 1969 as Amended* (21-3-101), June 1979.

——. "Wyoming School District Organization Law of 1969." *Wyoming Statutes 1977*.

Strang, William, Adrienne von Glatz, and Patricia Cahape Hammer. "Setting the Agenda: American Indian and Alaska Native Education Research Priorities." ERIC Clearinghouse on Rural Education and Small Schools, December 2002.

Sturm, Circe. *Blood Politics: Race, Culture, and Identity in the Cherokee Nation of Oklahoma*. Berkeley: University of California Press, 2002.

Szasz, Margaret Connell. *Education and the American Indian: The Road to Self-Determination since 1928*. Albuquerque: University of New Mexico Press, 1984.

Tippeconnic, John W., III. "Tribal Control of American Indian Education: Observations since the 1960s with Implications for the Future." In *Next Steps: Research and Practice to Advance Indian Education*, edited by Karen Gayton Swisher and

John W. Tippiconnic III, 33–52. Charleston WV: ERIC Clearinghouse on Rural Education and Small Schools, 1999.

Uchida, Yoshiko. *Desert Exile*. 1982; reprint, Seattle: University of Washington Press, 2002.

Ulrich, Roberta. *American Indian Nations from Termination to Restoration, 1953–2006*. Lincoln: University of Nebraska Press, 2010.

U.S. Congress. "An Act Authorizing the Secretary of the Interior to arrange with States or Territories for the Education, Medical Attention, Relief of Distress, and Social Welfare of Indians, and for Other Purposes (Johnson-O'Malley Act)." In *The Statutes at Large: Recent Treaties and Conventions, Executive Proclamations and Agreements*. 21st Amendment to the Constitution, 73rd Cong., 2nd sess. (from March 1933 to June 1934). Washington DC: GPO, 1934, vol. 48 (pt.1, ch. 147): 596.

——— . "For Support of Schools." In *The Statutes at Large and Recent Treaties, Conventions, and Executive Proclamations*. 51st Cong., 2nd sess. (from December 1889 to March 1891). Washington DC: GPO, 1891, vol. 26 (ch. 543): 1012–14.

——— . "For Support of Schools." In *The Statutes at Large*. 52nd Cong., 2nd sess. Washington DC: GPO, 1893, vol. 27 (ch. 209): 634–38.

——— . House. Hearings before the Committee on the Judiciary Pursuant to H. Res. 803. *Statement of Information: A Resolution Authorizing and Directing the Committee on the Judiciary to Investigate Whether Sufficient Grounds Exist for the House of Representatives to Exercise Its Constitutional Power to Impeach Richard M. Nixon President of the United States of America (and) Impoundment of Funds: Government Expenditures on President Nixon's Private Properties at San Clemente and Key Biscayne*. 93rd Cong., 2nd sess. Washington DC: GPO, May–June 1974, Book XII: 1–187.

——— . *No Child Left Behind Act of 2001—Title 3: Language Instruction for Limited English Proficient and Immigrant Students*. 107th Cong., 1st sess., December 13, 2001. Washington DC: National Clearinghouse for Bilingual Education, George Washington University, 268–315.

——— . "Public Law 92-318." In *The Statutes at Large: Laws and Concurrent Resolutions and Proposed Amendment to the Constitution and Proclamations*. 92nd Cong., 2nd sess. (1972). Washington DC: GPO, 1973, vol. 86 (in one pt.): 235–381.

——— . "Public Law 93-638." In *The Statutes at Large: Private Laws, Concurrent Resolutions and Proclamations, Public Laws 93-447 through 93-649*. 93rd Cong., 2nd sess. (1974). Washington DC: GPO, 1976, vol. 88 (pt. 2): 2203–17.

——— . "Public Law 97-451." Federal Oil and Gas Royalty Management Act of 1982. In *The Statutes at Large: Laws and Concurrent Resolutions*. 97th Cong., 2nd sess. (January 12, 1983). Washington DC: GPO, 1984, vol. 96 (pt. 2): 2447–66.

————. Senate. Committee on Labor and Public Welfare, Special Subcommittee on Indian Education. *Indian Education: A National Tragedy—A National Challenge.* 91st Cong., 2nd sess., Report No. 91-501. Washington DC: GPO, 1969, 1–220.

U.S. Department of Education, Office of Elementary and Secondary Education. *State of Wyoming Consolidated State Application Accountability Workbook,* 2005–2006 Revisions for State Grants under Title IX, Part C, Section 9302 of the Elementary and Secondary Education Act, Public Law 107-110. Revised submissions each year since 2003.

U.S. Environmental Protection Agency, Region 8. "Attachment 1: Legal Analysis of the Wind River Indian Reservation Boundary." https://www.epa.gov/sites /production/files/2013-12/documents/attachment2capabilitystatement.pdf (accessed July 10, 2018).

Ward, Carol J. *Native Americans in the School System: Family, Community, and Academic Achievement.* New York: Rowman and Littlefield Publishers, 2005.

Washakie Co. Sch. Dist. No. One v. Herschler, Wyo., 606 P.2d 310 (1980).

Washburn, Wilcomb E. *Red Man's Land—White Man's Law: A Study of the Past and Present Status of the American Indian.* New York: Charles Scribner's Sons, 1971.

Wax, Murray L., Stanley Diamond, and Fred O. Gearing, eds. *Anthropological Perspectives on Education.* New York: Basic Books, 1971.

Wells, Amy Stuart, Jennifer Jellison Holme, Anita Tijerina Revilla, and Awo Korantemaa Atanda. "How Society Failed School Desegregation Policy: Looking Past the Schools to Understand Them." In *Review of Research in Education,* edited by Robert E. Floden, 47–99. Washington DC: American Educational Research Association, 2004.

White, Theodore H. *Breach of Faith—The Fall of Richard Nixon.* New York: Atheneum Publishers, 1975.

Whiting, Jason B., et al. "Intergenerational Transmission of Violence: The Influence of Self-Appraisals, Mental Disorders and Substance Abuse." *Journal of Family Violence* 24 (July 2009): 639–48.

Wiles, Sara. "Indian Basketball: Two Films." *Visual Anthropology Review* 18, no. 1–2 (2002): 102–9.

Wilkins, David E. *American Indian Politics and the American Political System.* Lanham MD: Rowman and Littlefield Publishers, 2002.

Wilson, Richard H. Report of Agent. Shoshone Agency, Wyoming, August 25, 1897. In *Report of the Secretary of the Interior,* 54th Cong., 2nd sess., H. Executive Docs. (Washington DC, 1897).

Wilson, Roger. "Teachers for Indian Children." In *The Schooling of Native America,* edited by Thomas Thompson, 155–67. Washington DC: American Association of

Colleges for Teacher Education in collaboration with the Teacher Corps United States Office of Education, 1978.

Wisconsin v. Yoder et al., 406 U.S. 205 (May 15, 1972).

Wixon, Karen K., Elizabeth Dutro, and Ruth G. Athan. "The Challenge of Developing Content Standards." In *Review of Research in Education*, edited by Robert E. Floden, 69–107. Washington DC: American Educational Research Association, 2004.

Wolcott, Harry F. "The Teacher as an Enemy." In *Education and Cultural Process: Toward an Anthropology of Education*, edited by George Dearborn Spindler, 411–25. New York: Holt, Rinehart and Winston, 1974.

Wong, Kenneth K., Stephen J. Meyer, and Francis X. Shen. "Educational Resources and Achievement Gaps in High Poverty Schools: Findings from the Longitudinal Evaluation of School Change and Performance (LESCP) in Title I Schools." U.S. Department of Education Report EA96008001, August 2002.

Wright, Peter M. "Washakie." In *American Indian Leaders, Studies in Diversity*, edited by David R. Edmunds, 131–51. Lincoln: University of Nebraska Press, 1980.

Wright v. Council of City of Emporia, 407 U.S. 451 (June 22, 1972). http://laws.findlaw .com/us/407/451.html (accessed February 21, 2012).

Yehuda, Rachel, Sarah L. Halligan, and Robert Grossman. "Childhood Trauma and Risk for PTSD: Relationship to Intergenerational Effects of Trauma, Parental PTSD and Cortisol Excretion." In *Development and Psychopathology* 13, no. 3 (2001): 733–53.

Zerga, Victor George. "A Study of the Progress, Methods, and Opinions Concerning the Development of a Unified School District on the Wind River Indian Reservation." MA thesis, University of Wyoming, 1972.

INDEX

U.S. Supreme Court, 148

Vinich, John, 161

Ward, Alfred, 97, 101, 104, 145
Warden, Cleaver, 174
Washakie (Chief), 17, 20, 81
Washakie County lawsuit, 167
Washington Post, 109
Wax, Murray, 57
Wax, Rosalie, 57
Weed, Starr, 31, 103, 106, 108
white. *See* non-Indian education; non-
Indian teachers
White, Crawford, 29–30
White, Nelson, 28–29
"white-washed," 34
Wilkins, David E., 152
Wilkinson, Jan, 137
Williams, John H., 159
Wind River: and courts, 206; Elders,
21, 22; and employment, 202–3,
207–8; and income differential, 54,
102; and Indian Reorganization
Act, 22; Intertribal Council, 206;
Joint Business Council, 21, 130; and
land sale, 19, 20; and literacy test,
23; and revenues, 54, 102; and state
jurisdiction over schools, 36–37;
and strategy, 22, 38; Wyoming
Indian Leadership Council, 65, 66
Wind River Indian Education Association (WRIEA), 66; and AIM, 73; and
testimony in Cheyenne, 124–26, 128;
and U.S. Supreme Court, 148; and
Wyoming courts, 140, 143–44, 145–48
Wind River Indian Reservation (WRIR):
death rates at, 182–83; economic
needs of, 204; and employment, 208;

and encroachments, 4–5, 18–19, 55,
83; and land diminishment, 19, 98;
and Little and Big Wind Rivers, 15;
and oil and gas fields, 81, 83; and
taxation, 36–37, 82; topography of,
79; Upper and Lower areas of, 23.
See also Arapaho(s), Northern; Sho-
shone(s), Eastern
Wind River Native Advocacy
(WRNA), 204
Wind River Shoshone and Arapaho
Education Association (WRSAEA),
46, 65, 90; aspirations of, 64; and
BIA, 72, 108–9, 111; board members
of, 65–66; and CICSB, 72; and Episcopal buildings, 72; "Fact Sheet"
of, 46; lobbying of, 65, 67; and PIE,
101; and self-determination, 47; and
travel, 67, 107–8
Wind River Tribal College, 207
Wisconsin v. Yoder, 141
Wounded Knee, 41–42, 75–76. *See also*
American Indian Movement (AIM)
Wunder, John, 84, 96
Wyoming education laws: Education
Code (1969), 77–78, 83, 118–19, 176;
School District Organization Law
(1977), 161, 162–63, 168
Wyoming Indian High School (WIHS):
accreditation of, 115–16, 191; adult
returnees to,118; and advanced
education, 198, 205–6, 207–8;
affiliation of, 163; and artistic
projects, 198; and aspirations, 67,
201–2; audit of, 116; and basketball,
116–17, 169–72; and BIA contract,
67, 69, 111, 113; and BIA standards,
115; classes at, 113, 177; counseling
at, 176, 183; and culture, 176–77,